A STUDY
OF VERSIFICATION

BY

BRANDER MATTHEWS, *1852 - 1929.*

PROFESSOR IN COLUMBIA UNIVERSITY
MEMBER OF THE AMERICAN ACADEMY OF
ARTS AND LETTERS

BOSTON NEW YORK AND CHICAGO
HOUGHTON MIFFLIN COMPANY
The Riverside Press Cambridge

The Riverside Press
CAMBRIDGE, MASSACHUSETTS
U · S · A

TO

W. C. BROWNELL

CRITIC OF POETS AND

PROSE-MASTERS

PREFATORY NOTE

It is now about thirty years since I prepared an American edition of a little book by the younger Tom Hood, which purported to set forth the rules of rime (the "Rhymester," Appleton & Co., 1882); and it is just twenty years since I first gave a course in metrical rhetoric to a class of undergraduates in Columbia College. And I have long felt the need of a simple text-book for the beginner, which would serve as an introduction to the study of English versification. There are many volumes devoted to the analysis of poetry, but there are few which confine themselves wholly to the problems of prosody; and scarcely any one of these is exactly adapted to the needs of the novice who knows little or nothing about the principles of the metrical art. The subject is treated casually and cursorily in many grammars and in many rhetorics; but the main purpose of these books is to help the student to express himself accurately and satisfactorily in prose.

This is the simple text-book for the beginner that I have undertaken in the present volume. It is a text-book of metrical rhetoric. Its aim is to explain to the inquirer the technic of verse-making and to show him how the poets have been able to achieve their effects. It sets forth what I believe to be the fundamental principle of the art, — that all poetry is to be said or sung, and that its appeal is to the ear and not to the eye. This principle is here asserted, unhesitatingly; and from it all the practices of modern English versification are here derived. No other principle is even discussed, and all controversy has been rigorously eschewed. The student will not be confused by any attempt to refute any other theory; and his time will not be wasted by the confutation of any code long ago disestablished.

The main object of this book is to provide the student with an understanding of the mechanism of verse, that he may have a richer appreciation of poetry. The metrical mastery of Chaucer and of Milton, of Pope and of Tennyson, will be more keenly relished by the lover of poetry when he has attained to an insight into the methods whereby this mastery was achieved. But while this is its primary intent, the book has also a secondary purpose, to encourage teachers to give courses in metrical rhetoric, — not with any vain hope that they will be able to train poets, but with the firm belief that exercise in verse is the best possible aid to easy flexibility in prose-writing. Verse-making is an admirable gymnastic; and the necessity of mating his words in rime and of adjusting them to rhythm enriches the student's vocabulary and increases his control over it. Constant practice in composing in stanzas prescribed by the instructor will not tend to puff up the young writer with the conceit that he is a poet. On the contrary, it is likely to take down his vanity by showing him how easy it is to acquire the elements of verse-making and by calling his attention to the technical dexterity possessed by the great craftsmen in verse. Indeed, there is no better corrective of undue pride, there is no more potent inciter of modesty, than the frequent attempt to pattern ourselves on the masters and to discover how lamentably we fall short of our lofty and unapproachable models.

B. M.

COLUMBIA UNIVERSITY
IN THE CITY OF NEW YORK.

CONTENTS

A STUDY OF VERSIFICATION

CHAPTER I

THE STUDY OF VERSE

As logic does not supply you with arguments, but only defines the mode in which they are to be expressed or used, so versification does not teach you how to write poetry, but how to construct verse. It may be a means to the end, but it does not pretend to assure its attainment. Versification and logic are to poetry and reason what a parapet is to a bridge : they do not convey you across, but prevent you from falling over. — TOM HOOD : *The Rules of Rhyme.*

THIS is not a handbook of poetics; and its aim is not to consider the several departments of poetry, — epic and lyric and dramatic. It does not deal with simile and metaphor, nor does it seek to open the mind of the student to the nobler beauties of poetry. It is intended to be an introduction to the study of versification, of the metrical mechanism which sustains poetry, and which differentiates poetry from prose.

It is devoted solely to the technic of the art of verse. It is an examination of the tools of the poet's trade. Although poets are said to be born and not made, there is no doubt that they have to be made after they are born. It is not a fact that the born poet warbles native wood-notes wild ; he has to serve an apprenticeship to his craft ; he has to acquire the art of verse ; he has to master its technic and to spy out its secrets. The poet is like the painter, who, as Sir

Joshua Reynolds declared, "is a painter only as he can put in practice what he knows, and communicate those ideas by visible representation."

In his ignorance, the layman may be led to despise technic; but this is a blunder of which the true artist is never guilty. Indeed, the true artist cherishes technic; he is forever thinking about it and enlarging his knowledge of it. He delights in discussing its problems; and when he is moved to talk about his art, technic is ever the theme of his discourse. The treatises on painting, for example, written by painters, by Reynolds or by La Farge, are full of technical criticism; and so are the essays on poetry, written by the poets themselves. The processes of their art are considered with unfailing zest by Pope and Wordsworth, by Coleridge and Poe. In fact, the artists are all aware that technic is almost the only aspect of their art which can be discussed profitably; and every layman can see that it is the only aspect which the artists often care to talk about. The other part, no doubt the loftier part, the poet's message to humanity, — this is too ethereal, perhaps too personal, too intimate, too sacred, to bear debate.

Every work of art can be considered from two points of view. It has its content and it has its form. We may prefer to pay attention to what the artist has to say, or we may examine rather how he says it. The content of his work, what he has to say to us, is the more important, of course, but this must depend on his native gift, on his endowment; and it is more or less beyond his control. He utters what he must utter; and he voices what he is inspired to deliver. But the form in which he clothes this message, how he says what he has to say, — this is what he may choose to make it, no more and no less. This depends on him and on him alone; it is not a gift but an acquisition; it is the result of his skill, of the trouble he is willing to take, of his artistic integrity, of his desire to do his best always, and never to quit his work until he has made it as perfect as he can.

This technical dexterity can be had for the asking; — or, at least, it can be bought with a price. It is the reward of intense interest, of incessant curiosity, of honest labor. And it is worth all that it costs, since we cannot really separate form and content, as we sometimes vainly imagine. What the poet has to say is inextricably intertwined with the way in which he says it, and our appreciation of his ultimate message is enhanced by our delight in his method of presenting it. In fact, our pleasure in his work is often due quite as much to the sheer artistry of his presentation as it is to the actual value of his thought and of his emotion. We might even go further and venture the assertion that it is by style alone that the poet survives, since his native gift profits him little unless he so presents his message that we cannot choose but hear. And, as Professor Bradley declared in one of his "Oxford Lectures on Poetry," "when poetry answers to its idea and is purely or almost purely poetic, we find the identity of form and content, and the degree of purity may be tested by the degree in which we feel it hopeless to convey the effect of a poem or passage in any form but its own."

There is benefit, therefore, for all of us in an endeavor to understand the mechanism of the poet's art, to gain an elementary acquaintance with its processes, to learn as much as we may about its delightful mysteries, — just as we must acquire a certain acquaintance with the conditions of building before we can gain a real insight into the beauty of architecture. This knowledge will increase our enjoyment of poetry, for it will give us a twofold interest, in the manner as well as in the matter. The more we know about versification, the better equipped we are to perceive the skill with which the poet has wrought his marvels and also to feel deeply his charm and his power. The more we know, the better we shall understand the real nature of poetic inspiration. " It is very natural," so Reynolds declared in another of his " Discourses on Painting," " for those who are unacquainted with the cause of anything extraordinary to be astonished at the effect, and to consider it as a kind of magic. They who have never observed the gradation by which art is acquired, who see only what is the full result of long labor and application of an infinite number and infinite variety of acts, are apt to conclude, from their entire inability to do the same at once, that it is not only inaccessible to themselves, but can be done by those only who have some gift of the nature of inspiration bestowed upon them."

This book is intended, not so much for those who may desire to write verse, as it is for those who wish to gain an insight into the methods of the poets that they may have a keener and a deeper appreciation of poetry; and yet its suggestions are available also for those who may feel themselves moved to speak in numbers. Attention may be called to the fact that it never pretends to declare how verse ought to be written; all that it endeavors to do is to show how verse has

been written by the poets who have enriched our literature. If any laws emerge into view, these are the result of a modest attempt to codify the practice of the
poets themselves and to deduce the underlying principles. It is never the privilege of the critic to lay down
arbitrary rules for any art; it is his duty to examine
what the great artists have given us, and to discover,
if he can, the subtle means whereby they achieved
their masterpieces. And it is a humble examination
of this kind which is undertaken in this inquiry.

As this is the main object of the present volume,
the reader must not expect to find here things not
germane to this intent. He will not have his attention
distracted by any investigation into the origins of
English verse. He will not be called upon to consider
the conflicting theories of English prosody. He will
not be confused by constant references to the very different metrical system which was employed by the
Greek and the Latin poets. These things are discussed
at length in many other books; and in this book they
would be out of place. To consider them in these
pages would interfere with the main purpose of the
present volume, which is to provide the lover of poetry
with an elementary knowledge of the principles that
govern modern English versification.

Exact definition tends to precision of thought; and
an acquaintance with technical terms is necessary to
any scientific investigation. As Professor Mayor has
declared, " the use of Prosody is to supply a technical
language by which each specimen of verse is brought
before us; to distinguish the different kinds of verse,
to establish a type of each, by reference to which ex-
isting varieties may be compared; and, finally, to

state the laws of composition which have been observed by those whom the world recognizes as poets. Then from this we may draw practical rules of art for the poet or the reader."

An acquaintance with the technical terms, a knowledge of the rules of the art, will not suffice to make any one of us a poet. But an ignorance of the underlying principles of verse will prevent now any one, however gifted by nature, from attaining eminence as a poet. The earlier verse-writers had to work by instinct only at first, guided by their intuitive feeling for rhythm; in time their successors had the solid support of tradition; and to-day every poet can profit by a study of the means whereby his great predecessors wrought their marvels. No doubt, delicacy of ear still guides him more securely than any rule of thumb; and yet he will find assistance in a knowledge of the science of verse which underlies the art of poetry. Apprentice poets may now find this science set forth more or less accurately in the treatises of the critics, or they may absorb it for themselves by reverent study of the great masters of verse.

It is true that versification is only the carved vase which holds the precious wine of poetry; and yet without the vase the wine would be spilled and wasted. On the other hand, the vase itself stands empty unless the poet has within himself that which will fill it worthily. Amiel asserted that the group of French poets in the nineteenth century who were known as the Parnassians "sculptured urns of agate and of onyx; but what do these urns contain? Ashes!" Yet the blunder of these Parnassians was not in the curious care with which they carved their urns of agate and

of onyx; it was in their failure to fill the urns with
an elixir worthy of receptacles thus adorned. It was
their fault or their misfortune that they had nothing
better than ashes to pour into their urns.

Still, after all, the urns themselves had their own
beauty. Every lover of poetry could cite numberless
lyrics which delight him by their art alone, by their
melody, by their merely external fascination, without
regard to their content, to their ultimate meaning. Indeed, there are not a few lovely lyrics in our language
the meaning of which is doubtful or even vague and
intangible. They charm our ears with their music,
even if they fail to appeal to our intellect. They live
by melody, and almost by melody alone. And if this is
a fact, surely it is well worth our while to seek for an
understanding of the principles of an art which can
work these marvels.

If there are a few lyrics which survive by form
rather than by content, none the less is it true that
in poetry form and content are inseparable; and
poetry demands for its full appreciation an understanding of versification. Indeed, Professor Bradley
does not go too far when he asserts that " the value
of versification, when it is indissolubly fused with
meaning, can hardly be exaggerated. The gift for
feeling it, even more perhaps than the gift for feeling
the value of style, is the *specific* gift for poetry, as distinguished from the other arts." And Leigh Hunt went
even further, for he insisted that " versification itself
becomes part of the sentiment of a poem. . . . I know
of no very fine versification unaccompanied with fine
poetry; no poetry of a mean order accompanied with
verse of the highest."

CHAPTER II

RHYTHM

Our new empiricism, following where intuition leads the way, comprehends the functions of *vibrations*: it perceives that every movement of matter, seized upon by universal force, is *vibratory*; that vibrations, and nothing else, convey through the body the look and voice of nature to the soul; that thus alone can one incarnate individuality address its fellow; that, to use old Bunyan's imagery, these vibrations knock at the ear-gate, and are visible to the eye-gate, and are sentient at the gates of touch of the living temple. The word describing their action is in evidence; they "thrill" the body, they thrill the soul, both of which respond with subjective, interblending vibrations, according to the keys, the wave-lengths of their excitants. — EDMUND CLARENCE STEDMAN: *The Nature and Elements of Poetry*.

IN any consideration of versification, we need to begin by reminding ourselves that poetry is always intended to be said or sung. Its appeal is primarily to the ear and only secondarily to the eye. At first, poetry was certainly sung, because it came into being long before the invention of the art of writing. After a while, poetry was both said and sung; it was recited, either with or without the accompaniment of music. Only after long centuries, during which it survived on the tongue and in the ear, was it written down to reach the eye also. " To pass from hearing literature to reading it is to take a great and dangerous step," said Stevenson; " with not a few, I think, a large proportion of their pleasure then comes to an end, . . . they read thenceforward by the eye alone and hear never again the chime of fair words or the march of the stately syllable." Even now, the real approach of

poetry to the soul of man is through his ears; and
we do not feel its full force until we speak it ourselves or hear it from others. It might almost be asserted that poetry is like music, in which the notation
in black and white is only a device to preserve it and
to transmit it; and that like music, poetry does not
fully exist until it is heard. As a result of this re-
semblance to music, poetry is likely to lose something
of its power when the poet thinks rather of his readers
than of his hearers.

Therefore, the true principles of versification can
be seized only when we keep this fact always in mind,
that the poet has intended his lines to be heard by
the ear, to be spoken or chanted or sung by one for
the pleasure of others. His verses, lyric or dramatic
as they may be, are meant to be spoken and so they
must adjust themselves to the vocal organs of man;
and they are meant to be heard and so they must be
measured to the capacity of the human ear. Indeed,
nearly all the elements of the art of versification are
the direct result of this condition of oral delivery.

The most important of these elements is rhythm.
All nature is rhythmic. The tides rise and fall; day
follows night; and the seasons recur one after the
other, year by year. Human nature is rhythmic also;
and emotion, which is the subject-matter of poetry,
tends always to express itself rhythmically. Passionate
language has its marked beats. Primitive man casts
his war-songs and his love-songs into a rude but emphatic rhythm. The wail of the tribe over its dead is
rhythmic; and so is the crooning of the mother over
her babe in the cradle by her side. The chant of triumph has its rise and fall. In all these examples, the

character of the rhythm may be open to question, but the existence of the rhythm itself is beyond dispute. Lowell singled out for praise the song of Deborah and Barak: "Awake, awake, Deborah! Awake, awake, utter a song! Arise, Barak, and lead thy captivity captive, thou son of Abinoam!"

This rhythmic utterance in moments of poignant emotion is spontaneous even to-day in our children. A few years ago the young daughter of a friend of mine was stricken to the heart by the crushing of a cherished doll under a rocking-chair. When the mother returned she found the little girl so pitiful and pathetic that she took the child in her arms and asked what had happened. And then the little daughter broke out in this lament: —

> My dolly is dead! My dolly is dead!
> I loved my dolly, and I did n't want her to die!
> But she died, and I buried her.
> And I wanted to bury her
> In the worst place I could find;
> So I looked all over the flat
> For the very worst place I could find.
> And I buried her in the pail —
> In the pail under the sink in the kitchen,
> In the pail where we put the old dinners
> And the old breakfasts and my crusts when I won't
>   eat 'em:
> And I buried her there.
> It was the very worst place I could find.
> I buried her on top of the dinner
> And under the breakfast,
> And there 's oatmeal where her head ought to be.
> And Annie will put her on the dumbwaiter,
> And she 'll send her down to the janitor,
> And the janitor will put her into the barrel,
> And he 'll put the barrel out on the sidewalk;

> And the man will come along with the wagon,
> And he 'll empty her into the wagon,
> And he 'll drive her down to the dock,
> And he 'll dump her into the river,
> And she 'll go floating down the river
> Without any head and without any legs —
> And I did n't want her to die !
> My dolly, my dolly, my dolly,
> Is dead and I 've buried her,
> And I did n't want her to die !

This childish dirge is curiously like the bold and formless lyric outpourings of savages. It is wildly rhythmic, not regular, not artificial, instinctive rather than artistic. It has even the repetition and reduplication and overt cataloging which often characterize the chants of primitive races.

Even in the less spontaneous and more consciously artistic paragraphs of the great orators, we can often feel the rise and fall of rhythm, sometimes only in a single sentence and sometimes carried through a long passage. For instance, in a speech of John Bright's delivered during the Crimean war, he said that "the angel of death has been abroad through the land : we may almost hear the beating of his wings." It would be easy to adduce other examples from the orations which are charged with sweeping emotion.

Certain of the novelists have now and again availed themselves of this same device to enhance the pathos of the situation they were setting forth. Dickens, in particular, could rarely resist the temptation to drop into very obvious rhythm whenever he stood by the death-bed or the tomb of one of his characters. Here, for example, is the concluding paragraph of "Nicholas Nickleby": "The grass was green above the dead boy's grave, trodden by feet so small and light, that not a daisy drooped its head beneath their pressure. Through all the spring and summer-time garlands of fresh flowers, wreathed by infant hands, rested upon the stone."

In general, prose is for daily use in this workaday world; and it becomes rhythmic when it has to express emotion, — that is to say, only on special occasions. But even when it is properly rhythmic we do not like to have it encroach on the borders of actual verse. We feel that prose is one thing and that verse is another; and therefore a delicate ear is annoyed by the excessive regularity of the rhythm in Dickens's elegies. It is a little too obvious, and it offends us as out of place in prose. The fundamental difference between the rhythms appropriate to prose and those appropriate to verse lies in the fact that the latter conform to a simple pattern and that the former do not. If a writer of prose forces us to perceive his pattern by limiting it, as Dickens does, he loses the ample freedom proper to prose, and he suffers this loss without achieving the special merit of verse. In prose, our ear delights in the vague suggestion of a pattern, which is too large for us to grasp, even though we take pleasure in it. In verse, the poet spreads the pattern before us, invites our attention to it; he awakes in us the expectancy that its elements will recur at regular intervals; and it is partly by the gratification of this expectancy that he gives us pleasure. This pattern is the result of reducing rhythm to measure; and it is this metrical rhythm which the writer of prose must avoid unless he is willing to annoy our ears. The orator and the novelist may deal with the same subject-matter as the poet, but they must not infringe on his method. Their diction may be as impassioned as his, as lofty in phrasing, as elevated in imagination; but they must avoid that formal regularity which we hold to be the privilege of the poet alone.

This formal regularity is what constitutes English verse; and it is easy to analyze. When we read a line of English poetry we cannot help noticing that certain syllables are bolder or longer or more emphatic than others. In Longfellow's

> Tell me not, in mournful numbers,

these more important syllables are the first of every pair; and in Drake's

> When Freedom from her mountain height,

they are the second in every pair. We may indicate the rise and fall of these syllables in Longfellow's line by suggesting that it more or less resembles

> *Tumty, tumty, tumty, tumty,*

while in Drake's line it is

> *Titum, titum, titum, titum.*

In Byron's line

> And the sheen of their spears was like stars on the sea,

the more important syllables are the third in each group of three; and the scheme of the line is

> *Tititum, tititum, tititum, tititum.*

If we read as one line Hood's

> Make no deep scrutiny into her mutiny,

the important syllables are the first in each group of three; and the scheme is

> *Tumtity, tumtity, tumtity, tumtity.*

That these syllables have an importance superior to the other syllables in the same lines is undeniable. This importance may be due to the fact that they are either more emphatic or longer in time of utterance. But are these differences in tone or in accent the only difference between them? Here we enter on one of the most disputed questions in versification. The more important syllables may differ in length, in the time we take to utter them, that is to say, in quantity. They may differ also in emphasis, in stress, that is to say, in accent. They may differ further in pitch, in their melodic tone. Or the difference may sometimes be due to a combination of time, stress and pitch, for a syllable may be at once longer than the syllables which precede and follow, while it is also more sharply accented, as well as higher in pitch. We may be in doubt as to the cause of the superior importance of these syllables, but we never deny the fact that for some reason they are more important. And this superior importance of certain syllables over other syllables in the same line, whatever its cause may be, is the basis of English versification. There is no profit in here entering on the discussion as to the cause of this superior importance; and hereafter in this book these syllables of superior importance will be called *long*, even though they may owe their value to other elements than mere duration of time. In like manner, the syllables of inferior importance will be called *short*, even though they may contain long vowels. And for the sake of convenience a long syllable will be marked or indicated by the sign – and a short syllable by the sign ◡.

If now we substitute these signs for *tumty* and

tumtity, we find that Longfellow's line "Tell me not, in mournful numbers," may be represented thus : —

$$- \smile, - \smile, - \smile, - \smile$$

Drake's "When Freedom from her mountain height" will be translated into these symbols : —

$$\smile -, \smile -, \smile -, \smile -$$

Byron's "And the sheen of their spears was like stars on the sea" has this scheme : —

$$\smile \smile -, \smile \smile -, \smile \smile -, \smile \smile -$$

And Hood's "Make no deep scrutiny into her mutiny" has this : —

$$- \smile \smile, - \smile \smile, - \smile \smile, - \smile \smile$$

Thus we see that each of these lines is made by the fourfold repetition of the same unit. Each of these units we call a foot. In Longfellow's line this unit is $- \smile$, a long followed by a short ; and by tradition this foot is called a *trochee*. In Drake's line the unit is $\smile -$, a short followed by a long ; and this foot is called an *iamb* or *iambus*. In Byron's line the unit is $\smile \smile -$, two shorts followed by a long ; and the name of this foot is *anapest*. In Hood's line the unit is $- \smile \smile$, a long followed by two shorts, a foot which is known as a *dactyl*. These terms, trochee, iamb, anapest, and dactyl, have been taken over from Latin versification, although they there represent feet not really corresponding to the English feet which bear the same names. These four are probably the only feet possible in English versification, because in English, which is a strongly accented language, we seem to be unable to utter three syllables in succession without making one of them more important than the other two, longer or more emphatic. Doubtless a few examples of three short syllables in succession may be discovered by a diligent examination of the whole body of English poetry ; but they are very few.

In fact, our speech is so accentual that we find it almost impossible to give exactly equal emphasis to two syllables in the same foot; and we are therefore deprived of the use of the *spondee*, made up of two longs, – –, a foot which was most useful in the versification of the Greeks and Romans. More than one English word taken by itself seems to be a spondee, *baseball*, for instance, and *stronghold ;* but when such words are used in verse, either the first syllable or the second is likely to be so lengthened or emphasized that we have a trochee or an iambus. Spondees can be discovered in English verse, especially in Milton, but they are infrequent. Two other feet known to classic meter are the *amphibrach*, ◡ – ◡, a short, a long, and a short; and the *amphimacer*, – ◡ –, a long, a short, and a long. But neither of these has established itself in English verse; and when either of them has been attempted, the result is very doubtfully distinguishable from a sequence of dactyls or anapests. Even Coleridge, a master of metrics, was not able to construct an English amphibrach and an English amphimacer which should set itself off sharply from the anapest. Here is his ingenious attempt to exemplify the several feet : —

> Trochee trips from long to short ;
> From long to long in solemn sort
> Slow Spondee stalks, strong foot, yet ill able
> Ever to come up with Dactyl trisyllable.

Iambics march from short to long ;
With a leap and a bound, the swift Anapests throng ;
One syllable long with a short at each side
Amphibrachys hastes with a stately stride :
First and last being long, middle short, Amphimacer
Strikes his thundering hoofs like a proud high-bred racer.

To scan a line is to divide it into its constituent feet, to mark the longs and the shorts, to count the feet and to declare their character. All verse in the English language can be scanned with the aid of the trochee and the iambic, the anapest and the dactyl. When we scan Longfellow's line we find that it consists of four trochees ; and therefore we describe it as *trochaic tetrameter.* When a line has two feet we call it *dimeter ;* with three feet it is *trimeter ;* with four it is *tetrameter ;* with five, *pentameter ;* with six, *hexameter,* and with seven, *heptameter.* When Drake's line is scanned it is seen to be iambic tetrameter ; Byron's is anapestic tetrameter ; and Hood's is dactylic tetrameter. When we scan Gray's

> The curfew tolls the knell of parting day

we find this scheme —

$$\cup - \mid \cup - \mid \cup - \mid \cup - \mid \cup -$$

and we declare that the line is iambic pentameter. And if we examine the first line of Baring Gould's hymn,

> Onward, Christian soldiers !

we discover that the scheme is

$$- \cup \mid - \cup \mid - \cup \mid$$

and we decide that it is trochaic trimeter. Austin Dobson's

> Too hard it is to sing
> In these untuneful times !

declares itself at once as iambic trimeter : —

$$\cup - \mid \cup - \mid \cup -$$
$$\cup - \mid \cup - \mid \cup -$$

and Rudyard Kipling's

We have learned to whittle the Eden Tree to the shape of a
    surplice-peg

is obviously anapestic heptameter, although it contains
iambics as well as anapests, as the translation into
symbols discloses at once : —

$$\cup\cup - \mid \cup - \mid \cup\cup - \mid \cup - \mid \cup\cup - \mid \cup\cup - \mid \cup -$$

And this apparent irregularity, this commingling of
anapests and iambics, leads us to another point of
prime significance. Verse consists of a regular arrangement of feet, of a pattern which can be taken
in by the ear without undue tension. In any single
foot the ear permits many liberties with the short syllables ; but it tolerates only a little license with the
long syllable. If there are in a line the required number of long syllables, of emphatic beats, the ear is not at
all particular about the less important short syllables.
These may be inserted or even on occasion omitted
altogether, without interfering with the rhythm, with
the swing of the line as the ear expects to receive it.
For example, an iambic pentameter may have an added
syllable at the end almost without our noting it, as in
Shakspere's

To be, or not to be: that is the question.

Or the final short syllable of a terminal trochee may
be dropped without spoiling the expected pattern, as
in Longfellow's " Psalm of Life " : —

Tell me not, in mournful numbers,
  Life is but an empty dream!   [ᴗ]
For the soul is dead that slumbers,
  And things are not what they seem. [ᴗ]

Here the rhythm is trochaic; and its flow is not broken
by the dropping out of these short syllables at the end
of the second and fourth lines. We may translate
these lines into symbols, enclosing the dropped syllables in brackets.

$$- ᴗ \mid - ᴗ \mid - ᴗ \mid - ᴗ$$
$$- ᴗ \mid - ᴗ \mid - ᴗ \mid - [ᴗ]$$
$$- ᴗ \mid - ᴗ \mid - ᴗ \mid - ᴗ$$
$$- ᴗ \mid - ᴗ \mid - ᴗ \mid - [ᴗ]$$

These lines still retain their four emphatic beats; and
so long as the ear can perceive these beats it is satisfied. These beats carry the tune, so to speak. The ear
not only permits variation of feet inside the framework of beats, it is even delighted when this is so
adroitly done as to evade the monotony of strict regularity. For example, the ear authorizes the poet to substitute a trochee for an iambus in the first foot of an
iambic pentameter, as in Shakspere's

O for a Muse of fire, that would ascend.

$$- ᴗ \mid ᴗ - \mid ᴗ - \mid ᴗ - \mid ᴗ -$$

And it does not protest when a similar substitution is
made in one of the other feet, as in the fourth foot of
Shakspere's

A kingdom for a stage, princes to act.

$$ᴗ - \mid ᴗ - \mid ᴗ - \mid - ᴗ \mid ᴗ -$$

The ear does not protest because it is not sharply conscious of the substitution. It expects the five long syl-

lables to occur substantially in the established order; and if this expectation is fulfilled, it is more or less unconscious of the minor irregularity. In iambic meters, it allows not only the occasional substitution of a trochee but the frequent substitution of anapests. So in anapestic meters, it is willing to accept an occasional iambus. Indeed, in many ballads there is such an intermixture of the iambus and of the anapest that it is almost impossible to decide whether the rhythm is really iambic or anapestic. In the older traditional ballads, the iambus predominates, but there is a free infusion of anapests, as in this line from " Sir Patrick Spens " : —

> To send us out, at this time of the year.

> ∪ – | ∪ – | ∪∪ – | ∪∪ –

These traditional ballads were, many of them, composed early in the history of English poetry by unknown bards, who were guileless of critical theory, and who sang their stanzas into being to please the ears of their own artless contemporaries. The traditional nursery-rimes are equally spontaneous; and they cast an equal illumination upon the natural methods of English versification. If we examine certain of the primitive nursery-rimes we can see that the untutored lyrists unhesitatingly dropped out short syllables, never doubting that the ears of their young hearers would carry the tune securely in spite of this omission. One of the most familiar of nursery-rimes begins

> Hark ! Hark !
> The dogs do bark
> The beggars are come to town.

The second and the third lines reveal to us that the
rhythm is iambic; and this shows us that a short syllable has been suppressed in both of the feet of the first
line. If we translate the three lines into symbols we
have this : —

$$[\cup] - \mid [\cup] -$$
$$\cup - \mid \cup -$$
$$\cup - \mid \cup \cup - \mid \cup -$$

Take another nursery-rime quite as well known : —

> Pease porridge hot,
>   Pease porridge cold,
> Pease porridge in the pot
>   Nine days old.

We all remember how this is to be spoken, with its
marked pauses and with its accompanying clapping of
the hands. We see that the rhythm is trochaic; and
although many of the short syllables are missing, the
place of each one of them is taken by a pause, by a
silence, by a rest (as it would be called in musical notation). And yet our memory assures us that these
silences do not interfere with the carrying of the tune.
The four lines might be represented in this way : —

$$- [\cup] \mid - \cup \mid - [\cup]$$
$$- [\cup] \mid - \cup \mid - [\cup]$$
$$- [\cup] \mid - \cup \mid - \cup \mid - [\cup]$$
$$- [\cup] \mid - [\cup] \mid - [\cup]$$

Perhaps the omissions can be made more evident by
noting the omissions in the lines themselves : —

> Pease [$\cup$] | porridge | hot [$\cup$]
> Pease [$\cup$] | porridge | cold [$\cup$]
> Pease [$\cup$] | porridge | in the | pot [$\cup$]
> Nine [$\cup$] | days [$\cup$] | old [$\cup$]

An even more striking illustration of the instinctive ease with which short syllables may be suppressed, if their places are taken by pauses, by rests, can be found in another nursery-rime, — that which invites us to sing a song of sixpence. One line of this,

Now was n't that a dainty dish to set before the King ?

makes it plain that we have here an iambic heptameter

∪ – | ∪ – | ∪ – | ∪ – | ∪ – | ∪ – | ∪ –

And yet at the end of the little ballad we are told about the maid in the garden hanging out the clothes, and we are informed that

Down came a blackbird and snipt off her nose.

And we find ourselves forced to translate this thus : —

[∪] Down | [∪] came | a black | [∪] bird | and snipt | [∪] off | her nose.

[∪] – | [∪] – | ∪ – | [∪] – | ∪ – | [∪] – | ∪ –

Thus represented the line seems to the eye arbitrary, not to say awkward; and yet the untrained ear of a child has never had any difficulty in feeling the full force of the rhythm. If the emphatic syllables assert themselves, if the successive beats of the line are clearly perceptible, then the ear can carry the tune, even if the silences, the pauses, the rests, are frequent. The line is still divided into a series of equal periods; and it is this series of equal periods that the ear expects and demands. The eye may be puzzled; but the ear is satisfied.

This device of boldly dropping out a short syllable in order to add weight to the long syllable, which then

stands forth alone, has been utilized not only by the
simple makers of ballads and of nursery-rimes but also
by the greater poets of our language. Tennyson was
a devoted student of versification, and he found his
profit in all the ingenious devices of the adroit craftsmen who had preceded him. In one of his briefer lyrics,
he may have taken a hint from the unknown writer of
the nursery-rime about the beggars coming to town: —

> Break, break, break,
> On thy cold gray stones, O Sea !
> And I would that my tongue could utter
> The thoughts that arise in me.

In reading this stanza, with due regard to its intention, we feel that each of the four lines is equal in
the time of delivery and in the number of beats. Thus
there is a harmonious and satisfactory effect on the ear,
although the eye may inform us that there are only
three syllables in the first line while there are nine in
the third. The line with three syllables is equal to the
line of nine syllables because it has intervals of silence
equivalent in duration of time to the syllables it lacks.
The stanza is really anapestic trimeter; and it may be
thus represented: —

$$[\smile\smile]-\mid[\smile\smile]-\mid[\smile\smile]-$$
$$\smile\smile-\mid[\smile]\smile-\mid[\smile]\smile-$$
$$\smile\smile-\mid\smile\smile-\mid[\smile]\smile-\mid\smile$$
$$[\smile]\smile-\mid\smile\smile-\mid[\smile]\smile-$$

In one of his "Cavalier Tunes" called "Marching
Along," Browning got a series of vigorous effects by
the repeated use of this device of substituting rests for
actual syllables: —

> Kentish Sir Byng stood for his King,
> Bidding the crop-headed Parliament swing :

> And, pressing a troop unable to stoop
> And see the rogues flourish and honest folk droop,
> Marched them along, fifty-score strong,
> Great-hearted gentlemen, singing this song.

On examination, these lines are seen to be dactylic tetrameter, but with a free dropping out of the shorter syllables, which are not missed, since their places are taken by equivalent pauses, the rhythm therefore flowing on unbroken. Here is the translation into symbols: —

$$- \cup \cup \mid - [\cup \cup] \mid - \cup \cup \mid - [\cup \cup]$$
$$- \cup \cup \mid - \cup \cup \mid - \cup \cup \mid - [\cup \cup]$$
$$\cup \mid - \cup \cup \mid - [\cup] \cup \mid - \cup \cup \mid - [\cup \cup]$$
$$\cup \mid - \cup \cup \mid - \cup \cup \mid - \cup \cup \mid - [\cup \cup]$$
$$- \cup \cup \mid - [\cup \cup] \mid - \cup \cup \mid - [\cup \cup]$$
$$- \cup \cup \mid - \cup \cup \mid - \cup \cup \mid - [\cup \cup]$$

Another peculiarity is to be noted both in Tennyson's stanza and in Browning's : syllables that may seem to be suppressed in one line sometimes appear in another. At the end of Tennyson's third line, we find *utter*, which gives the line a short syllable too much ; but at the beginning of the fourth line we find that there is a short syllable too little. Perhaps the rhythm has been carried over from one line to the next. So at the beginning of Browning's third and fourth lines, we find a short syllable *and*, which is not needed in the first foot of either of these lines, but which stands instead of one of the two short syllables omitted at the ends of the lines preceding these two. This is evidence that the poets were not composing their lines one by one, and that they were thinking rather of their stanzas as wholes. These suppressions and insertions may seem abnormal to the eye which is looking for exact symmetry; but they are quite normal to the ear which is held by the swing of the rhythm.

It should always be remembered that poets compose their lyrics not only for the ear, but also by the ear. Sometimes a poet does not write down his song until he has made it up in his head, chanting it to himself and fitting it to the tune that is running in his own ears. Scott, for example, often beat out his bold ballads while he was on horseback. Tennyson composed in the open air on the slopes of the hills of Haslemere; afterwards he tested what he had done when he put it down in black and white; but it owed its rhythmic ease to the earlier labor far from his desk. Composing to please his own ear, first of all, and then the ears of all who might speak his lines, the poet does not care whether the printed poem happens to conform to academic rules which are the result of the mistaken belief that poetry should appeal primarily to the eyes, — a belief that no true poet has ever held. Professor Gummere has reminded us that Coleridge and Wordsworth, Scott and Tennyson, all read their verses in " a kind of chant " ; and Hazlitt has recorded that in the case of the three older poets, this " acted as a spell upon the hearer." And then Professor Gummere adds the needed explanation that " this chant was not singsong; singsong simply shows the feet, baldly asserts meter, while rhythmical reading does justice to cadence and the harmonious movement of the verse."

The poet may even choose to print his lines in a form which will possibly at first puzzle the eyes of those who seek to declare its metrical scheme; and this he does unhesitatingly if he has made sure that

the rhythm is easily apprehended by the ear. Here is
the opening stanza of one of Poe's most beautiful
lyrics, " For Annie ": —

> Thank Heaven ! the crisis,
>   The danger is past,
> And the lingering illness
>   Is over at last
> And the fever called "Living"
>   Is conquered at last.

The ear seizes the rhythm of this at once, and is perfectly satisfied with it, however much the eye may be
at a loss to declare just what the apparently irregular
meter really is. This perplexity is due to the fact that
the eye sees six lines as the poet has printed his poem,
whereas the ear catches only three, each of which is
an anapestic tetrameter. The transcription into signs
shows this clearly : —

$$[\smile]\; \smile - \;|\; \smile\smile - \;|\; \smile$$
$$\smile - \;|\; \smile\smile -$$
$$\smile\smile - \;|\; \smile\smile - \;|\; \smile$$
$$\smile - \;|\; \smile\smile \;|\; -$$
$$\smile\smile - \;|\; \smile\smile - \;|\; \smile$$
$$\smile - \;|\; \smile\smile -$$

The actual scheme is clearly revealed when we put
these symbols into three lines : —

$$[\smile]\; \smile - \;|\; \smile\smile - \;|\; \smile\smile - \;|\; \smile\smile -$$
$$\smile\smile - \;|\; \smile\smile - \;|\; \smile\smile - \;|\; \smile\smile -$$
$$\smile\smile - \;|\; \smile\smile - \;|\; \smile\smile - \;|\; \smile\smile -$$

In his suggestive essay on the " Rationale of Verse,"
Poe adduced a most striking example of a poet's lack

of regard for the eye of the reader. He quoted the
opening lines of Byron's "Bride of Abydos" (in which
the British bard was echoing Goethe): —

> Know ye the land where the cypress and myrtle
> Are emblems of deeds that are done in their clime,
> Where the rage of the vulture, the love of the turtle,
> Now melt into sorrow, now madden to crime?
> Know ye the land of the cedar and vine,
> Where the flowers ever blossom, the beams ever shine;
> Where the light wings of Zephyr, oppress'd with perfume,
> Wax faint o'er the gardens of Gúl in her bloom;
> Where the citron and olive are fairest of fruit,
> And the voice of the nightingale never is mute.

The American poet-critic then asked how these
lines are to be scanned. The first is obviously dactylic, but the last is as obviously anapestic, and more
than one of the others is doubtful in its apparent irregularity. If the lines are considered severally, we are
at a loss to declare the rhythm in which this beautiful
prelude is written. But Byron did not compose them
severally; he composed them continuously, or rather
he composed the passage as a whole regardless of its
division into lines. He was appealing to the ears of
the hearer and not to the eyes of the reader, certain
that the ears can carry the tune without regard to
any division into lines for the purposes of print. Considering the passage as a whole, we observe that the
rhythm is dactylic from beginning to end, even in
those lines which, taken by themselves, may seem to
be anapestic. The syllables which appear to be
missing at the end of the first line are to be found at
the beginning of the second; and those missing at
the end of the second are to be found at the beginning of the third; and so on.

In other words, the poet is free to select his pattern at will. He may choose a trochaic or an iambic rhythm, a dactylic or an anapestic. Having decided on the number of his beats, of his long syllables, he must accustom our ears to the pattern he has resolved upon. When this tune has rung in our ears he must sustain it with his long syllables, but he is at liberty to vary his short syllables at will, and even to suppress them, if these changes do not interfere with the tune of the verse. When we have once perceived the pattern, we are willing enough to allow the poet the privilege of any variation which does not interfere with the tune which he has given us to carry in our heads.

Sometimes he profits by this liberty at his peril because he cannot always make sure that we are going to take his lines in exact accordance with his metrical intent. He may have supposed that his suppression of a short syllable, his substitution of a trochee for an iambus would not interrupt the flow of the rhythm. And he may have been at fault in this supposition, since for some reason unforeseen by him, the suppression or the substitution may call attention to itself and thus break the current of the rhythm. If this happens the poet can find no excuse in pointing out that the license he took was authorized by the practice of some earlier master of verse. If the misfortune befalls him, he cannot claim exemption by citing precedents. It is by the result of his own work that the poet must be judged. If his lines fail to fall agreeably on the ear, then is the poet himself at fault.

The poet, no less than the prose-writer, is bound to observe what Herbert Spencer called the principle of

Economy of Attention. At any moment any one of us has just so much attention to give to the man who is addressing us. Some of this attention is necessarily taken up by the effort of seizing what he is saying; and therefore the less his manner attracts our notice, the more attention we shall have to bestow upon his matter. The more clearly and the more simply he can deliver his message, the more amply can we receive it. The poet has something to say to us and he employs verse to convey this to our ears; therefore whenever the verse itself arrests our attention we have just so much the less to bestow upon what he has to say. If he has once set the tune and aroused in us the interest of expectancy for a definite rhythm, then whenever he violates this accepted rhythm he forces us suddenly to consider his instrument, and our interest is thereby at once distracted from his meaning. Therefore, it is safer for the poet to vary his lines very cautiously and to keep in mind always the limitations of the human ear, since it is only through the ear that he can move the soul of his fellow-man.

And we as readers must do our part also. We must read verse aloud as the poet meant us to read it, as he read it himself when he sang it into being. "We must restore to poetry its primary intention as cadenced and melodious verse," so Professor Gummere has declared. "What is a lyric without its rhythmical values? What is the wild water of a brook when it is dammed into a duckpond? The very tropes and figures depend upon this charm of movement, like flashes of light thrown back by the hurrying waves. Yet we are so afraid of singsong, and even more afraid of the pathetic and sentimental, that we suppress all cadences, and come out triumphant with a hybrid sort of performance that reminds one of a bird which should flap its wings without flying."

CHAPTER III

METER

Here, at the outset, we find precisely what differentiates verse from prose. These two possess much in common. Their ideals are often similar; their subjects may be identical; their cadences sometimes coincide. Yet there is an essential difference, which has seldom been rightly stated, and which is a difference of mechanical method. The units of prose are diverse, irregular in length, rarely conformed to a common pattern. In verse, on the other hand, succession is continuous. Something recurs with regularity. This is the distinctive note of verse, making its structure differ from that of prose; no other absolute line of demarcation can be drawn. Typical recurrence, uniform repetition, is the prime postulate of meter. — T. S. Omond: *A Study of Meter.*

WE have seen that the habits of the English language are such as to make it practically impossible to write English verse except in one of the four rhythms which we call iambic, trochaic, anapestic and dactylic. And the practice of the poets reveals that any poem in our language must be in one or another of these rhythms. The poet, having accustomed our ear to the rhythm he has chosen, must keep to the pattern of his choice. He must give us the succession of beats in the order he has promised them to us. He may make varied substitutions and frequent suppressions inside his lines, but he must preserve always the expected framework of the chosen form. That is to say, he must decide once for all, whether he will compose in an iambic rhythm or a trochaic, an anapestic or a dactylic.

Of these four rhythms, the iambic has ever been the favorite. Indeed, there seem to have been periods when it was the only rhythm known. In King James' rules for writing verse, published in 1585, only the iambus is considered, as if it was the sole possible rhythm. Even in Greek, Aristotle held the iambic to be the most colloquial, since "conversational speech runs into iambic form more frequently than into any other kind of verse." Probably nine tenths of English poetry is iambic; this is the basis of the blank verse of Shakspere's plays and of Milton's epic, of most ballads old and new, of the heroic couplet of Dryden and of Pope, of the sonnet, and of a large majority of the hymns. Even in the nineteenth century, when poets were eager in devising new stanzaic arrangements, most of them clung to the iambus. Perhaps this immense popularity is due to the simplicity of the rhythm, with its short followed by a long, in accord with the rhetorical precept of putting the emphasis at the end. Perhaps it is due to the fact that when the iambic is once established in the ear of the listener, the poet can avoid monotony by a wide variety of substitutions and suppressions.

Although iambic and trochaic rhythms consist in a similar succession of alternating longs and shorts, the iambic is far bolder; it is more masculine; it has a direct vigor, which seems often to be lacking to the trochaic. The iambic apparently has a majesty of its own which fits it for loftier themes. The trochaic is gentler, sweeter, more feminine, adapted for consolation rather than for reinvigoration. It is inferior in terseness and in sharpness.

The anapestic rhythm had served chiefly for satire and for humor, until the nineteenth century, when English poets began to appreciate it and to employ it for nobler topics. It was the favorite of Swinburne, who handled it with superb freedom and mastery.

The dactylic rhythm is least used of the four, although Hood proved that it had advantages of its own, and although Browning employed it with clear understanding of its special characteristics.

In rimeless verse a poet might let any one of these rhythms flow on indefinitely, breaking off only when he had come to the end of his topic. But this un broken flow is too fatiguing for the ear; and therefore poems are divided into lines, so that the ear can have intervals of rest. When a rhythm is thus cut into sections we have meter, for we can measure every line by the number of times the foot happens to be repeated. In the verse of the modern languages, the ends of the lines are generally distinguished by rimes, a device unknown to the ancients. In some modern languages, especially in French which lacks boldness of accent, these terminal rimes are so important as to be almost essential. But in English, although rime is useful, it is not necessary; and the poets of our language have adventured themselves in many forms of unrimed verse.

Whether there is or is not a terminal rime, there is generally a pause of some sort to mark the end of the line; and there is often a full stop, although the more accomplished masters of meter reveal their dexterity in carrying over the sense from line to line while still keeping the structure distinct. Here again the appeal is to the ear and not to the eye; the poet may choose to print his lines to suit his own whim; but the way in which he presents them does not determine the metrical scheme. That is decided by the ear of the listener and not by the eye of the reader. We may even disregard the arrangement of the rimes in deciding what the meter really is. For example, Shelley chose to write this as six lines: —

> Arethusa arose
> From her couch of snows
> In the Acroceraunian mountains, —
> From cloud and from crag,
> With many a jag
> Shepherding her bright fountains.

And Scott chose to write this as four lines: —

> Who spilleth life, shall forfeit life,
> So bid my lord believe;
> That lawless love is guilt above,
> This awful sign receive.

While Macaulay was satisfied to set this down as only two lines: —

> Now glory to the Lord of Hosts, from whom all glories are;
> And glory to our sovereign liege, King Henry of Navarre.

But however different these three on the printed page may appear to the eye, the ear recognizes them at once as identical. They are all three of the iambic heptameter, modulated by occasional anapests. And when we translate them into symbols we see that Shelley's

$$\breve{}\breve{}- \mid \breve{}\breve{}-$$
$$\breve{}\breve{}- \mid \breve{}-$$
$$\breve{}\breve{}- \mid \breve{}\breve{}- \mid \breve{}\breve{}- \mid \breve{}$$
$$\breve{}- \mid \breve{}\breve{}-$$
$$\breve{}- \mid \breve{}\breve{}-$$
$$-\breve{} \mid \breve{}- \mid \breve{}- \mid \breve{}$$

and Scott's

$$\breve{}- \mid \breve{}- \mid \breve{}- \mid \breve{}-$$
$$\breve{}- \mid \breve{}- \mid \breve{}-$$
$$\breve{}- \mid \breve{}- \mid \breve{}- \mid \breve{}-$$
$$\breve{}- \mid \breve{}- \mid \breve{}-$$

are really the same as Macaulay's

```
∪ – | ∪ – | ∪ – | ∪ – | ∪ – | ∪ – | ∪ –
∪ – | ∪ – | ∪ – | ∪∪ – | ∪ – | ∪ – | ∪ –
```

The differing typographical presentations and the differing rime-schemes may be disregarded since the effect upon the ear is identical in all three cases. Other examples of the advisability of disregarding the way in which the poet may have written his lines have been given in the second chapter, — from Poe's " For Annie " and from Byron's " Bride of Abydos." In all these poems, the way in which the poet has preferred to present these lines to the eye of the reader is not really the way in which he composed them for his own ear and for the ears of his future readers.

There is no limit to the number of feet which may be included in a single line, except in so far as excessive length may impose an undue burden on the ear and make it more difficult to carry the tune. Swinburne wrote a ballade in anapestic hexameter : —

There are cliffs to be climbed on land, there are ways to be
    trodden and ridden ; but we
Strike out from the shore as the heart invites and beseeches,
    athirst for the foam.

And once he even ventured on a long-drawn anapestic octameter, which called for twenty-four syllables in every line : —

Ere frost-flower and snow-blossom faded and fell, and the
    splendor of winter had passed out of sight,
The ways of the woodland were fairer and stranger than dreams
    that fulfil us in sleep with delight.

Richard Hovey essayed a line of nine iambics: ——

Let him await Another who shall come and sit in the Siege
    Perilous,
And live. In Him shall he behold how light can look in dark-
    ness and forgive.

Yet in practice the poets have rarely chosen to employ any line longer than the heptameter; and the
pentameter has been used more often than any other
measure; it is the meter of the heroic couplet, of blank
verse and of the sonnet. The reason for the popularity
of these meters is physiological; the pentameter and
the heptameter adjust themselves to the normal
breathing and are delivered by the voice, easily and
without conscious effort. The tetrameter exactly ac-
cords with the rate of breathing of the average man;
and this accounts for its "fatal facility."

This principle was worked out by Oliver Wendell
Holmes in his suggestive paper on the "Physiology
of Versification." The average man breathes twenty
times a minute; and in a minute the average man
will read aloud about twenty lines of "Hiawatha"
or of "Marmion"; that is to say, he will probably
pronounce one line to each expiration of the breath,
taking advantage of the pause at its close to breathe
in again. "The only effort required is that of vocal-
izing and articulating; the breathing takes care of
itself, not even demanding a thought except where
the sense may require a pause in the middle of a line.
The very fault found with these octosyllabic lines is
that they slip away too fluently, and run easily into a
monotonous singsong." We need only recite a brief
passage from either Scott's poem or Longfellow's to

assure ourselves that this adverse criticism is well
founded. Here is an extract from " Marmion " : —

> Thin curling in the morning air,
> The wreaths of failing smoke declare
> To embers now the brands decayed,
> Where the night-watch their fires had made.
> They saw, slow rolling on the plain,
> Full many a baggage-cart and wain,
> And dire artillery's clumsy car,
> By sluggish oxen tugged to war.

In Longfellow's " Hiawatha," the singsong effect
is probably intensified by the trochaic rhythm and
also to some slight extent by the deliberate repetitions : —

> But the fearless Hiawatha
> Heeded not her woman's warning ;
> Forth he strode into the forest,
> At each stride a mile he measured ;
> Lurid seemed the sky above him,
> Lurid seemed the earth beneath him,
> Hot and close the air around him,
> Filled with smoke and fiery vapors,
> As of burning woods and prairies,
> For his heart was hot within him,
> Like a living coal his heart was.

The iambic pentameter line, so Holmes declared,
will probably be read at the rate of about fourteen
lines a minute. "If a breath is allowed to each line the
respiration will be longer and slower than natural, and
a sense of effort and fatigue will soon be the consequence "; but this is rarely felt because there is a
break or a pause generally about the middle of the
line, which serves as a breathing-place. "This gives a
degree of relief, but its management requires care in
reading." Probably the immense popularity of the

pentameter is in part due to the fact that it is not so easy that it slips into singsong, and in part that it can be adjusted readily to the natural processes of the vocal apparatus.

The iambic heptameter, which is the "common meter" of the hymn-books and the meter of most of the ballads, and which is perhaps the most popular of English meters after the pentameter, is also satisfactory from a physiological point of view, since the fourteen syllables of the normal iambic line subdivide themselves into sections of eight and six, allowing a longer pause at the end of the line. Even when a fair share of anapests has been substituted here and there for the normal iambs, there are still not more syllables in the section than can readily be uttered by a single breath, as can be observed by reading aloud the quotations from Shelley, Scott and Macaulay.

Since verse is written to be spoken and to be heard, to be read aloud and not merely to be read, it is not difficult to see why the iambic hexameter has never been a favorite with the poets of our language. Dr. Holmes declared that it was "almost intolerable, from its essentially unphysiological character. One can read the ten-syllable line in a single expiration without any considerable effort. One instinctively divides the fourteen-syllable line so as to accommodate it to the respiratory rhythm. But the twelve-syllable line is too much for one expiration and not enough for two." Here are a few lines from Drayton's "Polyolbion" which will serve to show the justice of these remarks: —

The naiads and the nymphs extremely overjoyed,
And on the winding banks all busily employed,

Upon this joyful day, some dainty chaplets twine:
Some others chosen out, with fingers neat and fine,
Brave diadems do make ; some baldrics up do bind :
Some garlands : and to some the nosegays were assigned.

Browning chose iambic hexameter for his " Fifine at the Fair " ; and perhaps the unfortunate meter is one reason why this poem has never attained an equal popularity with many of his other poems.

Dr. Holmes asserted that this critical test of poetry by the stop-watch, and its classification according to its harmonizing more or less exactly with a great vital function, is exactly scientific ; but he warned us that we must not overlook the personal equation. A man " of ample chest and of quiet temperament may breathe habitually only fourteen times a minute, and find the iambic pentameter to correspond with his respiratory rhythm, and thus easier than any other for him to read. A person of narrower frame and more nervous habit may breathe oftener than twenty times in a minute, and find the seven-syllable verse of Dyer's ' Grongar Hill ' fits his respiration better than " the tetrameter of Scott and Longfellow. In childhood, before we have attained to the full-lunged power of our maturity and when our breathing is quicker than it is later, we find the briefer meters easiest ; and perhaps this accounts for the frequency of dimeter and of trimeter in our nursery-rimes : —

Goosey, goosey, gander,
Where do you wander ?

and

Little Miss Muffet
Sat on a tuffet
Eating her curds and whey.

As these nursery-rimes are artfully adjusted to the undeveloped breathing apparatus of the very young, so the patriotic chants of the several nations are never too long in meter, being gaged to the average of human respiration, as we perceive when we consider " Yankee Doodle " and " God Save the King," the " Marseillaise " and " What is the German Fatherland?" "Nothing in poetry," Dr. Holmes insisted, " is widely popular that is not calculated with strict reference to the respiratory function." And then he made the striking suggestion that " the unconscious adaptation of voluntary life to the organic rhythm is perhaps a more pervading fact than we have been in the habit of considering it. One can hardly doubt that Spenser breathed habitually more slowly than Prior, and that Anacreon had a quicker respiration than Homer. And this difference, which we conjecture from their rhythmical instincts, if our conjecture is true, probably, almost certainly, characterized all their vital movements." It would be interesting to push this suggestion further and to consider how much light the favorite meters of Tennyson and of Browning, of Swinburne and of Longfellow, of Whitman and of Kipling, may shed on their physiological organization. A French student of versification has insisted that the hexameter of the Greeks and Latins and the so-called alexandrine of the French (iambic hexameter) mark the limit of single expiration of the human voice; and that therefore no longer line can ever succeed in winning a wide popularity.

When the poet has chosen his meter and when he has established in our ears the expectancy proper to it, he is free to vary the strict monotony of the line, by additions, by substitutions, by suppressions, and by shifting his central pause. He may do these things at his pleasure for our pleasure, within the sole restriction that he must not disappoint our ear of its expectancy. He must not violently force us to read any line unnaturally, by misplacing a normal accent or by unduly prolonging a syllable. He must so compose that when we read for the meaning we are reading also for the meter. Emerson declared that it was the secret of Shakspere's verse "that the thought constructs the tune, so that reading for the sense will best bring out the rhythm." If a line satisfies the ear, when it is read naturally with full regard to its content, then it is a good line prosodically ; since there can be no other test. If it fails to satisfy the ear, as we read it aloud, then the fault might be ours, for we may have read it wrong ; but on the other hand the fault might be the poet's, for he may not have been able to impose on us the rhythmic sequence he intended. It is the poet's duty not only to feel his rhythm himself, but so to transmit it that we cannot fail to feel it also. If he does not succeed in this, he violates the principle of Economy of Attention ; he interrupts the current of sympathy ; he throws us off the track. Herbert Spencer notes that we are put out by halting versification : " Much as at the bottom of a flight of stairs, a step more or less than we counted upon gives us a shock, so, too, does a misplaced accent, or a supernumerary syllable," in the wrong place. And this is in accord with the advice given by Boileau in his " Art of Poetry " : —

> Write what your reader may be pleased to hear,
> And for the measure have a careful ear :

On easy numbers fix your happy choice;
Of jarring sounds avoid the odious noise;
The fullest verse, and the most labored sense —
Displease us if the ear once take offence.

We have seen already that in the iambic pentameter the poet is at liberty to add a short syllable at
the end of his line : —

To be, or not to be: that is the question.

We have seen also that he can substitute a trochee
for an iambus in the opening foot : —

Ō fŏr a Muse of fire, that would ascend,

or in almost any other foot in the line : —

A kingdom for a stage, prīncĕs to act.

He may also substitute a spondee for an iambus, as
Milton often does : —

O'er bog or steep, through strait, rōūgh, dēnse, or rare,
With head, hānds, wīngs or feet, pursues his way ;
And swims, or sinks, or wades, or creeps, or flies.

So strongly accentual is our language that two consecutive long syllables in any iambic line are likely to be
read as an iambus by our unconscious shortening of
the first of the two or by our unconscious lengthening
of the second. And yet in these lines of Milton's it is
almost impossible not to feel that the foot is really a
spondee, infrequent and unnatural as that foot may be
in English verse. If we read for the meaning only,
without in any way forcing the rhythm, *rough* and
dense in the first line and *hands* and *wings* in the
second, are long syllables, of equal weight. Milton is
ever a marvelous metrist, bending sounds to do his

bidding as no other English poet has ever been able to do.

Milton, Pope and Tennyson are the three English poets whose artistry in verse is most certain. Their theories of poetry were very different; but each of them was a deliberate and conscious artificer. "Again and again," wrote Wordsworth in a letter, "I must repeat that the composition of verse is infinitely more of an art than men are prepared to believe, and absolute success in it depends upon innumerable minutiæ. . . . Milton talks of pouring easy his unpremeditated verse. It would be odious and untrue to say there is anything like cant in this, but it is not true to the letter and tends to mislead. I could point out five hundred passages in Milton upon which labor has been bestowed." In nothing is Milton's art more obvious than in the skill with which he modulates his lines, keeping the tune intact for the ear of the listener and yet delighting this ear by the delicately chosen variations of accent. Without breaking his rhythm he can substitute trochees and spondees for iambs; and he can change the march of his line to accommodate it more expressively to his thought, making the sound echo the sense. There is no English poet whose versification better repays the most careful study; and it is wonderful to discover how he can achieve massive effects by apparently simple devices. His verse justifies itself to the ear; but it is so dextrously adapted to the ear that it has often puzzled the eyes of the theorists who have sought to apply an arbitrary method of syllable-counting, into which Milton's large and free lines frequently fail to fit.

While Milton is the mighty master, the verse of

many other poets rewards analysis. Especially to be
noted is the pleasure the poet gives our ears when he
modifies his tempo to accord with a change in the
thought he is expressing. Emerson, for example, is often
careless in his versification, not bestowing on it the
unhasting and unresting attention which characterizes
Milton's composition. Yet, on occasion, Emerson attains to a lofty level of lyric beauty : —

> Thou canst not wave thy staff in air,
> Or dip thy paddle in the lake,
> Bŭt ĭt cārves the bow of beauty there,
> Aňd thĕ rĭppleš iň rīme the oar forsake.

A part of the ease and melody of the last line of this
quatrain is the result of the substitution of the two
lighter anapests for the more sedate and stately iambs.
There are fourteen feet in the quatrain and all but
three are emphatically iambic. The three anapests
occur at exactly the right intervals to lighten the
movement most felicitously. And consider also this
quatrain of Browning's : —

> Ōvĕr the sea our galleys went,
> With cleaving prows in order brave,
> Tŏ ă spēeding wind and ă bōunding wave,
> A gallant armament.

Something of the buoyancy of the first line is due
to the substitution of a trochee for an iambus in the
first foot; and the two anapests in the third line, so a
critic has declared, "give life and rapidity to the motion
which the first two lines picture as vigorous and steady."
The return to strict iambics in the final line "restores
the original impression and enriches it with the added
notion of security."

Attention has been called in the preceding chapter to the fact that the short syllables of a foot may be omitted at the beginning of a line or at the end or even within the line. It may be well to adduce other examples. Especially in dactylic rhythm either one or both of the short syllables at the ends of the lines may be suppressed with the result of enriching the verse by a variety which pleases the ear. We may take, for example, this stanza of Hood's " Bridge of Sighs," written in dactylic dimeter:—

> One more Unfortunate,
>   Weary of breath, [◡ ◡]
> Rashly importunate,
>   Gone to her death ! [◡ ◡]
> Take her up tenderly,
>   Lift her with care ; [◡ ◡]
> Fashioned so slenderly,
>   Young, and so fair ! [◡ ◡]

The suppression of the two final short syllables which is only casual in Hood's poem may be consistent, as in this stanza of Austin Dobson's " On a Fan," written in dactylic trimeter:—

> Ah, but things more than polite [◡ ◡]
>   Hung on this toy, *voyez-vous !* [◡ ◡]
> Matters of state and of might, [◡ ◡]
>   Things that great ministers do ; [◡ ◡]
>   Things that, may be, overthrew [◡ ◡]
> Those in whose brains they began ; [◡ ◡]
>   Here was the sign and the cue, — [◡ ◡]
> This was the Pompadour's fan ! [◡ ◡]

Although the short syllables of the iambus and of the dactyl are those which are most likely to be suppressed, sometimes even the long syllable of the iambus may be omitted, its place being taken by an equivalent

rest. Of this as good an example as any may be found
in one of Macaulay's stirring ballads: —

And how can man die better [-] than facing fearful odds,
For the ashes of his fathers, and the temples of his gods ?

Another example, from Austin Dobson, shows the
suppression of the long syllable in three lines out of
four: —

> The ladies of St. James's [-]
>   Go swinging to the play ;
> Their footmen run before them, [-]
>   With a " Stand by ! Clear the way ! "
> But Phyllida, my Phyllida !
>   She takes her buckled shoon,
> When we go out a-courting [-]
>   Beneath the harvest-moon.

One frequently employed method of lightening verse
is to add a short syllable at the end of an iambic line,
thereby permitting a double rime, which relieves the
monotony of the emphatic termination of the ordinary
iamb. Sometimes this added syllable is at the end of
the first and third lines, as in this stanza of Pea-
cock's "Love and Age": —

> You grew a lovely roseate maiden,
>   And still our early love was strong ;
> Still with no care our days were laden,
>   They glided joyously along;
> And I did love you very dearly —
>   How dearly, words want power to show;
> I thought your heart was touched as nearly ;
>   But that was fifty years ago.

Or the extra syllable which makes the double rime
may be appended to the second and fourth lines, as in
this stanza of Praed's " Belle of the Ball-room ": —

She smiled on many, just for fun, —
   I knew that there was nothing in it !
I was the first — the only one
   Her heart had thought of for a minute, —
I knew it, for she had told me so,
   In phrase which was divinely molded;
She wrote a charming hand, — and oh !
   How sweetly all her notes were folded !

The methods of avoiding monotony most often to be observed are the use of double and treble rimes, the shifting of the pause which occurs toward the middle of a line and the interchange of one foot for another at exactly that point in the line where the substitution helps to bring out the thought. Sometimes — as we have already seen — these substitutions may be so free and so frequent that we are almost in doubt whether a rhythm is really iambic or anapestic, — as in this stanza from a ballad of Scott's : —

Oh ! I lo'e weel my Charlie's name,
   Though some there be that abhor him;
But oh ! to see the deil gang hame
   Wi' a' the whigs before him !
[ᴗᴗ] Over the water, and over the sea,
   And over the water to Charlie;
Come weal, come wo, we 'll gather and go,
   And live and die with Charlie.

Here there is no question but that the result is pleasing to the ear ; and while we may choose to mark off the iambs and the anapests for our own information, their intermingling matters little. As King James declared more than three centuries ago, " your ear must be the only judge and discerner." What the poet needs above all else is a natural ear for the tunes of verse. Without this, he will unceasingly blunder and annoy us with the harshness of his lines. With it, he has the root of the matter in him; and he can then go forward resolutely to acquire an added skill in handling the subtleties of metrical technic. "For if Nature be not the chief worker in this art," to quote from King James once more, "rules will be but a band to Nature, and will make you within a short space weary of the whole art; whereas if Nature be chief and bent to it, rules will be a help and staff to Nature."

CHAPTER IV

RIME

> Whate'er you write of, pleasant or sublime,
> Always let sense accompany your rime;
> Falsely they seem each other to oppose, —
> Rime must be made with reason's law to close;
> And when to conquer her you bend your force,
> The mind will triumph in the noble cause;
> To reason's yoke she quickly will incline,
> Which, far from hurting, renders her divine.
>
> BOILEAU, *Art of Poetry* (as translated by Soame).

IN all modern languages poetry is generally rimed; and even in English, in spite of our possession of blank verse, a metrical instrument of surpassing power and variety, most of our verse is in rime. Although there is not yet any absolute agreement upon its rules, we may venture to define rime in English as an identity of the vowel-sound in the last long foot and of all the sounds that follow it, preceded by a difference in the consonant sound that comes before this final long vowel. Thus *charm* and *alarm* are rimes, *charming* and *alarming*, *charmingly* and *alarmingly*. There must be a distinct difference in the consonant sound that precedes; *cent* and *descent*, *meant* and *lament* are not generally accepted in English as good rimes. Although it would not be difficult to cite from distinguished poets examples of the effort to pass off as rimes pairs of words in which there is no change in the consonant preceding the vowel of the final long syllable, there is an almost unanimous opinion that this is contrary to the best traditions of English poetry. Yet it is only fair to note that Lowell links *recompense* and *expense*, Austin Dobson unites *Mentor* and *tormentor*, Byron ties together *philanthropic* and *misanthropic*. It may be well to mention also that the principle that the accord shall be on the vowel of the final long syllable is violated by Walt Whitman who mates *exulting* and *daring*, *crowding* and *turning*, and by Poe who conjoins *dead* and *tenanted*.

A rime on one syllable only, *turn* and *discern*, is called single, or masculine. A rime on two syllables, *turning* and *discerning*, is called double, or feminine. A rime on three syllables, *beautiful* and *dutiful*, is called triple.

A single rime is the natural termination of iambic and of anapestic rhythms : —

> Here was a type of the true elder race,
> And one of Plutarch's men talked with us face to face;

and

> The Assyrian came down like a wolf on the fold ;
> His cohorts were gleaming in silver and gold.

The double rime is the natural termination of trochaic rhythms : —

> And the people — ah, the people,
> They that dwell up in the steeple.

And the triple is the natural termination of dactylic rhythms : —

> Ere her limbs frigidly
> Stiffen too rigidly.

But the iambic and anapestic rhythms may have an

added short syllable, and in this case they have double rimes: —

> The time I've lost in wooing,
> In watching and pursuing;

and

> Let the wind take the green and the gray leăf
> Cast forth without fruit upon air ;
> Take rose-leaf and vine-leaf and bay-leăf
> Blown loose from the hair.

In like manner the short syllable may be dropped at the end of a trochaic rhythm, and then we have a single rime : —

> Lives of great men all remind us
> We can make our lives sublime, [◡]
> And departing leave behind us
> Footprints on the sands of time. [◡]

And in a dactylic rhythm either one or both of the short syllables at the end of the line may be omitted, with the result that in the first case we have a double rime and in the second a single rime: —

> Still, for all slips of hers,
> One of Eve's family —
> Wipe those poor lips of hers
> Oozing so clammily.
> Loop up her tresses [◡]
> Escaped from the comb, [◡ ◡]
> Whilst wonderment guesses [◡]
> Where was her home ? [◡ ◡]

Since poetry must be considered always as something to be said or sung, there should be absolute identity of sound in the vowels and consonants which make up a rime. The ear is the judge, not the eye, and therefore identity of spelling is not sufficient. *Height* does not rime with *eight ;* but it does rime with

sight, bite, indict and *proselyte. One* does not rime
with *gone* or with *tone* or with *shone ;* but it does
rime with *son* and with *dun. Tomb* is no rime for
comb or *bomb* or *rhomb ;* but it mates perfectly with
doom and *spume* and *rheum.* Our English orthography is chaotic in its disregard of the proper phonetic
representation of the sounds of our language ; and
therefore it is the worst of guides for the poet who
seeks to delight our ears. If he is tempted to link together two words which lack the needful identity of
sound, whether they are or are not identical in spelling,
he violates at once the principle of Economy of Attention. He fails to provide the listeners with the specific
pleasure he has led them to anticipate. He has with-
drawn their interest for a moment from his meaning
to his machinery. While they are asking themselves
whether what he has given them was meant for a
rime or not, and whether it really is a rime, the
current of their sympathy is cut off. He may feel that
he is forced by the paucity of pairing words at his
command to take the nearest approach to a rime
that he can lay his hand on ; but he does this at his
peril. The listeners may forgive this, if the poem as a
whole appeals to them and pleases them ; but none the
less are they likely to feel that this false rime is a
blemish, just as they would resent his forcing the accent upon some syllable where it does not naturally
belong. A false rime affects a sensitive ear like a
false note in music.

It may be that this insistence upon rigid identity
of sound is a counsel of perfection, and that it sets
up too exalted a standard. And it is a fact that many
poets of high distinction have on occasion fallen from

grace and descended to marry pairs of words which protested more or less violently against the wedding. Poe linked *valleys* and *palace;* Mrs. Browning conjoined *remember* and *chamber;* Bret Harte tied together *rarest* and *heiress;* Whittier united *Eva* and *give her;* Kipling weds *abroad* and *lord;* Browning coupled *windows* and *Hindus,* as well as *spider* and *consider;* Keats combined *critics* and *prickets;* Tennyson put together *pair* and *her;* and Emerson went so far as to join in matrimony *woodpecker* and *hear.*

It cannot be denied that these poets are great in their several degrees in spite of these atrocious rimes, more or less resented by every one who has a sensitive ear for the melody of verse. The moment we admit that the appeal of poetry is primarily to the ear, we must confess that " a rime to the eye " is an absurdity. Rime is a uniformity of sound; and as the younger Tom Hood aptly remarked, " You do not match colors by the nose or sounds by the eye."

There is something to be said, however, in behalf of certain inadequate rimes which are traditional, which have been employed by poets in every generation, and which may be said to be accepted by convention. These are pairs of words like *ever* and *river,* *shadow* and *meadow,* *heaven* and *even,* *love* and *prove.* Of course, they are not really rimes at all; and yet unless some such pairing is allowed, *ever* and *shadow,* *heaven* and *love* are likely to go often unmarried, because of the lack of fit mates in our language for these words which are a necessary part of the poet's vocabulary. The only exact rimes to *love* are *glove* and *dove, above* and *shove;* and the only exact rimes to *heaven* are *leaven* and *seven* and *eleven.* Now *shove* is not a fit bride for *love ;* and in serious verse it is not often that *heaven* will mate itself spontaneously either with *seven* or *eleven.* There is a certain cogency in the plea that the union of *shadow* and *meadow* and these other marriages of reason have been " legitimated by custom," as has been claimed by one writer, who asserted that " *river* has just got to rime with *ever* or the game cannot be played." Yet it might be urged in rebuttal that this plea could be advanced only by a lover of poetry long familiarized with the custom he defends, and that young readers, generation after generation, will feel a certain shock of dissatisfaction the first time these unhappy marriages are announced to them. The one safe rule is to abide by the rigor of the game and to avoid anything which may offend the ear of any one.

For if we once abandon the belief that rimes ought to be rigorously exact to the ear of the listener, if we once accept any heresy of "allowable rimes," then we have lost the true faith and we have parted with the sole compass that can guide us. At first we may wink at the minor infraction of the letter of the law and accept the tying together of *ever* and *river*, for example, and of *love* and *prove ;* and then we shall find it harder to resist the insidious claim of the " rime to the eye," which would permit the mating of *eight* and *sleight.* Having gone so far on the wrong road, there is little to prevent us from ending our unfortunate journey in a state of mind which might at last allow us to tolerate the pairing of *bean* and *ocean* and of *plague* and *ague*, because of their identity of orthography. That way madness lies. And we shall do well to keep to the strait and narrow path. " A barbarous phrase," so Ben Jonson once declared, and perhaps he would have included a barbarous rime, "hath often made me out of love with a good sense, and doubtful writing hath wracked me beyond my patience."

When we set up the test of exact repetition of sound, we should be willing to abide by it, and to be satisfied with a rime which is perfect in our ordinary pronunciation, not insisting upon pedantic precision of speech. Our unfortunate spelling is continually suggesting to us that it is our duty to strive for an exactness of articulation which we none of us attain and which indeed we could hardly achieve without an absurd over-insistence on trifles. For example, Tennyson has been censured for riming *flower* and *hour* on the theory that *flower* is a dissyllable and *hour* a monosyllable. Now, whether either or both of these words can be called monosyllabic or dissyllabic is beside the question, since the average man of cultivated speech pronounces them in such manner that they rime perfectly.

Swinburne has linked *riot* and *quiet* : —

> Here, where the world is *quiet*,
> Here, where all trouble seems
> Dead winds' and spent waves' *riot*,
> In doubtful dream of dreams.

To the eye *quiet* and *riot* seem to differ in the vowel-sound ; but in the ear both of them take an obscure sound for which we have no exact symbol in our alphabet. This same obscure sound occurs again in Tennyson's riming of *Devon* and *Heaven ;* and any objection to this may be dismissed as merely pedantic purism.

Perhaps Browning was a little too colloquial when he chose to rime *barret* and *parrot:* —

> Margheritone of Arezzo,
> With the grave-clothes garb and swaddling *barret,*
> Why purse up mouth and beak in a pet so,
> You bald old saturnine poll-clawed *parrot?*

Barret is an unusual word, an anglicization of the Italian *barretta,* and some of us would be inclined to give it a sharp *e,* like that in *let,* whereas the *o* in parrot has another obscure sound in normal speech, a sound which, whatever it is, is certainly not identical with the *e* in *let.* In the same poem Browning undertakes to rime *scaffold* with *baffled:* —

> Shall I be alive that morning the *scaffold*
> Is broken away, and the long-pent fire,
> Like the golden hope of the world, *unbaffled*
> Springs from its sleep, and up goes the spire?

Here again it is a question as to exactly what our normal pronunciation is. Do we really sound the *o* in *scaffold* or do we so obscure it that the word is a fit mate for *baffled?* As to this, opinions will undoubtedly differ; and if this is the case, Browning has risked the possibility of diverting our attention from his story to his rime. The principle to be borne in mind always is that rime should seem natural and easy, that it should appear absolutely effortless, and even inevitable. It should resemble the attire of a well-bred woman, or the style of a strong writer, in that it never attracts attention to itself. This principle Browning seems to have violated when he rimes *mistress* and *this tress:* —

> Nay but you, who do not love her,
>   Is she not pure gold, my *mistress?*
> Holds earth aught — speak truth — above her ?
>   Aught like this tress, all, and *this tress.*

Here we may detect a certain forcing of the words for the sake of the rime; and the same strain is to be observed in a stanza of Tennyson's : —

> Came wet-shod alder from the wave,
>   Came yews, a dismal *cotery ;*
> Each plucked his one foot from the grave,
>   Pousseting with a *sloe-tree.*

Especially to be avoided is any rime which suggests vulgarity of pronunciation. When Holmes links *Elizas* and *Advertisers*, we cannot help wondering whether he was in the habit of pronouncing the former *Elizers ;* and when Whittier rimes *Eva* with *receive her*, we feel that this is possible only to one who is willing to pronounce *Eva* as though it was *eever.* This same unfortunate slip of taste was made by Mrs. Browning : —

> Now grant my ship some smooth haven *win her ;*
> I follow Statius first, and then *Corinna.*

Browning himself once rimed *I* and *enjoy*, which might tempt a hostile critic to suggest that the poet was in the habit of consorting with Yankee rustics, some of whom still say *enjy.* Wordsworth, who insisted that the vocabulary of everyday life should serve as the diction of poetry, once so far forgot himself as to rime *brethren* with *tethering.* The dropping of the final *g* of the present participle is not uncommon in literary circles in London to-day ; and yet it has a flavor of rusticity. It suggests not the poet careful of his utterance, but the villager, careless of his speech. To those who are in the habit of sounding the final *g* in words ending with *ing*, this dropping of the *g* is distinctly offensive. It is an annoying vulgarism, wholly out of place in poetry of serious intent. Yet it may be found again and again in any anthology of the British poets of the nineteenth century, although it is far less frequent in American verse. Scott puts together *Hevellyn* and *yelling;* Rossetti has *laughing* and *half in;* and Wordsworth descends to *coming* and *omen* — which is as inexcusable as *brethren* and *tethering*. Poe protested against the length of the license Mrs. Browning allowed herself in the vain effort to conjoin *Eden* and *succeeding, taming* and *overcame him, coming* and *woman, children* and *bewildering*.

Of course, the dropping of the final *g* is perfectly proper in dialect verse, wherein the poet has proposed to reproduce the exact pronunciation of the uneducated. And it is not out of place in broadly comic verse, — although even here it would be better to indicate the intended pronunciation to the reader's eye by substituting an apostrophe for the final *g* which is not to be spoken, — *invitin'* and *come right in*, for example. Possibly some of us would make this correction for ourselves when we read aloud the lilting lyric in praise of the Bells of Shandon,

> That sound so grand on
> The pleasant waters
> Of the river Lee,

and we might almost attempt an Irish brogue, so convincingly Hibernian is the tone of the poem: —

I 've heard bells *tollin'*
Old Adrian's *mole in*,
Their thunder *rollin'*
    From the *Vatican*.
And cymbals glorious
Swinging uproarious
In the gorgeous turrets
    Of Notre *Dame*.

Here we are asked to receive the final syllable of *Vatican* as a rime to *Dame*. There is no need to inquire whether the *a* in *can* and the *a* in *Dame* are properly mated, for what is most obvious is that the first word ends with the sound of *n* and the second with the sound of *m*. And earlier in the same lyric we find

Those Shandon bells
Whose sounds so *wild would*
In the days of *childhood*
Fling round my cradle
Their magic spells.

Here we are asked to receive as a double rime *wild would* and *childhood*, in spite of the substitution of an *h* for a *w* in the final short syllable of the second line. Apparently the lyrist was satisfied by the actual identity of the vowel-sound and was careless of the consonants that followed it. Strictly speaking, this is not rime but assonance, that is, identity of the long vowel of the final foot with liberty to modify the consonant at will. The use of assonance instead of rime is of high antiquity; we can find it in a proverbial couplet like

See a pin and pick it *up*
All day long you 'll have good *luck*.

We can discover it frequently in nursery-rimes : —

> Leave them *alone*,
> And they will come *home*.

And again : —

> Little Tommy *Tucker*,
> Singing for his *supper*,
> What shall he have ?
> Brown bread and *butter*.

It is to be found also in the traditional bacchanalian lyric which begs the landlord to fill the flowing bowl, and which asks us to accept *over* as a rime for *October*.

We can observe it even in Shakspere, in the "Comedy of Errors" : —

> So thou, who hast no unkind mate to *grieve thee*,
> With urging helpless patience would *relieve me*.

And again in a play which is generally attributed to Shakspere, in "Pericles," in the opening couplet of the speech of Gower as *Prologue :* —

> To sing a song that old was *sung*,
> From ashes ancient Gower is *come*.

In one sonnet Shakspere matches *open* and *broken*, and in another *remembered* and *tendered*.

We can find it in Scott : —

> Heaven send it happy dew,
> Earth lend it sap anew.

We can note it again in Whittier's uniting *main land* and *train band*. But where it still flourishes freely is in the comic song of the violently funny musical song-piece. So long as the final long vowel gets

across the footlights boldly, neither the writers of the
words of the song nor the hearers seem to care whether
there is any kinship in the consonants. A satirist has
held these negligent rimesters up to scorn in a
parody of their own method: —

> There seems not to be a *man*
> In this comic opera *land*
> Who is mindful of a *rime ;*
> Anything, they say, is *fine.*
> Don't they sing of all the *happy*
> Days they spent in *Cincinnati?*
> And, with rare poetic *feeling,*
> Carol of a boyhood *fleeting ;*
> Lyric-writers, will you *answer*
> Where you get your rime for *transfer?*
> *Some* and *done* — and always *war*
> Makes the proper rime to *saw.*
> Can you think a rime to *pie-fork?*
> No, you cannot ? Well, it's *high talk.*

It is interesting to note that this primitive assonance, possibly of Celtic origin and surviving in
nursery-rime and street-lyric, is exact in mating its
vowels and slovenly in matching its consonants ; and
it is thus precisely the reverse of the so-called "allowable rimes," which poets of high literary pretension
have permitted themselves, *river* and *ever, shadow*
and *meadow,* in which the consonants are exactly
mated and the vowels are matched in more slovenly
fashion. The unliterary ear of the populace is satisfied if it can catch the repetition of the bold vowel,
while the sophisticated ear of the dilletant may even
find a certain perverted pleasure in a slight variation
of this vowel, accompanied by exact identity of the
consonants. Perhaps it is not going too far to suggest

that here the unsophisticated taste of the unpretending crowd is wiser than the overcultivated taste of the dilletants, since the vowel supplies the dominant carrying sound to a rime, and the identity of the vowel is therefore more important than the identity of the consonants. Of course, there is no really adequate rime which has not the double identity of vowel and of consonant.

Rime should be so exact as not to attract attention to itself, just as meter should not attract attention to itself. Rime and meter might be likened to the two rails along which the poet invites us to glide with him; and the more smoothly we move forward, the less we have occasion to consider the track itself, the better pleased we are, and the more completely can we bestow our interest upon the passengers in the car or upon the landscape glimpsed through the windows. Rime and meter must work together unobtrusively to this end. What Lowell said of meter is true also of rime, although in a less degree: " Meter, by its systematic and regular occurrence, gradually subjugates and tunes the senses of the hearer, as the wood of the violin arranges itself in sympathy with the vibration of the strings, and thus that predisposition to the proper emotion is accomplished which is essential to the purpose of the poet. You must not only expect, but you must expect in the right way; you must be magnetized beforehand in every fiber by your own sensibility in order that you may feel what and how you ought."

The principle here laid down by Lowell is often deliberately violated by Browning, in not a few of whose serious poems we find the poet consciously striving for ingenious and far-fetched rimes which attract attention to themselves and thereby more or less distract us. There is an obvious shock to our sensibility when we come to a couplet like this : —

> I, that have haunted the dim San *Spirito,*
> Patient on altar-step planting a *weary toe ;*

or to another like this : —

> Oh, what a face ! One by *fits eyed*
> Her and the horrible *pitside.*

Or to a quatrain like this : —

> Image the whole, then execute the parts —
> Fancy the *fabric*
> Quite, ere you build, ere steel strikes fire from quartz,
> Ere mortar *dab brick.*

These rimes are perfect, no doubt, but they are artificial. They are too clever, too ingenious, too witty, to be in keeping with the somber tone of the poems in which we find them. Browning's practice was condemned in advance by Coleridge, who asserted that " double and trisyllable rimes form a lower species of wit, and, attended to exclusively for their own sake, may become a source of momentary amusement." Here Coleridge seems to have gone a little too far, since Hood, for one, proved in the " Bridge of Sighs " that double and treble rimes may be employed effectively. The difference between Browning's use of these rimes and Hood's lies in this, that the latter employs natural rimes, instantly recognizable as ordinary words and evoking no start of surprise, whereas the former invents novel and arbitrary combinations which are continually compelling notice.

This witty ingenuity in devising unexpected rimes,

which appears out of place in serious poetry, is wholly
appropriate in comic verse, where we expect the writer
to amuse us with his unfailing cleverness. We find a
" source of momentary amusement " in the unexpected
matings which justify themselves in the " Ingoldsby
Legends " and in the " Fable for Critics." Humorous
verse of this kind gets part of its fun out of difficulty
vanquished ; and when we hear the troublesome syllables at the end of the first line of a couplet, we take
pleasure in guessing, or at least in wondering, how
the poet is going to satisfy us at the end of the second
line. Here the manner perhaps is almost as important
as the matter ; and the mere mechanism of the light
poem can be paraded without our losing any of its
less significant meaning. No one can help feeling the
fun in this couplet of Barham's : —

> There's Setebos storming because *Mephistopheles*
> Dashed in his face a whole cup of *coffee-lees*.

No one can help smiling at the wit in this couplet
of Byron's " Don Juan ": —

> O ye lords of ladies *intellectual*,
> Inform us truly, have they not *henpecked you all ?*

And every one must appreciate the affluence of
ingenuity which we discover in Lowell's " Fable for
Critics ": —

> Quite *irresistible*
> Like a man with eight trumps in his hand at a *whist-table*
> (I bethought me at first that the rime was *untwistable*,
> Though I might here have lugged in an allusion to *Cristabel*).

To get the full effect of this clever solving of a
self-imposed difficulty, the normal word should end
the first line and the artificial combination must fol-

low. This is a minor detail, of course, and it has not
always been kept in mind by luxuriant rimesters.
Barham, for example, disregarded it in this couplet:—

> Should it even set fire to the castle and *burn it, you're*
> Amply insured both for buildings and *furniture.*

And Browning frequently refused to consider it, as
in this couplet: —

> Here we get peace and *aghast I'm*
> Caught thinking war the true *pastime.*

And again in this quatrain: —

> Blue-black, lustrous, thick like *horsehairs,*
> — Can't I see his dead eye glow?
> Bright, as 't were a Barbary *corsair's?*
> (That is, if he 'd let it show!)

Perhaps it is not too much to say that in comic
verse it is permissible to violate accent, to play tricks
with meter or to alter orthography. There is an element of absurdity in Canning's deliberate splitting of
a word to make his rime : —

> Sun, moon, and thou, vain world, *adieu,*
>   That kings and priests are plotting in;
> Here doomed to starve on *water-gru-*
> el, never shall I see the *U-*
>   -niversity of Gottingen,
>   -niversity of Gottingen.

And this exaggerated device is carried a step farther
in " Lewis Carroll's " : —

> Who would not give all else for *two p-*
> -ennyworth only of beautiful *soup?*

We will forgive the humorous bard also if he
achieves his rime only by deliberate misspelling : —

> A stingy old man of *Malacca*,
> Who wore clothes of the thinnest *alpacca*,
>   Would remark with a groan:
>   "I've a match of my own;
> Will you lend me a pipe and *tobacca*?"

Thus far rime has been considered as terminal only, as an ornament at the end of a pair of lines. But it may also be internal, appearing within the lines, to give an added and unexpected pleasure to the ear. This internal rime is often quite distinct from the terminal rime that plays along the edges of the stanza. As satisfactory an example as any is this of Scott's:—

> There was *racing* and *chasing* on Cannobie Lee.

Or this of Swinburne's:—

> With changes of *gladness* and *sadness* that cheer and chide.

Or this of Swinburne's again:—

> From *afar* to the *star* that recedes, from anear to the wastes of the wild shore.

Or this of Poe's:—

> *Thrilled* me, *filled* me, with fantastic terror never felt before.

Internal rime is more elaborately employed in these lines of Kipling's "McAndrews' Hymn":—

> An' home again, the Rio run; it's no child's play to *go*
> Steamin' to bell for fourteen days o' *snow* an' *floe* an' *blow*—
> The bergs like kelpies overside that *girn* and *turn* an' shift
> Whaur grindin' like the Mills o' God, goes by the big South drift.

Here we have the independent internal rimes *girn* and *turn*, and also the internal rimes *snow* and *floe* that echo and intensify the terminal rimes *go* and *blow*.

Sometimes the internal rimes are in different lines, as in this couplet of Hood's: —

> *Mad* from life's history,
> *Glad* to death's mystery.

Or in this quatrain of Poe's "For Annie," which is metrically only two lines, although printed as four: —

> My tantalized spirit
> Here blandly reposes,
> *Forgetting*, or never
> *Regretting* its roses.

Or again in this quatrain of Locker-Lampson's "Serenade": —

> Arise then, and lazy
> Regrets from thee fling,
> For *sorrows* that hazy
> *To-morrows* may bring.

In the stanza of Rossetti's "Love's Nocturn" there is an internal rime in the last line which mates with three earlier rimes: —

> Poets' fancies all are *there:*
> There the elf-girls flood with wings
> Valleys full of plaintive *air;*
> There breathe perfumes; there in rings
> Whirl the foam-bewildered springs;
> Siren *there*,
> Winds her dizzy *hair* and sings.

Browning once employed the same internal rime three times in a single line: —

> And stood by the rose-wreathed gate. Alas,
> He loved sir, — used to meet:
> How *sad* and *bad* and *mad* it was —
> But then, how it was sweet!

And this same rime Swinburne chose to repeat four times in a single line of a ballade, and as this line was the refrain, it had to be repeated four times.

> Villon, our *sad bad glad mad* brother's name.

This does not commend itself to the ear; it sounds freakish and self-conscious. It is a glaring patch of wilful repetition which almost shrieks aloud for recognition. It is aggressively inartistic in a serious poem, although it might be tolerated and even accepted willingly in a comic poem. Probably we should not be moved to protest if we found it in a lilting lyric of humorous intent like that in which Eugene Field pretended to tell the " Truth about Horace " and in which we find this specimen of ultra-ingenuity in riming : —

> With a *massic-laden* ditty,
> And a *classic maiden* pretty,
> He painted up the city,
>   And Mæcenas paid the freight.

Even more complicated is the congeries of internal and external rimes in Joaquin Miller's " Lost Love" : —

> *Thatch* of *palm*, and *patch* of *clover*,
>   Breath of *balm*, in a field of brown;
> The clouds *blew* up and the birds *flew over*.
>   And I looked upward, but who looked down ?
>
> Who was true in the test that tried us ?
>   Who was it mocked ? Who now may mourn
> The *loss* of a love that a *cross* denied us,
>   With folded hands and a heart forlorn ?

Sometimes the poet shortens his lines and multiplies his rimes, external and internal, to correspond to the theme he is treating ; and sometimes he lengthens his lines and eschews internal rime altogether. Sometimes he contrasts his riming vowels in successive lines to give variety; and sometimes he may prefer to compose a whole poem on the same rime. This is what H. C. Bunner did in his humorously pathetic "One, Two, Three,"[1] in which he adds to the effect of this recurring terminal open vowel by leaving the alternate lines entirely without rime: —

It was an old, old, old, old lady,
  And a boy who was half-past three;
And the way that they played together
  Was beautiful to see.

She couldn't go running and jumping,
  And the boy, no more could he,
For he was a thin little fellow,
  With a thin little twisted knee.

They sat in the yellow sunlight,
  Out under the maple tree;
And the game that they played I'll tell you,
  Just as it was told to me.

It was Hide-and-go-Seek they were playing,
  Though you'd never have known it to be —
With an old, old, old, old lady,
  And a boy with a twisted knee.

The boy would bend his face down
  On his one little sound right knee,
And he'd guess where she was hiding,
  In guesses One, Two, Three!

"You are in the china closet!"
  He would cry and laugh with glee —
It wasn't the china closet:
  But he still had Two and Three.

[1] By permission from *Rowen, Second Crop Songs*, copyright, 1892, by Charles Scribner's Sons.

" You are up in papa's big bedroom,
      In the chest with the queer old key ! "
And she said: " You are warm and warmer,
      But you 're not quite right," said she.

" It can't be the little cupboard
      Where mamma's things used to be —
So it must be the clothes press, gran'ma,"
      And he found her with his Three.

Then she covered her face with her fingers,
      They were wrinkled and white and wee,
And she guessed where the boy was hiding,
      With a One and a Two and a Three.

And they had never stirred from their places,
      Right under the maple tree —
This old, old, old, old lady,
      And the boy with the lame little knee —
This dear, dear, dear old lady,
      And the boy who was half-past three.

This monotony of rime in the second and fourth
lines and this absence of rime in the first and third,
must not be ascribed to any poverty of resource on
the poet's part; we can hardly fail to perceive the
unity of tone which has been attained by these devices.
Bunner felt instinctively the riming effect that would
best suit his theme. The work of the poet must be
conscious to some extent, but it must also be largely
unconscious, the result of intuitive impulse. In " One,
Two, Three," the result proves that the poet was justified in his feeling that he would do well for once to
ring the changes on a single rime. But so much can
scarcely be said for Browning's " In the Metidja,"
where we find the same device less happily employed.

Dr. Holmes once declared that " when a word comes
up fit to end a line with, I can *feel* all the rimes in

the language that are fit to go with it without naming
them. I have tried them all so many times, I know
all the polygamous words, and all the monogamous
ones, and all the unmarrying ones — the whole lot
that have no mates — as soon as I hear their names
called. Sometimes I run over a string of rimes, but
generally speaking it is strange what a short list it is
of those that are good for anything. This is the pitiful side of all rimed verse. Take such words as *home*
and *world*. What can you do with *chrome* or *loam* or
gnome or *tome?* You have *dome, foam* and *roam*,
and not much more to use in your *pome*, as some of
our fellow countrymen call it. As for *world*, you know
that in all human probability somebody or something
will be *hurled* into it or out of it; its clouds may be
furled or its grass *impearled ;* possibly something may
be *whirled* or *curled* or *swirled*."

Here Dr. Holmes is following in the footsteps of
Pope, who asserted in his "Essay on Criticism" that
the poetasters have little variety in their verse : —

> While they ring round the same unvaried chimes,
> With sure returns of still expected rimes ;
> Where'er you find "the cooling western breeze,"
> In the next line it " whispers through the trees " :
> If crystal streams " with pleasing murmurs creep,"
> The reader's threatened — not in vain — with " sleep."

As yet no one has drawn up a complete catalog of
what Dr. Holmes called the monogamous rimes, those
which are fated to marry the same one again and again,
because there is absolutely no other mate for them
in our language, such as *anguish, blackness, mountain,* and *winter*. Of those words which are condemned to absolute celibacy, the old maids of poetry,

because there is not a single suitor for them, there must be two or three score at least. Here are some of them: *April, August, chimney, coif, crimson, forest, kiln, microcosm, month, nothing, open, poet, rhomb, scarce, scarf, silver, statue, squirrel, temple, widow, window.*

CHAPTER V

TONE-COLOR

We must not only choose our words for elegance, but for sound, — to perform which a mastery in the language is required; the poet must have a magazine of words, and have the art to manage his few vowels to the best advantage, that they may go the farther. He must also know the nature of the vowels — which are more sonorous, and which more soft and sweet — and so dispose them as his present occasions require. — DRYDEN: *Discourse on Epic Poetry.*

THE province of rime is twofold; its primary purpose is to emphasize the architecture of the poem, to indicate the ends of the lines, and to bind up the couplet, the quatrain or the longer stanza into a harmonious unit; and it has the secondary duty of pleasing the ear by its own sound. The ear finds unending delight in the melody which is the result of the adroit commingling of rhythm and rime so as not merely to carry the meaning of the poet, but also to intensify this meaning by the choice and by the contrast of the sounds which convey it. As Pope asserted in his "Essay on Criticism" : —

> True ease in writing comes from art, not chance,
> As those move easiest who have learned to dance.
> 'T is not enough no harshness gives offence,
> The sound must seem an echo to the sense.
> Soft is the strain when zephyr gently blows,
> And the smooth stream in smoother numbers flows ;
> But when loud surges lash the sounding shore,
> The hoarse rough verse should like the torrent roar ;
> When Ajax strives some rock's vast might to throw,
> The line, too, labors, and the words move slow.

Not so, when swift Camilla scours the plain,
Flies o'er the unbending corn, and skims along the main.

Here Pope artfully conformed his practice to his preaching. This adjustment of the sound to the sense can be accomplished by a variety of devices; and it is now generally known as tone-color. It will be noted that Pope was careful in the selection of his rimes, ever the most salient words. *Roar* and *shore*, *throw* and *slow*, at the ends of two of his couplets are exactly the right words to convey the desired impression.

But it is not enough that the rimes shall be well chosen; they ought to be varied one from the other. A quatrain or a stanza has a weak, thin effect upon the ear if the vowel-sounds in the several rimes are either identical or too clearly akin. For example, *sight* and *light*, *glide* and *abide* would not be satisfactory rimes in the same quatrain, since the ear would have to strain to distinguish sharply between the two pairs of words. "The result," as Lanier declared, "is like two contiguous shades of pink in a dress; one of the rimes will seem faded." This is a defect which we can discover even in Swinburne, who is a master metrist, commanding sounds at will to work his magic: —

Where shall we find her, how shall we *sing to her*,
    Fold our hands round her knees and *cling?*
O that man's heart were as fire and could *spring to her*,
    Fire, or the strength of the streams that *spring*.

Here, in fact, there is not only identity of rime, but identity of the actual riming word in the third and fourth lines, *spring to her* and *spring*.

Set this with its monotony beside another chorus from the same dramatic poem, "Atalanta in Calydon," and observe how much force is gained by the opposition of the vowel-sounds in the rimes: —

> Before the beginning of the years,
>   There came to the making of man
> Time, with a gift of tears;
>   Grief, with a glass that ran.
>
> .   .   .   .
>
> Strength without hands to smite;
>   Love that endures for a breath;
> Night, the shadow of light,
>   And life, the shadow of death.

Sometimes the tone-color is aided by shortening one of the two successive riming lines so that the echo of the sound is more immediate. Here is an example in single rime taken from Browning's " Love among the Ruins " : —

> Where the quiet-colored end of evening smiles
>   Miles and miles
> On the solitary pastures where our sheep
>   Half asleep
> Tinkle homeward through the twilight, stray or stop
>   As they crop.

And here is another example in double rime by Austin Dobson, written really in anapestic tetrameter, but so divided that it falls on our ears as alternating trimeter and monometer riming together, and gaining much of its buoyancy from the dexterity of its double rimes : —

> In our hearts is the Great One of Avon
>   Engraven,
> And we climb the cold summits once built on
>   By Milton.
> But at times not the air that is rarest
>   Is fairest ;

And we long in the valley to follow
    Apollo.
Then we drop from the heights atmospheric
    To Herrick,
Or we pour the Greek honey, grown blander,
    Of Landor;
Or our coziest nook in the shade is
    Where Praed is,
Or we toss the light bells of the mocker
    With Locker.
Oh, the song where not one of the Graces
    Tight-laces, —
Where we woo the sweet Muses not starchly,
    But archly, —
Where the verse, like a piper a-Maying,
    Comes playing —
And the rime is as gay as a dancer
    In answer, —
It will last till men weary of pleasure
    In measure !
It will last till men weary of laughter . . .
    And after !

In Browning's "Love among the Ruins," the rimes
were all single, and in Austin Dobson's "Jocosa Lyra,"
the rimes were all double; and in both cases this
decision was justified by the result. Often, however, an
admirable effect is attained by alternating single and
double rimes, with due regard to the rich contrast
of the vowel-sounds that are interlinked, as in this
stanza of Swinburne's: —

The songs of dead seasons, that wander
    On wings of articulate words;
Lost leaves that the shore-wind may squander,
    Light flocks of untamable birds;
Some sang to me dreaming in class time
    And truant in hand as in tongue;
For the youngest were born of boy's pastime,
    The eldest are young.

In this there is an added felicity in the unexpected
shortening of the final line of the stanza. Sometimes
however a poet gains an effect by ending his stanza
with a full line terminating in a bold single rime,
preceded by shorter lines with double rimes. Here
is an illustration from Longfellow's " Seaweed " which
exemplifies the superb mating of sound and sense : —

> When descends on the Atlantic
>   The gigantic
> Storm-wind of the equinox,
> Landward in his wrath he scourges
>   The toiling surges,
> Laden with seaweed from the rocks ;
>
> From Bermuda's reefs ; from edges
>   Of sunken ledges,
> In some far-off, bright Azore;
> From Bahama, and the dashing,
>   Silver-flashing
> Surges of San Salvador ;
>
> From the tumbling surf, that buries
>   The Orkneyan skerries,
> Answering the hoarse Hebrides ;
> And from wrecks of ships, and drifting
>   Spars, uplifting
> On the desolate, rainy seas ; —
>
> Ever drifting, drifting, drifting
>   On the shifting
> Currents of the restless main ;
> Till in sheltered coves, and reaches
>   Of sandy beaches,
> All have found repose again.

Often there is advantage in not having the riming words too closely alike; *light* and *slight*, for example, are perfectly proper rimes; but there would

be more variety if *light* were linked with *sight* and *slight* with *fright*. And yet sometimes the poet finds his effect in using rimes which have just this similarity, as in a stanza of the " Village Blacksmith " : —

> Week in, week out, from morn till night,
> You can hear his bellows *blow;*
> You can hear him swing his heavy sledge,
> With measured beat and *slow,*
> Like a sexton ringing the village bell,
> When the evening sun is *low.*

Perhaps something of the largeness of this stanza of Longfellow's is due to the triple repetition of the same riming vowel and to the absence of rime in the first, third and fifth lines, whereby he avoids a jingling jigginess.

As the skilful lyrist may rime all his lines or may refuse to rime some of them in accord with his instinct for the better way, and as he may commingle double and single rimes, placing each just where he feels that it will be most effective, so he varies his choice, now using words of a single syllable and then preferring ampler vocables. In Pope's day, there was a prejudice against the monosyllable which is voiced in a line of the " Essay on Criticism " : —

> And ten low words oft creep in one dull line.

But more than one poet has been able so to handle lines composed almost wholly of monosyllables that he has not only avoided dulness but attained to a massive dignity of utterance. Consider, for example, these lines of Milton's : —

> Tell me, how may I know Him, how adore,
> From whom I have that thus I move and live ?

And also this simple speech of Shakspere's where King John is suggesting the murder of Arthur : —

> Good friend, thou hast no cause to say so yet ;
> But thou shalt have ; and creep time ne'er so slow,
> Yet it shall come, for me to do thee good.
> I had a thing to say ; — but let it go.

Professor Corson, dwelling on Shakspere's mastery of the monosyllable, declared that " deep feeling of every kind expresses itself through, and indeed, attracts to itself, the monosyllabic words of the language ; not only because such words are, for the most part, Anglo-Saxon, and therefore more consecrated to feeling than to thought, but because the staccato effect which can be secured through them rather than through dissyllabic and trisyllabic words, subserves well the natural movement of impassioned speech."

Addison Alexander once composed two sonnets in which he set forth, and at the same time exemplified, the " Power of Short Words " : —

> Think not that strength lies in the big round word,
>   Or that the brief and plain must needs be weak.
> To whom can this be true who once has heard
>   The cry for help, the tongue that all men speak,
> When want or woe or fear is in the throat,
>   So that each word gasped out is like a shriek
> Pressed from the sore heart, or a strange wild note
>   Sung by some far-off fiend ? There is a strength
> Which dies if stretched too far or spun too fine,
>   Which has more height than breadth, more depth than length.
> Let but this force of thought and speech be mine,
>   And he that will may take the sleek fat phrase
> Which glows and burns not, though it gleam and shine, —
>   Light, but no heat, — a flash, but not a blaze !
>
> Nor is it mere strength that the short word boasts :
>   It serves of more than fight or storm to tell,

The roar of waves that dash on rock-bound coasts,
    The crash of tall trees when the wild winds swell,
The roar of guns, the groans of men that die
    On blood-stained fields. It has a voice as well
For them that far off on their sick beds lie ;
    For them that weep, for them that mourn the dead ;
For them that laugh and dance and clap the hand ;
    To joy's quick step, as well as grief's slow tread,
The sweet, plain words we learnt at first keep time,
    And though the theme be sad, or gay, or grand,
With each, with all, these may be made to chime,
    In thought, or speech, or song, or prose, or rime.

In Gascoigne's " Certain Notes of Instruction concerning the Making of Verse," we are told that " the
most ancient words are of one syllable, so that the more
monosyllables you use, the truer Englishman you shall
seem, and the less you shall smell of the ink-horn."

On the other hand, there is strength also in the polysyllable, as when Shakspere writes: —

> No, this my hand will rather
> The multitudinous seas incarnadine.

In comic verse, the use of the polysyllable is often
most amusing, as in the couplet of a humorous ballad
about a certain hypocritical lord whom his attendants
found

> beneath the table sunk,
> Problematically pious but indubitably drunk.

There is profit in varying words of one syllable and
of two with infrequent words of three syllables, as in
this stanza of " A Revolutionary Relic " by Austin
Dobson : —

> Did she turn with sight swift-dimming,
>   And the *quivering* lip we know,
> With the full, slow eye-lid brimming,
> With the *languorous* pupil swimming
>   Like the love of Mirabeau ?

In another stanza of the same lyric, we find only one trisyllable in the five lines, the rest of the words having been almost equally divided between monosyllables and dissyllables: —

> Wailing, wailing, as the plover
> Waileth, wheeleth, *desolate,*
> Heedless of the hawk above her,
> While as yet the rushes cover,
> Waning fast, her wounded mate.

And in this last stanza there is another point to be observed — the repetition of the sound which begins the first, second and fifth lines, the sound of *way.* We may remark also that in the third line two words, both of them long, *heedless* and *hawk,* begin with the same letter. This is the device which is known as alliteration, the repetition of the same initial consonant. Alliteration, as an aid to rhythm, is historically earlier than rime; indeed, it is a kind of incomplete rime at the beginning of a line. It is very prevalent in primitive poetry; and it was accepted by Wagner as preferable to rime for lyrics intended to be set to music. Wagner held that " rime is useless in music because it implies identity not only of vowel-sounds but also of the succeeding consonants," which are lost to the listener by the singer's need of dwelling on the vowel alone, whereas the initial consonant cannot be lost, " because it is that which stamps its physiognomy on a word." As the repetition of the same sound in a series of initial consonants creates " a sort of musical cadence which is agreeable to the ear," Wagner desired alliteration to be substituted for rime. For this preference the composer had a reason sufficient to himself; but in poetry, which is sup-

posed to be spoken rather than sung, rime is held to
be more effective; and alliteration has been reserved
as an occasional accessory to be employed sparingly
and unobtrusively.

Here are two striking examples of the obtrusive use
of alliteration, taken from Poe and from the British
poet who learned much from the American lyrist, and
who often bettered his teaching. In his " Ulalume "
Poe informs us that his shadowy heroine has

> Come up through the *lair* of the *lion,*
> With *love* in her *luminous* eyes.

And in one of his earlier lyrics, Swinburne contrasts
violently

> The *lilies* and *languors* of *virtue,*
> The *raptures* and *roses* of *vice.*

In another lyric, " A Child's Daughter," the same
British poet " hunts the letter" even more emphatically : —

> All the *bells* of heaven may ring,
> All the *birds* of heaven may sing,
> All the *wells* on earth may spring,
> All the *winds* on earth may bring
> All *sweet sounds* together ;
> Sweeter far than all things *heard,*
> *Hand* of *harper,* tone of bird,
> *Sound* of *woods* at *sundawn stirred,*
> *Welling waters, winsome word,*
> *Wind* in *warm, wan weather.*

Here our attention is taken from off the matter and
called strenuously to the manner. Our ear begins to
count the number of alliterations, to expect them and
to wonder at them; and while it is doing this, it is
likely to fail to catch the poet's meaning. If we once
begin to notice tricks of method, we shall not appre-

hend the message. If we fall to admiring the poet's
dexterity in juggling with sounds, we shall not really
listen to what he is talking about—and perhaps we
shall not care. If this is the case, the verbal artist has
plainly overreached himself. He has constructed his ornament instead of ornamenting his construction. He
has allowed the minor matter of style to interfere with
the major matter of substance. As Sir Joshua Reynolds
said, "the value and rank of every art is in proportion
to the mental labor employed in it or the mental pleasure produced by it. As this principle is observed or
neglected a profession becomes either a liberal art or a
mechanical trade." And in another place Reynolds insisted that " art in its perfection is unostentatious; it lies
hid and works its effects, itself unseen."

When we seek to discover why Poe's lines and Swinburne's produce this unforeseen and unfortunate effect,
we perceive that the four l's in the American poem and
the two r's, the two l's and the two v's in the British
poem are all of them initials of long syllables, of syllables which have an emphatic accent, so that they impress themselves most forcibly upon the ear. Contrast
the two lines of Poe and the two lines of Swinburne
with these two lines of Tennyson:—

> The moan of doves in immemorial elms
> And murmur of innumerable bees.

Here are actually eight m's; and yet they achieve
their soothing effect without projecting themselves into
our consciousness and without in any way arresting the
current of our interest. There they are, and we may
count them at our leisure if we choose; but they do
not cry aloud for immediate recognition when the lines

fall on our ears. While some of these *m*'s are initials
of long feet, most of them are more cunningly commingled with the three *l*'s, with the three repetitions
of the *u* sound (for that is heard also in *doves*), and
with the two long *o*'s in the first line. Where Poe and
Swinburne have vaunted their virtuosity, proudly pa-
rading it, Tennyson has subtly hidden his far more
delicate art. Sometimes Tennyson, when he feels the
need, dares a bolder alliteration: —

> Where with puffed cheek the belted hunter blew
> His wreathed bugle-horn.

And Browning makes use of like words for a like
purpose: —

> That bubble they were bent on blowing big,
> He had blown already till he burst his cheeks.

In the following four lines Bunner has only two initial
l's and *w*'s, but another *l* and another *w* are unobtrusively effective while the third line is sustained by three
long *o*'s contrasted with *r*'s: —

> I *dwell* in a *land* of *winter*,
> From my *love* a *world* apart —
> But the snow blooms over with roses
> At the thought of her in my heart.

The result justified frank initial alliteration in these
lines of Shakspere's: —

> The churlish chiding of the winter wind.

> In maiden meditation, fancy free.

And also in these of Coleridge's: —

> The fair breeze blew, the white foam flew,
> The furrow followed free.

Yet in this last example the repeated *f*'s, all at the beginning of long syllables, are perilously near to the danger-line where they might divert the reader's mind from the story he was hearing to the technic of the story-teller. There is profit in setting this by the side of a marvelously adroit interweaving of complementary and contrasted sounds in this exquisitely musical passage of Tennyson's "Princess":—

> The babe that by us,
> Half-lapt in glowing gauze and golden brede,
> Lay like a new-fall'n meteor on the grass,
> Uncared for, spied its mother and began
> A blind and babbling laughter, and to dance
> Its body, and reach its fatling innocent arms
> And lazy ling'ring fingers.

This fragment of Tennyson's is more elaborately wrought than this of Milton's, in which however there is the same intermittent play of alliteration, changing its letter from line to line:—

> And ever, against eating cares,
> Lap me in soft Lydian airs,
> Married to immortal verse,
> Such as the meeting soul may pierce,
> In notes with many a winding bout
> Of linkèd sweetness long drawn out
> With wanton heed and giddy cunning,
> The melting voice through mazes running,
> Untwisting all the chains that tie
> The hidden Soul of Harmony.

Perhaps there is no passage of Shakspere more cunningly contrived with a varied play of repeated and contrasted consonants than the description of Cleopatra's descent of the Nile:—

The barge she sat in, like a burnished throne,
Burn'd on the water: the poop was beaten gold;
Purple the sails, and so perfumed that
The winds were love-sick with them ; the oars were silver,
Which to the tune of flutes kept stroke, and made
The water which they beat to follow faster,
As amorous of their strokes.

If we reserve alliteration to describe the recurring of the same sound as the initial of words or of long syllables, then we need another term for the recurrence of the same sound in the less emphatic places in the line. " Colliteration," a word which has been proposed by Bliss Carman, seems to be excellent for the purpose, since it suggests at once the close relation between it and alliteration and yet points out the difference. Colliteration, then, has this advantage over alliteration, that it is less obvious, that it forces itself less upon the hearer's attention, that it conveys a gentler pleasure to the ear while concealing the source of this gratification. Alliteration braves the spotlight of publicity, while colliteration modestly shrinks from the glare of self-display. These two lines of Browning's have been used to illustrate the delicate effects of adroit colliteration : —

But I know not any tone
So fit as thine to falter forth a sorrow.

As Richard Hovey pointed out, the repeated *f*'s (*fit*, *falter*, *forth*) are a true alliteration in that they are the initials of long syllables and get the full force of three beats out of the five in the line. The *t*-sounds (*t* in *but*, *not*, *tone*, *fit*, *to* and *-ter*, and *th* in *thine* and *forth*) are scattered indiscriminately, three falling in short syllables, three on the ends of long syllables, and two only (and these not exactly the same, *t* in *tone* and *th* in *thine*) on the beginnings of long syllables. " The result of this scattering is that they do not catch the ear as the alliterating *f*'s do ; but they do unconsciously impress the mind with a sense of a prevailing color." Again, the *n*'s (*know*, *not*, *any*, *tone*, *thine*) form a colliterating group with a slight associated alliteration (the final *n*'s of *tone* and *thine*, which strongly affect the beat).

It needs to be noted that alliteration and colliteration have nothing to do with spelling, since our chaotic orthography allows almost every single sound of our language to be represented by a variety of different symbols. The sound of *u* in *burn*, for example, is represented by every other vowel in *earn*, *journey*, *firm*, *myrrh*. To the ear this is true alliteration, although the eye may not always discover the identity of sound.

The too frequent recurrence of the same vowel-sound may be fatiguing, as Lanier illustrated by two lines which he made as atrocious as possible in order to set the fault forth clearly : —

'Tis May-day gay ; wide-smiling skies shine bright,
Through whose true blue cuckoos do woo anew.

The assertion has been made that Browning strove ever to avoid the repetition of the same vowel-sound in a single line. If he did act on this principle, he deprived himself of a valuable means of securing tone-color. We may feel that the reëcho of the same vowel-sound in Byron's

Oh, we 'll *go no more* a-*roving*

is perhaps a little too bold and direct. But Poe's in-

tentional repetition of the same sound in three lines
of " The Bells " is admirable in its carrying out of the
purpose of the poem : —

> From the *molten-golden notes,*
>   And all in tune,
> What a liquid ditty *floats.*

And there is the same bold use of the same open
vowels, a luxurious symphony, in two quatrains of
Andrew Lang's " Twilight on Tweed " : —

> A mist of memory broods and *floats,*
>   The *border* waters *flow ;*
> The air is full of ballad *notes,*
>   *Borne* out of long *ago.*
>
> *Old songs* that sung themselves to me,
>   Sweet through a boy's day-dream,
> While trout *below* the *blossom'd* tree
>   Plashed in the *golden* stream.

There is a deliberate expressiveness not otherwise
attainable in Tennyson's

> Lab*o*rious *o*rient iv*o*ry sphere in sphere.

Not in the same line, indeed, but in three consecutive lines, does Shakspere employ a triple repetition
of the long *i* sound : —

> In such a *night*
> Stood *Di*do with a willow in her hand,
> Upon the *wi*ld sea banks, and waft her love
> To come again to Carthage.

Here we may note also the alliteration of the three
w's (*willow, wild,* and *waft*) and of the two *c*'s (*come*
and *Carthage*), as well as the colliteration of the *u*
sound (*love* and *come*). And Pope got a certain effect

by repeating a vowel-consonant combination in his
second line : —

> If nature *thun*dered in our opening ears
> And *stunned* us with the music of the spheres.

The same kind of imitative harmony is to be found
in Whitcomb Riley's "When the Frost is on the
Punkin," especially in these two lines : —

> The husky, rusty rustle of the tossels of the corn,
> And the rashin' of the tangled leaves, as golden as the morn.

English is a language sibilant beyond all others ;
and it is not easy for our poets to avoid making lines
which hiss unpleasantly. It was in the effort to escape
from this danger that an anonymous bard was moved
to compose this " Song without a Sibilant " :—

> Oh ! come to-night ; for naught can charm
>   The weary time when thou 'rt away.
> Oh ! come ; the gentle moon hath thrown
>   O'er bower and hall her quivering ray.
> The heatherbell hath mildly flung
>   From off her fairy leaf the bright
> And diamond dewdrop that had hung
>   Upon that leaf — a gem of light.
>   Then come, love, come !
>
> To-night the liquid wave hath not —
>   Illumined by the moonlit beam
> Playing upon the lake beneath,
>   Like frolic in an Autumn dream —
> The liquid wave hath not, to-night,
>   In all her moonlight pride, a fair
> Gift like to them that on thy lip
>   Do breathe and laugh, and home it there.
>   Then come, love, come !
>
> To-night, to-night, my gentle one,
>   The flower-bearing Amra tree

> Doth long, with fragrant moan, to meet
> The love-lip of the honey-bee.
> But not the Amra tree can long
> To greet the bee, at evening light,
> With half the deep, fond love I long
> To meet my Nama here to-night.
> Then come, love, come !

Tennyson held it essential that the poet should have a fine ear for vowel-sounds and an ability to kick "the geese out of the boat," that is, to avoid sibilations. He declared that he "never put two *s*'s together in any verse of mine. My line is not, as often quoted,

> And freedom broaden*s* *s*lowly down,

but

> And freedom slowly broadens down."

In laying down this rule, Tennyson was refining upon the practice of Shakspere, who unhesitatingly ends one word with an *s* and begins the next with the same sound : —

> The multitudinou*s* *s*eas incarnadine.
>
> The air bite*s* *s*hrewdly ; it is very cold.
>
> But that our loves and comfort*s* *s*hould increase.
>
> I am thy father'*s* *s*pirit.

This liberty of Shakspere's is the more significant, because these quotations are all taken from his plays, where every line was intended to be spoken. Yet Tennyson's insistence upon the high standard of avoiding the succession of *s*'s is evidence that he kept in mind always the effect of his lines upon the ear. Tennyson lacks the large affluence of Shakspere ; his

art is more timid; but it is ever worthy of the most
careful study. He was what he called Catullus, a
"consummate metrist," avid of experiment and untir-
ing in search of ultimate perfection. Consider, for another example, how skilfully he colliterates the short
i sound with thin *t*'s and *k*'s to gain an effect of
insignificance : —

> The little rift within the lover's lute,
> Or little pitted speck in garnered fruit,

in which there are eight varied *t*'s and seven *i*'s.

The precept and the practice of Tennyson have left
a deep impress upon the technic of all the later verse-
writers of our language. His influence was beneficial
in raising the level of technical accomplishment. It
has made the average versifier ashamed of negligent
work. The lyrists of to-day may have only a few burning words to utter and the torch of poesy may be
dimmer than a generation ago, because our bards have
now no message tipped with flame ; but they see clearly
while the lamp holds out to burn. They know how to
say what little they may have to say. As Tennyson
himself asserted late in life,

> All can grow the flower now,
> For all have got the seed.

Of course, there is an ever-present danger that
manner may come to be more highly esteemed than
matter. Stedman was not overstating the case when
he asserted that certain " non-creative writers lavish
all their ingenuity upon decoration until it becomes a
vice. You cannot long disguise a lack of native vigor
by ornament and novel effects. Over-decoration of late

is the symptom of over-prolonged devotion to the technical side of poetry. All of the countless effects of technic are nothing without that psychical beauty imparted by the true vitality — are of less value than faith and works without love. The *vox humana* must be heard. That alone can give quality to a poem ; the most refined and artistic verse is cold and forceless without it. A soulless poem is a stained glass window with the light shining on and not through it."

Yet it is well to have the instruments of the art kept fit for the service of the truly creative poet when he shall come. The bugle will be ready to his hand, when he arrives to blow a mighty blast. No artist can have too great technical dexterity ; and every artist must serve his apprenticeship in the workshop, learning his trade. In default of the major poet, with his message for all men, we can find delight in the dexterity of the minor poets and in the skill with which they carve their cameos. We can take a keen pleasure in the measured movement of this stanza of Aldrich's "Voice of the Sea," with its certainty of touch, its effective repetitions, and its perfect adjustment of sound to sense : —

> In the hush of the autumn night
> I hear the voice of the sea,
> In the hush of the autumn night
> It seems to say to me —
> Mine are the winds above,
> Mine are the caves below,
> Mine are the dead of yesterday
> And the dead of long ago.

We can enjoy also the skilful interweaving of rimes, the delicate play of alliteration and of colliteration,

the artful selection of thin vowel-sounds and thin
consonants, in these quatrains of Riley's:—

> When chirping crickets fainter cry,
> And pale stars blossom in the sky,
> And twilight's gloom has dimmed the bloom
> And blurred the butterfly ;
>
> When locust-blossoms fleck the walk,
> And up the tiger-lily stalk,
> The glow-worm crawls and clings and falls
> And glimmers down the garden walls.

And it is well now and then to study a masterpiece
of poetry, like Tennyson's "Crossing the Bar," and
examine its workmanship, if we wish to convince ourselves anew that content and form are Siamese twins,
after all, and that one cannot exist without the other,
born at the same moment:—

> Sunset and evening star,
>   And one clear call for me !
> And may there be no moaning of the bar,
>   When I put out to sea,
>
> But such a tide as moving seems asleep,
>   Too full for sound and foam,
> When that which drew from out the boundless deep
>   Turns again home.
>
> Twilight and evening bell,
>   And after that the dark !
> And may there be no sadness of farewell,
>   When I embark ;
>
> For tho' from out our bourne of Time and Place
>   The flood may bear me far,
> I hope to see my Pilot face to face
>   When I have crost the bar.

It would be difficult to set a more profitable task before any student than to ask him to take this lovely

lyric apart and to discover how much of its ineffable and intangible beauty is due to the poet's artistry, to his mastery of alliteration and colliteration, to his exquisite feeling for vowel-sounds, to his firm control over contrasting consonants, to his intuitive sense of rhythm, and to his perfect understanding of the value of an adroitly varied refrain, — to the antithesis of "Sunset and evening star" with "Twilight and evening bell," and to the final recurrence of the figure of the bar to be crossed which is suggested in the first quatrain.

Perhaps the refrain is not fairly to be classed under tone-color; and yet it may as well be considered here as later. The refrain may be defined as a phrase, often filling a whole line, which recurs again and again at intervals, sometimes absolutely unchanged and sometimes artfully modified in meaning. This device, which we use now for sustaining and reawakening the interest of the hearer, is of very high antiquity; and it is frequent in the folksongs of various peoples. Macaulay employed it in the stirring stanzas in which he sought to recapture the swiftness of the primitive ballad; and in the "Battle of Ivry" he ends off again and again with "King Henry of Navarre." Tennyson chose to set his refrain at the beginning of every stanza of his "Lady Clara Vere de Vere." Kipling makes us feel its stark power in his gruesome "Danny Deever" and he forced it to lend weight to his lofty "Recessional." Walt Whitman seized it for once in his noble lament for Lincoln, where every stanza begins with

O Captain, my Captain !

and every stanza ends with

Fallen cold and dead.

The refrain is the backbone of Longfellow's " Excelsior " and of his " Old Clock on the Stairs " ; and
he modified it pathetically in his " Chamber over the
Gate." It is adroitly handled in Riley's " There, little
girl, don't cry." It is the heart of Tennyson's " Lady
of Shalott " ; and it is dramatically varied in his
ballad of the " Sisters," in which all the six stanzas
end with the same line : —

O, the earl was fair to see !

While in the third line of the successive stanzas he
rings the changes on

The wind is blowing in turret and tree,

which becomes

The wind is howling in turret and tree

and

The wind is raving in turret and tree,

only to return in the final stanza to the original form.
Tennyson also employed it most effectually in his
" May Queen " and again, a little insistently, in his
" Oriana."

In the essay on the " Philosophy of Composition,"
wherein Poe pretended to set forth the successive
steps which he took in order to write the " Raven,"
he asserted that no artistic effect had been more often
employed in verse than the refrain. " The univer-
sality of its employment sufficed to assure me of its
intrinsic value, and spared me the necessity of sub-
mitting it to analysis. I considered it, however, with
regard to its susceptibility of improvement, and soon
saw it to be in a primitive condition. As commonly

used, the refrain or burden, not only is limited to lyric verse, but depends for its impression upon the force of monotone — both in sound and thought. The pleasure is deduced solely from the sense of identity — of repetition. I resolved to diversify, and so heighten, the effect by adhering in general to the monotone of sound, while I continually varied that of thought; that is to say, I determined to produce continuously novel effects by the variation of the application of the refrain — the refrain itself remaining for the most part unvaried." Whether Poe knew it or not, this exact repetition of the refrain with a shifting meaning of the repeated word or phrase was not really a novelty of his, since it can be found — to search no further — in the ballade and the rondeau and the triolet.

Poe then went on to consider the proper length of the refrain itself; and here his acuteness has full play. "Since its application was to be repeatedly varied, it was clear that the refrain itself must be brief, for there would have been an unsurmountable difficulty in frequent variations of application in any sentence of length. In proportion to the brevity of the sentence would of course be the facility of the variation. This led me at once to a single word as the best refrain." And as the refrain was properly to close the several stanzas, "such a close, to have force, must be sonorous and susceptible to protracted emphasis." These considerations "inevitably led me to the long *o* as the most sonorous vowel in connection with *r* as the most producible consonant." So he selected for his refrain the single word *Nevermore*.

It may be doubted whether Poe is quite candid in

his explanation of the processes of his composition of the " Raven," for if the poem is solely the result of his analytic determination of the proper constituent elements of a pathetic lyric, there would be reason for wonder why he did not start up the machinery again and manufacture a succession of similar poems. Yet few poets have ever taken us so satisfactorily into the workshop as Poe did in this paper, laying bare the artistic motives which guided his creation. Poe declared these motives to have been conscious, and such they may have been in some measure, although probably not to the degree he claims. A true poet has always built better than he knew ; and conscious craftsman as Tennyson was, we may doubt whether the half of the verbal and metrical felicities which we can detect in " Crossing the Bar " were deliberately intended and foreseen by the poet. They were the result of Tennyson's lifelong attention to technic, until his hand had become subdued to what it worked in and until he wrought his marvels almost unconsciously.

The refrain is closely akin in effect to the repetition of a thought in other words — as Tennyson returned in his last line to the crossing of the bar, first mentioned in the fourth line of his first stanza. Sometimes this can be attained by the recurrence of a single striking word, as in this " Parable " [1] by Anna Reeve Aldrich : —

> I made the cross myself whose weight
>> Was later laid on me.
> This thought is torture as I toil
>> Up life's steep Calvary.

[1] By permission from *Songs about Love, Life and Death,* by Anna Reeve Aldrich, copyight, 1892, by Charles Scribner's Sons.

To think mine own hands drove the nails !
  I sang a merry song,
And chose the heaviest wood I had
  To build it firm and strong.

If I had guessed — if I had dreamed
  Its weight was meant for me,
I should have made a lighter cross
  To bear up Calvary.

And this repetition of the vital word or phrase need not occur at the end of the poem or even of the stanza. Indeed, there is sometimes a special emphasis in placing it earlier, as in Landor's exquisite lyric, which has a classic grace in its delicate force. In this poem a beautiful proper name serves to tie the two quatrains together: —

Ah, what avails the sceptered race,
  Ah, what the form divine !
What every beauty, every grace !
  Rose Aylmer, all were thine.

Rose Aylmer, whom those wakeful eyes
  May weep, but never see,
A night of memories and of sighs
  I consecrate to thee.

This same transposition of the refrain from the end of the stanza is to be seen in Gilder's "Sherman," where it opens each of the first three stanzas to reappear paraphrased but undisguised in the third line of the final stanza: —

Glory and honor and fame and everlasting laudation
For our captains who loved not war, but fought for the life of
    the nation;
Who knew that, in all the land, one slave meant strife, not peace;
Who fought for freedom, not glory; made war that war might
    cease.

Glory and honor and fame; the beating of muffled drums;
The wailing funeral dirge, as the flag-wrapped coffin comes;
Fame and honor and glory; and joy for a noble soul,
For a full and splendid life, and laureled rest at the goal.

Glory and honor and fame; the pomp that a soldier prizes;
The league-long waving line as the marching falls and rises;
Rumbling of caissons and guns; the clatter of horses' feet,
And a million awe-struck faces far down the waiting street.

But better than martial woe, and the pageant of civic sorrow;
Better than praise of to-day, or the statue we build to-morrow;
Better than honor and glory, and History's iron pen,
Was the thought of duty done and the love of his fellow-men.

Perhaps it is not needful to draw attention to what
all must have felt — the imitative ingenuity of the

Rumbling of caissons and guns

and the imagination and picturesqueness of

The league-long waving line as the marching falls and rises.

Poe also made use of another device which has a
certain likeness to the refrain. He repeated the
final line of his stanza with a modification of one or
more words, thus gaining the emphasis of reiteration
while avoiding the monotony of exact repetition. In
" For Annie," for example, not a little of the vibrating
intensity of the lyric is due to these terminal echoes : —

> The moaning and groaning,
>   The sighing and sobbing,
> Are quieted now
>   With that horrible throbbing
> At heart: — ah, that horrible,
>   Horrible throbbing !
> .   .   .   .   .   .
> When the light was extinguished
>   She covered me warm,

And she prayed to the angels
To keep me from harm,
To the queen of the angels
To shield me from harm.

The same method is to be observed also in " Annabel Lee ": —

For the moon never beams, without bringing me dreams
Of the beautiful Annabel Lee;
And the stars never rise, but I feel the bright eyes
Of the beautiful Annabel Lee;
And so, all the night-tide, I lie down by the side
Of my darling, my darling — my life and my bride,
In her sepulchre there by the sea,
In her tomb by the sounding sea.

And in " Ulalume," the principle seems to have
been carried to an even further extreme: —

Our talk had been serious and sober,
But our thoughts they were palsied and sere,
Our memories were treacherous and sere,
For we knew not the month was October,
And we marked not the night of the year,
(Ah, night of all nights in the year !)
We noted not the dim lake of Auber
(Though once we had journeyed down here),
Remembered not the dank tarn of Auber
Nor the ghoul-haunted woodland of Weir.

This stanza has a magic melody, even if its meaning is vague and uncertain; it steals over us like a
strain of music. And its insinuating charm is due to
dexterity of rhythmic variation, to adroitness in invention of rime, and, above all, to tone-color, to the choice
and to the contrast of the mere sounds.

Perhaps this chapter cannot end better than with
a pregnant quotation from Stevenson's most illumi-

native essay on "Style in Literature": "Each phrase in literature is built of sounds, as each phrase in music consists of notes. One sound suggests, echoes, demands, and harmonizes with another; and the art of rightly using these concordances is the final art in literature. It used to be a piece of good advice to all young writers to avoid alliteration; and the advice was sound, in so far as it prevented daubing. None the less for that, was it abominable nonsense, and the merest raving of the blindest of the blind who will not see. The beauty of the contents of a phrase, or of a sentence, depends implicitly upon alliteration and upon assonance. The vowel demands to be repeated. The consonant demands to be repeated; and both cry aloud to be perpetually varied. You may follow the adventures of a letter through any passage that has particularly pleased you; find it perhaps denied a while, to tantalize the ear; find it fired at you again in a whole broadside; or find it pass into congenerous sounds, one liquid or labial melting away into another."

CHAPTER VI

THE STANZA

Verse — to the true poet — is no clog. It is idly called a trammel and a difficulty. It is a help. It springs from the same enthusiasm as the rest of his impulses, and is necessary to their satisfaction and effect. Verse is no more a clog than the condition of rushing upward is a clog to fire, or than the roundness and order of the globe is a clog to the freedom and variety that abound within its sphere. Verse is no dominator over the poet, except inasmuch as the bond is reciprocal, and the poet dominates over the verse. — LEIGH HUNT: *What is Poetry?*

EPIC, idyllic and narrative poems, as well as didactic, descriptive and satiric verse, are usually written continuously without subdivision into minor parts of a rigid length. They may be set off into books or cantos; but they are not cut up into stanzas. That is to say, they may have a series of chapters, but they are not measured off into equal paragraphs. Lyric poetry, including the ballad and often also the story in verse, is generally composed of a succession of stanzas identical in structure and uniform in length. Thus the stanza is the unit, of which the sequence constitutes the poem. It is a part of the whole; and yet it is complete in itself. It resembles the paragraph of prose-composition, except that it has uniformity of length and of structure.

In the majority of the poems written in the modern languages, rime is employed to make the framework of the stanza clearly perceptible to the ear. Rime not only marks off the ends of the several lines, it serves also to organize and to coördinate the stanza itself. It sustains the architecture of the often elaborate form. This is an added reason why rime should be exact and perfect, so that the ear may the more readily perceive the scheme of the stanza, however complex this may be. And as this apprehension and retention of the skeleton of the structure imposes more or less burden upon the ear, there is a certain disadvantage in a stanza which is too protracted in length, or too complicated in arrangement. This must ever be borne in mind, in spite of the fact that some stanzaic constructions which are neither short nor simple, have a sweeping amplitude gratefully welcomed by the ear.

The stanza may be any length, from two lines to a dozen or more. A succession of couplets, each complete in itself, might seem to be unduly monotonous to carry a story satisfactorily. Yet the couplet is the simple form chosen by Whittier to tell about "Maud Muller" and "Barbara Frietchie." In the first, the sense is generally coincident with the couplet: —

> Maud Muller on a summer's day
> Raked the meadow sweet with hay.

> Beneath her torn hat glowed the wealth
> Of simple beauty and rustic health.

In the second, the poet sometimes lets the thought run on from couplet to couplet: —

> Up from the meadows rich with corn,
> Clear in the cool September morn,

> The clustered spires of Frederick stand
> Green-walled by the hills of Maryland.

The couplet is also the form preferred by Austin Dobson for his " Ballad of Beau Brocade": —

> Seventeen hundred and thirty-nine —
> That was the date of this tale of mine.
>
> First great George was buried and gone ;
> George the Second was plodding on.

The British bard, it must be noted, allowed himself the liberty of an occasional triplet to interrupt the current of his couplets: —

> Out spoke Dolly the chambermaid,
> (Tremulous now and sore afraid,)
> " Stand and deliver, O Beau Brocade !"
>
> Firing then, out of sheer alarm,
> Hit the Beau in the bridle arm.
>
> Button the first went none knows where,
> But it carried away his solitaire ;
>
> Button the second a circuit made,
> Glanced in under the shoulder-blade ; —
> Down from the saddle fell Beau Brocade.

The triplet has also served as a stanza, generally tied together by a single rime, as in Longfellow's " Maidenhood": —

> Maiden ! with the meek, brown eyes,
> In whose orbs a shadow lies
> Like the dusk in evening skies !
>
> Thou whose locks outshine the sun,
> Golden tresses, wreathed in one,
> As the braided streamlets run !
>
> Standing, with reluctant feet,
> Where the brook and river meet,
> Womanhood and childhood fleet !

Longfellow's triplets are trochaic tetrameters with the final short syllable dropped. In "A Toccata of Galuppi's," Browning employs triplets of trochaic octameter, also cutting off the final short syllable : —

As for Venice and her people, merely born to bloom and drop,
Here on earth they bore their fruitage, mirth and folly were the
    crop :
What of soul was left, I wonder, when the kissing had to stop ?

Sometimes the poet has chosen to avoid the triple repetition of the same sound in leaving the middle line of the three unrimed ; and sometimes he has carried over into the second triplet the terminal sound of this second line. This is what Browning has done in the " Statue and the Bust " : —

There 's a palace in Florence, the world knows well,
    And a statue watches it from the square,
And this story of both do our townsmen tell.

Ages ago, a lady there,
    At the farthest window facing the East
Asked, " Who rides by with the royal air ? "

The bridesmaids' prattle around her ceased;
    She leaned forth, one on either hand ;
They saw how the blush of the bride increased —

This same method of linking the triplets together into a chain is to be found also in Morris's " Defence of Guinevere " : —

But, knowing now that they would have her speak,
    She threw her wet hair backward from her brow,
Her hand close to her mouth, touching her cheek,

As though she had there a shameful blow,
    And feeling it shameful to feel ought but shame
All through her heart, yet felt her cheek burn so,

> She must a little touch it: like one lame,
>   She walked away from Gauwaine, with her head
> Still lifted up ; and on her cheek of flame.

A massive and sweeping triplet-stanza is that employed by Kipling in the dedication of his book of verses to his dead brother-in-law, Wolcott Balestier. It owes much of its weight and largeness to the length of the several lines, which are iambic heptameter: —

Beyond the path of the outmost sun through utter darkness
   hurled —
Further than ever comet flared or vagrant star-dust swirled —
Live such as fought and sailed and ruled and loved and made
   our world.

They are purged of pride because they died, they know the
   worth of their bays,
They sit at wine with the Maidens Nine and the Gods of the
   Elder Days,
It is their will to serve or be still as fitteth our Father's praise.

This large triplet-stanza is appropriate to the full-blown eulogy which is here Kipling's intent. But it is not fitter for its special purpose than the more reserved triplet-stanza that Tennyson chose for his " Two Voices ": —

> And all so variously wrought,
> I marvell'd how the mind was brought
> To anchor by one gloomy thought.

Of all possible stanzas the quatrain is the most frequent in English verse. Generally the first and third lines rime together, and the second and fourth, — as in Emerson's " Concord Hymn ": —

> By the rude bridge that arched the flood,
>   Their flag to April's breeze unfurled,
> Here once the embattled farmers stood,
>   And fired the shot heard round the world.

This form of the quatrain may be varied by the alternation of double and single rimes, as in Byron's : —

> When a man hath no freedom to fight for at home,
>   Let him combat for that of his neighbors;
> Let him think of the glories of Greece and of Rome,
>   And get knocked on the head for his labors.

And in this of Shelley's : —

> I fear thy kisses, gentle maiden,
>   Thou needest not fear mine;
> My spirit is too deeply laden
>   Ever to burden thine.

Some poets have found an advantage in leaving the first and third lines unrimed, as in this quatrain of Coleridge's : —

> All thoughts, all passions, all delights,
>   Whatever stirs this mortal frame;
> All are but ministers of love,
>   And feed his sacred flame.

But although this is here printed as four lines, it may be questioned whether the ear does not really receive it rather as two long lines, in consequence of the absence of the rime. In this case there is a certain strain imposed on the hearing. This is probably the reason why careful versifiers rarely leave any pair of lines unrimed in a poem which is otherwise rimed. A single unrimed line in a quatrain, the other three lines of which rime together, is often restful ; and this is the form of the quatrain chosen by Fitzgerald for his translation of Omar Khayyám : —

> A book of verses underneath the bough,
> A jug of wine, a loaf of bread, and thou
>   Beside me singing in the wilderness —
> Oh, wilderness were Paradise enow !

Another disposition of the unrimed line is to be found in Byron's familiar epistle to his publisher, which consists of a riming triplet, with an unrimed refrain: —

> To thee, with hope and terror dumb,
> The unfledged MS. authors come;
> Thou printest all — and sellest some —
>   My Murray.
>
> Along thy sprucest bookshelves shine
> The works thou deemest most divine —
> The "art of cookery," and mine,
>   My Murray.

This same arrangement of the quatrain, which Byron employed jocularly, serves also for the massive and resonant "Battle-Hymn of the Republic": —

> Mine eyes have seen the glory of the coming of the Lord:
> He is trampling out the vintage where the grapes of wrath are
>   stored;
> He hath loosed the fateful lightning of his terrible swift sword:
>   His truth is marching on.

In this lofty lyric, the refrain always ends with "marching on," but the rest of the line is sometimes varied: —

>   His day is marching on,

and

>   Since God is marching on.

This is a form of the quatrain closely akin to a triplet; and there is also a form of the quatrain which is composed of two consecutive couplets. Here is an example, from Byron's "Stanzas written on the Road from Florence to Pisa": —

> Oh, talk not to me of a name great in story;
> The days of our youth are the days of our glory;
> And the myrtle and ivy of sweet two-and-twenty
> Are worth all your laurels, though ever so plenty.

In this quatrain, the two couplets come one after the other. In the quatrain which Tennyson chose for " In Memoriam" a couplet is inserted between the lines of another couplet : —

> Who loves not Knowledge ? Who shall rail
> Against her beauty ? May she mix
> With men and prosper ! Who shall fix
> Her pillars ? Let her work prevail.
>
> But on her forehead sits a fire;
> She sets her forward countenance
> And leaps into the future chance,
> Submitting all things to desire.

As it is customary to represent iambs and trochees by symbols, $\smile$ – and – $\smile$, so it is traditional to indicate the riming scheme of any stanza by alphabetical symbols, a–a representing one pair of rimes, b–b another and x–x standing for lines without rime. Translating into these alphabetic symbols the several forms of the quatrain, we see that the alternating rimes, all single or single and double, as in the examples from Emerson and Shelley, are arranged thus, a, b, a, b. In Coleridge's quatrain we have x, a, x, a; in Fitzgerald's a, a, x, a and in Byron's flippant address to Murray, a, a, a, x. In Byron's quatrain composed of a pair of couplets, we have a, a, b, b; and in Tennyson's " In Memoriam " we have a, b, b, a. These are not all the ways in which rimed and unrimed lines can be arranged in a quatrain, but they are the most frequently used. And these forms of the quatrain may be made infinitely various by lengthening or shortening one or more lines of the four. The rime-scheme of Bryant's " To a Waterfowl " is a, b, a, b, the same as that of Emerson's " Concord Hymn"; and yet the effect upon the ear is totally different in consequence of the metrical variation : —

> Whither, midst falling dew,
> While glow the heavens with the last steps of day,
> Far, through their rosy depths, dost thou pursue
> Thy solitary way ?

The same also is the rime-scheme of Hood's " Haunted House," wherein the difference is accentuated by the double rime : —

> The wood-louse dropped and rolled into a ball,
> Touched by some impulse, occult or mechanic.
> And nameless beetles ran along the wall
> In universal panic.

Just as the quatrain may be composed by the union of two couplets, one following the other, so two quatrains of any of these forms may be combined into an eight-line stanza. The stanza of the ordinary ballad is simply a double quatrain, riming a, b, a, b, c, d, c, d, or else with the first, third, fifth and seventh lines left unrimed, x, a, x, a, x, b, x, b, as in Kipling's " Merchantmen " : —

> King Solomon drew merchantmen
> Because of his desire
> For peacocks, apes, and ivory,
> From Tarshish unto Tyre :
> With cedars out of Lebanon
> Which Hiram rafted down,
> But we be only sailormen
> That use in London Town.

The noble stanza in which Drayton composed his superb and sonorous " Battle of Agincourt " is simply two triplets with the fourth and eighth lines riming together, a, a, a, b, c, c, c, b : —

> Fair stood the wind for France,
> When we our sails advance,
> Nor now to prove our chance
> Longer will tarry ;
> But putting to the main,
> At Caux the mouth of Seine,
> With all his martial train
> Landed King Harry.

Herrick, who is a master of metrical effect, in his lively " To Violets " uses a shorter line than Tennyson chose for his stately " In Memoriam," but employs the same arrangement of rimes, *a, b, b, a, c, d, d, c* : —

> Welcome, maids of honor !
> You do bring
> In the Spring,
> And wait upon her.
> She has virgins many
> Fresh and fair;
> Yet you are
> More sweet than any.

Another effective eight-line stanza is that which Byron handles wittily in "Don Juan." The rime-scheme is *a, b, a, b, a, b, c, c*, the final couplet coming like the crack of a whip : —

> If ever I should condescend to prose
> I 'll write poetical commandments, which
> Shall supersede beyond all doubt all those
> That went before; in these I shall enrich
> My text with many things that no one knows,
> And carry precept to the highest pitch:
> I 'll call the work " Longinus, o'er a Bottle,
> Or, Every Poet his *own* Aristotle."

Yet another arrangement of rimes, pleasing to the ear and binding the stanza into compact unity, is that in which a quatrain is followed by a triplet, the added eighth line riming with the second and fourth, *a*, *b*, *a*, *b*, *c*, *c*, *c*, *b*, as in Swinburne's "Garden of Proserpine":—

> We are not sure of sorrow,
>   And joy was never sure;
> To-day will die to-morrow,
>   Time stoops to no man's lure;
> And love, grown faint and fretful,
> With lips but half-regretful,
> Sighs, and with eyes forgetful
>   Weeps that no loves endure.

Also excellent in its tying of the two quatrains together is the form found, for example, in Chaucer's "Monk's Tale," *a*, *b*, *a*, *b*, *b*, *c*, *b*, *c*, the second rime of the first quatrain continuing as the first rime of the second quatrain, thus setting a couplet in the middle of the stanza:—

> Cenobia, of Palymerie queene —
> As writen Persies of hir noblesse, —
> So worthy was in armes, and so kene,
>   That no wight passed hir in hardynesse,
>   Ne in lynage, ne in other gentilesse.
> Of Kinges blood of Percs is she descended;
>   I seye not that she had moost fairnesse,
> But of hire shape she myghte not been amended.

Not only can almost numberless combinations of rimes be essayed in the eight-line stanza, but any combination which may be adopted can be modified to suit the theme, and can be made to take on an aspect of novelty by shortening certain lines and lengthening others, and by the interlinking of double rimes with single or by leaving certain lines unrimed. The choice of types at the command of the poet is practically inexhaustible; and he reveals his intuitive feeling for verse by the certainty with which he selects the type that is best suited to his subject, and by the skill with which he so modifies this as to serve his immediate purpose.

After the quatrain, the stanza of eight lines has been the most popular with the poets of our language. Yet they have chosen to write also in stanzas of many another length; and it is only proper to give a few specimens of the more significant of these other stanzas. The stanza of five lines, for example, has advantages of its own. Sometimes it resembles one of the quatrain-forms already considered with the addition of an extra line; and sometimes it takes on a special quality of its own. The younger Hood considered it "one of the most musical forms of the stanza," since "it is capable of almost endless variety, and the proportions of rimes, three and two, seem to be especially conducive to harmony." The rime-scheme may be *a*, *a*, *b*, *b*, *x*, the *x* representing a refrain, as in Longfellow's "Excelsior":—

> The shades of night were falling fast,
> As through an Alpine village passed
> A youth, who bore, 'mid snow and ice,
> A banner with the strange device,
> Excelsior!

Or it may be *a*, *b*, *a*, *b*, *b*, as in Waller's "To a Rose":—

> Go, lovely rose!
> Tell her that wastes her time and me,
> That now she knows,
> When I resemble her to thee,
> How sweet and fair she seems to be.

Here the final couplet seems to sum up and reinforce the stanza, giving it a sharper point. The same

rime-scheme with the use of double rimes is found in
Shelley's "Skylark" : —

> Higher still and higher
> From the earth thou springest
> Like a cloud of fire ;
> The blue deep thou wingest,
> And singing still dost soar, and soaring ever singest.

Here the lengthening of the fifth line strengthens
the stanza. Perhaps it was Shelley's use of this effect
in lyric which suggested to Swinburne the type he
employed more than once, in which the fifth line is as
long as all the four lines which precede it : —

> First life on my sources
> First drifted and swam;
> Out of me are the forces
> That save it or damn;
> Out of the man and woman and wild-beast and bird; before God
> was, I am.

If we analyze this metrically, we perceive it to be
really an anapestic heptameter couplet, of which the
first line is divided into four parts by the use of
double and single rhymes, gaining weight and mass
by the full flow of the final line, unencumbered by internal rime. But this is a form to be handled satisfactorily only by a master; and it lends itself easily
to parody, because of the obvious peculiarity of its
structure. It was borrowed by Bret Harte for his
"Plain Language from Truthful James" :—

> Which I wish to remark,
> And my language is plain,
> That for ways that are dark
> And for tricks that are vain,
> The heathen Chinee is peculiar,
> Which the same I would rise to explain.

In one of the lyrics of "The Foresters," Tennyson
has a five-line stanza, x, a, b, a, b, in which he obtains
an effect of ease and freedom by leaving the first line
without rime: —

> Love flew in at the window
> As Wealth walked in at the door.
> "You have come as you saw Wealth coming," said I.
> But he fluttered his wings with a sweet little cry,
> "I 'll cleave to you rich or poor."

And in "A Serenade at the Villa," Browning is
content with five lines of equal length, rimed alternately, a, b, a, b, a, perhaps the simplest possible
arrangement of this stanza: —

> That was I, you heard last night,
> Where there rose no moon at all,
> Nor, to pierce the strained and tight
> Tent of heaven, a planet small:
> Life was dead, and so was light.

It may be thought that Mrs. Browning was a little
too negligent of the possibilities of the five-line form,
when she was content to use only one rime, leaving
two lines unrimed, — x, a, x, a, a; but there is indisputable strength in the lengthening of the final
line, although this is not paraded as in Swinburne's
stanza already quoted: —

> Oh, a lady might have come there,
> Hooded fairly like her hawk
> With a book or lute in summer,
> And a hope of sweeter talk.
> Listening less to her own music than for footsteps on the walk.

When we analyze this, we discover that it is really a
triplet of trochaic octameter, although presented to the

eye as five lines, — much as Swinburne's stanza revealed itself as a couplet. In fact, both Swinburne's and Mrs. Browning's are not really in the five-line form, since they assume this outer shape only to the eye. To the ear Swinburne's is only a couplet of long lines, and Mrs. Browning's is only a triplet. In Mrs. Browning's case the absence of more than the absolutely necessary three rimes makes this fairly obvious, even to a careless ear; whereas the two pairs of rimes inside Swinburne's first line may be held to give his stanza more claim to be considered as actually made up of five lines, in spite of the metrical equivalence of the first four to the final one.

Longfellow employed an effective five-line stanza in his " Enceladus," *a, b, b, a, b* : —

> Under Mount Etna he lies,
> It is slumber, it is not death ;
> For he struggles at times to arise,
> And above him the lurid skies
> Are hot with his fiery breath.

Just as two quatrains can be combined into an eight-line stanza, so two five-line stanzas can be united to make a ten-line type. Sometimes, indeed, the five-line stanzas may even be printed separately, although the rime goes over from the first to the second and from the third to the fourth, as in Longfellow's " The Goblet of Life," in which the rime-scheme is *a, a, a, a, b,* — *c, c, c, c, b* : —

> Filled is Life's goblet to the brim ;
> And though my eyes with tears are dim,
> I see its sparkling bubbles swim,
> And chant a melancholy hymn
> With solemn voice and slow.

No purple flowers, — no garlands green,
Conceal the goblet's shade or sheen,
Nor maddening drafts of Hippocrene,
Like gleams of sunshine, flash between
Thick leaves of mistletoe.

This is one of Longfellow's earlier lyrics and he did not employ this type again, probably feeling that the fourfold repetition of the rime in prompt succession was a little monotonous, and that the long wait for the rime of the fifth line to recur in the tenth was perhaps a little fatiguing to the ear.

The two five-line stanzas may be merely conjoined, as in Moore's "The Time I've lost in wooing," wherein the rime-scheme is $a, a, b, b, a, c, c, d, d, c$: —

The time I've lost in wooing,
In watching and pursuing
    The light that lies
    In woman's eyes,
Has been my heart's undoing.
Though wisdom oft has sought me,
I scorned the love she brought me.
    My only books
    Were woman's looks,
And folly's all they taught me.

A better arrangement of the ten-line stanza is that we find in Gray's "On a Distant Prospect of Eton College," wherein he ties together by a middle couplet two quatrains, the first with interlinked rimes and the last with rimes arranged, as in Tennyson's "In Memoriam," $a, b, a, b, c, c, d, e, e, d$: —

Ye distant spires, ye antique towers,
    That crown the watery glade,
Where grateful Science still adores
    Her Henry's holy shade ;

And ye, that from the stately brow
Of Windsor's heights the expanse below
    Of grove, of lawn, of mead survey,
Whose turf, whose shade, whose flowers among
Wanders the hoary Thames along
    His silver-winding way.

There is an effective ingenuity in the ten-line stanza which Bret Harte employed in "Miss Blanche Says." The rime-scheme is *a, b, a, b, c, d, c, c, c, d*; and the quadruple repetition of one riming sound is relieved by the use of double rimes in four of the other lines : —

And you are the poet, and so you want
    Something — what is it ? — a theme, a fancy ?
Something or other the Muse won't grant
    To your old poetical necromancy ;
Why, one half you poets — you can't deny —
    Don't know the Muse when you chance to meet her,
But sit in your attics and mope and sigh
For a faineant goddess to drop from the sky,
When flesh and blood may be standing by
    Quite at your service, should you but greet her.

It is needless to attempt to catalog all the possible forms of the ten-line stanza, since it is capable of unending variations in the rime-scheme. But no one of its several types is quite as large and sweeping as the nine-line stanza which Spenser employed in the "Faery Queen" and which is usually called the Spenserian : —

So pure and innocent as that same lamb,
She was in life and every virtuous lore ;
And by descent from royal lineage came
Of ancient kings and queens, that had of yore
Their scepters stretcht from east to western shore.
And all that world in their subjection held ;
Till that infernal fiend with foul uproar
Forwasted all their land, and them expelled ;
Whom to avenge she had this Knight from far compelled.

This Spenserian stanza is one of the most melodious instruments that ever a great poet played on, and we need not wonder that Byron and Burns, Keats and Hood borrowed it in turn and evoked delicious music from it. Holmes described it as

> The sweet Spenserian, gathering as it flows,
> Sweeps gently onward to its dying close,
> Where waves on waves in long succession pour,
> Till the ninth billow melts along the shore.

Lowell had the same figure of speech in one of those critical papers of his which were always informed with the insight of a poet into the mechanism of his art. "There is no ebb and flow in the meter more than on the shores of the Adriatic, but wave follows wave with equable gainings and recessions, the one sliding back in fluent music to be mingled with and carried forward by the next. In all this there is soothingness, indeed, but no slumberous monotony; for Spenser was no mere metrist, but a great composer. By the variety of his pauses — now at the close of the first or second foot, now of the third, and again of the fourth — he gives spirit and energy to a measure whose tendency certainly is to become languorous. He knew how to make it rapid and passionate at need."

Three other nine-line stanzas may be mentioned here. One of them is Chaucer's, of which the rime-scheme is *a, a, b, a, a, b, b, c, c*. A second is that which we find in Poe's "Ulalume," where the rimes are arranged *a, b, b, a, b, a, b, a, b*, the final *a, b*, consisting of a repetition of the riming words of the preceding *a, b*. The third is that employed by Tennyson in "The Lady of Shalott," *a, a, a, a, b, c, c, c, b,* the two *b* rime-words being always *Shalott* and *Camelot*, which thus serve as a double refrain, so to speak. This nine-line stanza of Tennyson's may be compared with Longfellow's ten-line stanza in "The Goblet of Life": —

> On either side the river lie
> Long fields of barley and of rye,
> That clothe the wold and meet the sky;
> And through the field the road runs by
>   To many-towered Camelot;
> And up and down the people go,
> Gazing where the lilies blow
> Round an island there below,
>   The island of Shalott.

Although many poets have written in stanzas of more than ten lines, few of these longer forms have justified themselves. Ten is apparently the utmost limit of the lines, the rimes of which the ear can receive without undue strain on the attention. Moore employed a thirteen-line stanza in "Fly not yet"; Francis Mahoney used sixteen short-lines in his "Bells of Shandon," ending every stanza with a refrain; and Swinburne, ever confident in his strength of wing, strove to soar aloft in a stanza of twenty-four lines in his "Last Oracle."

The consideration of the combination of quatrains into the eight-line stanza and of five-line stanzas into ten-line stanzas led to the temporary overlooking of a shorter stanza, which now demands consideration. This is the six-line stanza. It is found very early in English verse, as in this "Christmas Carol," where the rime-scheme is *x, a, x, a, x, a*: —

> God rest you merry, gentlemen,
> Let nothing you dismay,

> Remember Christ our Savior
> Was born on Christmas day:
> To save us all from Satan's power
> When we were gone astray.

This is the same rime-scheme as we find in Longfellow's " The Village Blacksmith," in Willis's " Unseen Spirits," and in Poe's " Annabel Lee." With the first, third, and fifth lines riming together, the form seems to be rare.

Sometimes the six-line stanza is made up of three consecutive couplets, *a, a, b, b, c, c*, as in Bunner's " Forfeits " [1] : —

> They sent him round the circle fair,
> To bow before the prettiest there.
> I 'm bound to say the choice he made
> A creditable taste displayed;
> Although — I can't say what it meant —
> The little maid looked ill-content.
>
> His task was then anew begun —
> To kneel before the wittiest one.
> Once more that little maid sought he,
> And went him down upon his knee.
> She bent her eyes upon the floor —
> I think she thought the game a bore.
>
> He circled then — his sweet behest
> To kiss the one he loved the best.
> For all she frowned, for all she chid,
> He kissed that little maid, he did.
> And then — though why I can't decide —
> The little maid looked satisfied.

Sometimes it is composed of a quatrain with alternate rimes followed by a couplet, *a, b, a, b, c, c*, as in this " Song " of Shelley's : —

Rarely, rarely comest thou,
  Spirit of Delight !
Wherefore hast thou left me now
  Many a day and night ?
Many a weary night and day
'T is since thou art fled away.

One of the most effective arrangements of rimes in the six-line stanza is that which we see in Longfellow's "Seaweed," in Hood's "Progress of Art," and in Holmes's "The Last Leaf." The scheme is *a, a, b, c, c, b*: —

I saw him once before,
As he passed by the door,
    And again
The pavement stones resound,
As he totters o'er the ground
    With his cane.

Effective also is the restriction to two rimes only, as in Longfellow's "Prelude," *a, b, a, a, a, b*: —

Before me rose an avenue
  Of tall and sombrous pines ;
Abroad their fan-like branches grew,
And, when the sunshine darted through,
Spread a vapor, soft and blue,
  In long and sloping lines.

The six-line stanza was a special favorite of Longfellow's. In "The Cumberland" he essayed still another rime-scheme, *a, b, a, c, c, b*: —

Next morn, as the sun rose over the bay,
  Still floated our flag at the mainmast head.
Lord, how beautiful was Thy day !
    Every waft of the air
    Was a whisper of prayer,
  Or a dirge for the dead.

Burns made frequent use of another six-line stanza with only two rimes, *a, a, a, b, a, b,* as in his lines "To a Mouse" : —

> Still thou art blest, compared wi' me !
> The present only toucheth thee:
> But, och! I backward cast my e'e
>   On prospects drear !
> An' forward, though I cannot see,
>   I guess an' fear !

The seven-line stanza is not frequently found, — far less frequently than the stanza of five lines. It may be a quatrain and a couplet with a final line riming with either pair of the lines of the quatrain, as in Swinburne's resonant invocation "To Walt Whitman in America" : —

> Till the motion be done and the measure
>   Circling through season and clime,
> Slumber and sorrow and pleasure,
>   Vision of virtue and crime;
> Till consummate with conquering eyes,
> A soul disembodied, it rise
>   From the body transfigured of time.

The seven-line stanza may, of course, have many other arrangements of its rime-scheme. Rossetti, for example, in "Love's Nocturn," chose to limit himself to two rimes, *a, b, a, b, b, a, b* : —

> Master of the murmuring courts
>   Where the shapes of sleep convene! —
> Lo ! My spirit here exhorts
>   All the powers of my demesne
>   For their aid to woo my queen.
>   What reports
>   Yield thy jealous courts unseen.

Tennyson, in his "Fatima," rimes his first four lines together and his last three, — *a, a, a, a, b, b, b* : —

> O Love, Love, Love! O withering might!
> O sun, that from thy noonday height
> Shudderest when I strain my sight,
> Throbbing thro' all thy heat and light,
> Lo, falling from my constant mind,
> Lo, parch'd and wither'd, deaf and blind,
> I whirl like leaves in roaring wind.

But the fourfold repetition of the first rime and the threefold repetition of the second combine to give the stanza an air of artificiality. There is a lack of the apparent ease and spontaneity, which most easily capture our interest. Indeed, "Fatima," for all its poetic and psychologic power, seems to be one of Tennyson's less successful experiments.

CHAPTER VII

THE SONNET

In the most successful pieces of poetical composition, the struggle between matter and form is not visible. Expression and thought are adapted and mutually helpful. But even single lines . . . of this perfection are rare. What we usually find is metrical skill surpassing power of thought . . . or, on the other hand, expression laboring with an idea which it is unable to embody. This conflict, which takes place in that part of poetic effort which falls within the domain of Art, is most perceptible in the sonnet, for the reason that this is the one form, which, in our language, has been brought within the control of fixed rules. — MARK PATTISON, *Introduction to Milton's Sonnets.*

THE stanza has been considered in the previous chapter as a constituent part of a longer poem, as a single link of a lengthening chain. Yet it may be independent; it may stand forth alone as a poem complete in itself. There are very brief lyrics in a single stanza of ten lines, or of five or even of two. The couplet is the shortest possible form of the stanza, and it has often served for epigram. There is, for example, Gay's epitaph on himself: —

> Life is a jest, and all things show it.
> I thought so once, and now I know it.

And here is the inscription which Pope wrote for the collar of a dog that belonged to the Prince of Wales:—

> I am his Highness' dog at Kew;
> Pray, sir, tell me, — whose dog are you?

These are pretty trifles only, crackling with wit; but the couplet has also served to present airier fancies or sterner thoughts, as in these two lines of Herrick's "Tears and Laughter": —

> Knewest thou one month would take thy life away,
> Thou 'dst weep ; but laugh, should it not last a day.

And in these two by the same dextrous lyrist, on "Dreams": —

> Here we are all, day by day ; by night we 're hurled
> By dreams, each into a several world.

The couplet has sufficed also for a sterner purpose in Emerson's "Inscription for a Well in Memory of the Martyrs of the War": —

> Fall, stream, from Heaven to bless ; return as well ;
> So did our sons ; Heaven met them as they fell.

So may the single triplet be adequate for the clear presentation of the poet's feeling at the moment, as in this three-line poem, also by Herrick, "On Himself": —

> Lost to the world, lost to myself, alone
> Here now I rest under this marble stone,
> In depth of silence, heard and seen of none.

Landor chose the triplet once for the modest contribution "Written on the First Leaf of an Album": —

> Pass me ; I only am the rind
> To the rich fruit that you will find,
> My friends, at every leaf behind.

Of all the briefer stanza forms, the one which has most often been chosen for the expression of a single thought or for the record of a single mood or feeling is the quatrain. Many poets have found that they could phrase a fleeting impression better in four lines than in six or eight. They have relished the sober compactness of this form which imposes a stern condensation. They have profited by the possible variety within the limitations of the four lines — the choice of any one of three rime-schemes, *a, b, a, b,* or *a, a, b, b,* or *a, b, b, a*; the option between any one of the four rhythms, and the privilege of lengthening or shortening the meter of any line. The English quatrain has slowly come to be recognized by the lyrists of our language as a fit instrument for special occasions, — for the epitaph, for the memorial inscription, for any brief utterance which would gain by an Attic concision and an Attic elevation of tone.

Thus Lowell chose the quatrain for the inscription which he was asked to compose for the Soldiers' and Sailors' Monument in Boston : —

> To those who died for her on land and sea,
> That she might have a country great and free,
> Boston builds this : build ye her monument
> In lives like theirs, at duty's summons spent.

Gilder sent a quatrain to Lowell himself on the latter's birthday : —

> Navies nor armies can exalt the state, —
> Millions of men, nor coined wealth untold :
> Down to the pit may sink a land of gold ;
> But one great name can make a country great.

For two memorial windows in St. Margaret's, Westminster, Lowell and Whittier prepared quatrains. The former had to commemorate Raleigh : —

> The New World's sons, from England's breasts we drew
> Such milk as bids remember whence we came ;
> Proud of her Past, wherefrom our Present grew,
> This window we inscribe with Raleigh's name.

And the latter did homage to Milton : —

> The New World honors him whose lofty plea
>   For England's freedom made her own more sure,
> Whose song, immortal as its theme, shall be
>   Their common freehold while both worlds endure.

The quatrain has been found fit for other purposes than inscriptions and congratulations, as is made plain in Aldrich's "Pessimist and Optimist" : —

> This one sits shivering in Fortune's smile,
>   Taking his joy with bated, doubtful breath ;
> This other, gnawed by hunger, all the while
>   Laughs in the teeth of Death.

Aldrich maintained that the quatrain was "a surprisingly difficult form of poem," with a "difficulty out of all proportion to its brevity. A perfect quatrain is as rare as a perfect sonnet. The quatrain has laws as imperative as those of the sonnet, not to be broken with impunity. Four lines do not necessarily constitute a quatrain proper any more than fourteen lines necessarily constitute a sonnet. If your little stanza ends with a snap, it becomes an epigram and ceases to be a poem. The idea or thought expressed must be so fully expressed as to leave no material for a second stanza. The theme that can be exhausted in the space of four lines is not easy to light upon. Landor was a master in this field."

It may be well to illustrate this last assertion by citing two of Landor's quatrains. Here is one written on his seventy-fifth birthday : —

> I strove with none, for none was worth my strife;
>   Nature I loved, and next to Nature, Art;
> I warmed both hands before the fire of life,
>   It sinks, and I am ready to depart.

And here is another, apparently composed even later : —

> Death stands above me, whispering low
> I know not what into my ear ;
> Of his strange language all I know
> Is, there is not a word of fear.

Like the couplet, the quatrain has served also for the purposes of satire ; and then it is likely to end with a snap and to become an epigram rather than an epigraph. Here are the vivacious four lines which Byron wrote on his wedding-day, January the second : —

> Here 's a happy New Year ! but with reason,
> I beg you 'll permit me to say —
> Wish me many returns of the season,
> But as few as you please of the day.

The noblest fixed form of English verse, far more valuable than the couplet or the quatrain, which have voiced satire more often than not, is the sonnet. Although it is not English in its origin, but borrowed from the Italian, it has been firmly established in our language for more than three centuries. It has proved itself a superb instrument for the supreme masters of English poetry ; and in no other tongue is there a more splendid collection of sonnets than in our own. And yet there is no final agreement on its exact form. The sonnets of Shakspere are written in an arrangement of rimes far easier than that in which the sonnets of Milton are composed. Indeed, most of those who have set forth the theory of this form are inclined to deny that the so-called sonnets of Shakspere are justly entitled to the name. All are agreed that the sonnet is a stanza of fourteen iambic pentameter lines, complete in itself, containing a single thought and ex-

pressing this adequately and amply. Most critics would
demand more than this; they would insist that the true
sonnet conforms to a special scheme of rimes, and that
no fourteener which does not conform to this scheme
is fairly to be termed a sonnet.

The stanza which satisfied Shakspere consisted simply of three quatrains followed by a couplet. Each of
the three quatrains rimes *a*, *b*, *a*, *b*, and the rimes in
each of the three are distinct; and distinct also are the
pair of rimes in the final couplet. This is the form prescribed by George Gascoigne, who has defined it as " a
poem of fourteen lines, every line containing ten syllables, the first twelve riming in staves of four lines
by cross meter, and the last two riming together."
It is this prescription that Shakspere chose to follow.
Here is his one hundred and thirty-ninth sonnet, as
characteristic as any : —

> O, call me not to justify the wrong
> That thy unkindness lays upon my heart;
> Wound me not with thine eye but with thy tongue,
> Use power with power and slay me not by art.
>
> Tell me thou lov'st elsewhere, but in my sight,
> Dear heart, forbear to glance thine eye aside:
> What need'st thou wound with cunning when thy might
> Is more than my o'er-press'd defence can bide ?
>
> Let me excuse thee : ah ! my love well knows
> Her pretty looks have been mine enemies,
> And therefore from my face she turns my foes,
> That elsewhere they might dart their injuries:
>
> Yet do not so, but since I am near slain,
> Kill me outright with looks and rid my pain.

In this poem we note that every quatrain is complete in itself, being in fact almost an independent

stanza, and that the couplet winds up the brief lyric with a sharp snap which is almost epigrammatic in its temper. If Shakspere, with all his instinctive feeling for technic, preferred this laxer form to the stricter and more limited arrangement of the true Italian sonnet, it was not because he was unacquainted with that, since it had been already attempted by not a few of his elder contemporaries. His choice was probably due to his belief that the three quatrains and the couplet were better suited for his own immediate purpose. As an acute critic has declared, Shakspere must have been convinced "that the classic symmetry of the Petrarchan sonnet was in English too difficult of attainment; that it cramped invention, and imposed too many sacrifices and concessions; and that the artistic end could better be achieved by the looser arrangement he adopted." Perhaps it may be suggested also that with his Elizabethan liking for points and conceits and antitheses, he felt that he wanted the final couplet with its epigrammatic suggestion. The same sharp critic noted also that Keats wrote his earlier sonnets in one of the stricter Italian forms, but in his later relapsed into the freer English arrangement which Shakspere had glorified. The most marked peculiarity of the Shaksperian fourteener is that there is likely to be a break in the sense at the end of each of the three quatrains, and that the couplet is thus sharply set off by itself. This is wholly contradictory to the theory of the more rigid Italian form, where the division occurs at the end of the second quatrain, leaving a large opportunity to the sestet for the application of the thought presented in the octave.

Having chosen his form for reasons sufficient to

himself, Shakspere revealed his keen insight into its possibilities. Commonly he developed " the subject in three stages, putting the conclusion into the final couplet." In the sixty-seventh sonnet, for example, three questions are asked, one in each quatrain; and the answer is given in the concluding pair of lines.

> Ah! wherefore with infection should he live,
>   And with his presence grace impiety,
> That sin by him advantage should achieve
>   And lace itself with his society ?
> Why should false painting imitate his cheek,
>   And steal dead seeing of his living hue ?
> Why should poor beauty indirectly seek
>   Roses of shadow, since his rose is true ?
> Why should he live, now Nature bankrupt is,
>   Beggar'd of blood to blush through lively veins ?
> For she hath no exchequer now but his,
>   And, proud of many, lives upon his gains.
> O, him she stores, to show what wealth she had
> In days long since, before these last so bad.

In other sonnets, Shakspere varied his method. It has been pointed out that in the eighty-third sonnet, " the poet's apology for silence is presented as an argument in three clauses, the salient fact being put in the couplet as strongly as possible " ; and that in the ninety-seventh " the second quatrain puts in an objection to the first, which is met by the third, the couplet in this case being treated as an extension of the third quatrain." Now and again, the triple division of the theme into the three quatrains is emphasized " by the repetition of the same or similar words at the beginning of each quatrain," as in the forty-ninth and the hundredth.

In spite of the weight of Shakspere's example, the large majority of English poets have preferred to

adopt a stricter form, more in accord with the Italian
model, although not a few of them have clung to the
final couplet. This Italian model resembles the Shaksperian form in that it is a stanza of fourteen iambic
pentameter lines; and it differs in that it has only two
quatrains and that instead of seven rimes it has at
most five and often only four. The two quatrains have
only two rimes between them, arranged $a, b, b, a,$
$a, b, b, a.$ The final six lines are allowed more liberty;
indeed there is no agreement as to the number of the
rimes or as to their order. Sometimes they are but
two, alternating c, d, c, d, c, d; and sometimes they are
three, $c, d, e, c, d, e.$

Milton's massive sonnet "On the Late Massacres in
Piedmont" may be taken as an example of the form
which has only four rimes:—

> Avenge, O Lord, thy slaughtered Saints, whose bones
>   Lie scattered on the Alpine mountains cold ;
>   Even them who kept thy truth so pure of old,
> When all our fathers worshiped stocks and stones,
> Forget not : in thy book record their groans
>   Who were thy sheep, and in their ancient fold
>   Slain by the bloody Piedmontese, that rolled
> Mother with infant down the rocks. Their moans
> The vales redoubled to the hills, and they
>   To heaven. Their martyred blood and ashes sow
> O'er all the Italian fields, where still doth sway
>   The triple Tyrant ; that from these may grow
> A hundredfold, who, having learnt thy way,
>   Early may fly the Babylonian woe.

This has a sweeping unity of theme and a weighty
austerity of thought. Its effect is intensified by the long
open vowel-sounds ay and o which end the final lines.
Its unity is so complete that it does not comply with
the requirement sometimes laid down that the thought

shall be stated in the first eight lines; that there shall
be a break at this point; and that then the thought
shall recoil on itself in the last six lines. This condition is fulfilled in Gilder's sonnet, "The Sonnet," in
which there are five rimes, two in the quatrains, *a, b, b, a,
a, b, b, a*, and three in the tercets, *c, d, e, c, d, e* : —

> What is a sonnet? 'T is the pearly shell
>> That murmurs of the far-off murmuring sea;
>> A precious jewel carved most curiously :
> It is a little picture painted well.
> What is a sonnet? 'T is the tear that fell
>> From a great poet's hidden ecstasy ;
>> A two-edged sword, a star, a song — ah me !
> Sometimes a heavy tolling funeral bell.
> This was the flame that shook with Dante's breath ;
>> The solemn organ whereon Milton played,
>>> And the clear glass where Shakespere's shadow falls :
> A sea this is — beware who ventureth !
>> For like a fiord the narrow floor is laid
>>> Mid-ocean deep sheer to the mountain walls.

These are the only two forms of the sonnet which
are admitted to be absolutely correct by the purists
and precisians. In both, the quatrains have only two
rimes, arranged *a, b, b, a, a, b, b, a*; and in one,
the final six lines have also only two rimes, each repeated alternately three times, *c, d, c, d, c, d*, while
in the other the final six lines are allotted three
rimes, each recurring twice in regular succession,
c, d, e, c, d, e. But if we seek to deduce the principle
from the practice of the masters of verse, we find that
there this rigid rule is not supported. The immense
majority of English sonnet-writers are found to cling
to the accepted arrangement of the octave; but they
are unwilling to be bound by any law which shall
limit the sequence of the rimes in the sestet. Often

they accept one or the other of the approved arrangements; but often also they reject these, for reasons of their own, unwilling to spoil their poem for the sake of an arbitrary rule, the validity of which they do not feel bound to acknowledge. Here again the test is the ear of the hearer. It is easy for the ear to follow the strict arrangement of the rimes in the two quatrains; but it is not easy for the ear to keep up the counting in the later lines, especially since it has been trained to accept either of two arrangements. So long as the rimes in the final six lines are two or three, and so long as the final couplet is avoided, the ear is satisfied. The sonnet is an arbitrary and artificial form, appealing especially to the cultivated ear, and most of those who appreciate its merits are likely to possess more or less acquaintance with the accepted rules of its composition; therefore any failure to follow these rules is likely to disappoint these hearers and to distract their interest.

Yet it seems to be only an unjustifiable hypercriticism which would object to the couplet that occurs in the middle of the final six lines of Lang's admirable sonnet on "The Odyssey":—

> As one that for a weary space has lain
>   Lulled by the song of Circe and her wine
>   In gardens near the pale of Proserpine,
> Where that Ægean isle forgets the main,
> And only the low lutes of love complain,
>   And only shadows of wan lovers pine,
>   As such an one were glad to know the brine
> Salt on his lips, and the large air again,—
> So gladly, from the songs of modern speech
>   Men turn, and see the stars and feel the free
>   Shrill wind beyond the close of heavy flowers,
> And, through the music of the languid hours,

> They hear like ocean on a western beach
> The surge and thunder of the Odyssey.

If fault must be found with this sonnet, it would not be that the lyrist has departed from the strict sequence of rimes, *c, d, e, c, d, e,* substituting his own arrangement, *c, d, e, e, c, d;* but rather that he has been a little careless of tone-color, in ending both of the rimes of his quatrains with the sound of *n, lain* and *wine,* and that he has also employed the sound of long *e* in two of the three rimes of his sestet, *speech* and *free.* A similar carelessness is to be discovered, also, in Wordsworth's "Scorn not the Sonnet," in which two of the rimes of the sestet are too closely akin, *lamp, land, damp, hand,* since the same vowel-sound of *a* occurs in both of them, intensified by the phonetic relation of the *m* to the *n.* To those who apply the test of the ear this will seem a more regrettable lapse from ultimate perfection than the use of a final couplet : —

> Scorn not the Sonnet; Critic, you have frowned,
> Mindless of its just honors; with this key
> Shakspere unlocked his heart; the melody
> Of this small lute gave ease to Petrarch's wound;
> A thousand times this pipe did Tasso sound;
> With it Camöens soothed an exile's grief;
> The Sonnet glittered a gay myrtle leaf
> Amid the cypress with which Dante crowned
> His visionary brow; a glow-worm lamp
> It cheered mild Spenser, called from Faery-land
> To struggle through dark ways; and, when a damp
> Fell round the path of Milton, in his hand
> The thing became a trumpet ; whence he blew
> Soul-animating strains — alas, too few.

It must needs be noted also that Wordsworth has here allowed himself the license of changing the pair of rimes in the middle of the second quatrain. Instead of *a, b, b, a, a, b, b, a,* he has *a, b, b, a, a, c, c, a.* And yet although he ventured upon his departure from the form, he retained the same vowel-sound in the middle of both quatrains, *key* and *melody* in the first, and *grief* and *leaf* in the second. It seems dimly possible that as he had emphasized the long *e* sound in the first quatrain, he may have thought that the ear would catch this same long *e* in *grief* and *leaf*, and that he was satisfied with this repetition, neglecting or unwittingly eliminating the insignificant *f* which follows the long *e* in the second quatrain. It was hard always for Wordsworth to put on the fetters of any fixed form ; he had a tendency to lawlessness of structure ; he was wilful in going his own way in his own fashion ; and it may be that he had a vague consciousness of this, which, as Lowell suggested, made him welcome the restraint of the sonnet. Nobility of thought was his by gift of nature, and elevation of outlook ; but in the minor matters of technic he needed some outside stimulus to keep him up to the mark of his highest achievement.

To the two sonnets on the sonnet already quoted here may be added a third by Rossetti, inferior to Wordsworth's in its imagination no doubt, but superior in its technic : —

A Sonnet is a moment's monument, —
  Memorial from the Soul's eternity
  To one dead deathless hour. Look that it be,
Whether for lustral rite or dire portent,
Of its own arduous fulness reverent:
  Carve it in ivory or in ebony,
  As Day or Night may rule; and let Time see
Its flowering crest impearl'd and orient.
A Sonnet is a coin; its face reveals
  The soul, — its converse, to what power 't is due: —

> Whether for tribute to the august appeals
>   Of Life, or dower in Love's high retinue,
> It serve; or, 'mid the dark wharf's cavernous breath,
> In Charon's palm it pays the toll of Death.

It is especially in the sonnet that Longfellow revealed his mastery of verse ; and he was prone to keep to the strict letter of the law, taking no liberties with the form, and preferring to use three rimes in the sestet, as he did in this on " Nature " : —

> As a fond mother, when the day is o'er,
>   Leads by the hand her little child to bed,
>   Half willing, half reluctant to be led,
> And leave his broken playthings on the floor,
> Still gazing at them through the open door,
>   Nor wholly reassured and comforted
>   By promises of others in their stead,
>   Which, though more splendid, may not please him
>   more;
> So Nature deals with us, and takes away
>   Our playthings one by one, and by the hand
> Leads us to rest so gently, that we go
> Scarce knowing if we wish to go or stay,
>   Being too full of sleep to understand
> How far the unknown transcends the what we know.

Longfellow's intuitive feeling led him to avoid the terminal couplet. Probably he would have agreed with Aldrich in holding that the strict Italian arrangement "with its interwoven rimes, its capacity for expressing subtle music is an instrument as superior to the English form as the harp or the guitar is superior to the banjo; and I fancy that most workers in this kind of verse will agree with me. The alternate lines riming, and closing with a couplet, gave the poet the command of some of the richest melodic effects within the reach of English versification. The sonnet that ends with a couplet misses that fine unrolling of music which belongs to the sonnet proper. The couplet brings the reader up with a jerk. In ninety-nine cases out of a hundred, the couplet has the snap of a whip-lash, and turns the sonnet into an epigram. To my thinking, this abruptness hurts many of Shakspere's beautiful poems of fourteen lines — for they are simply that. One must go to Milton, and Wordsworth, and Keats (in three instances) in order to find the highest development of the English sonnet."

In fact, it seems to be the opinion of most of the later poets of our language that if the game is to be played at all, it is best to follow the rules without cavil and without claiming any license to depart from them. There is no obligation on any poet to make use of the sonnet framework; and if he would express himself without restraint he has at his command the large liberty of all the other lyrical forms. It is in the rigidity of its skeleton that the charm of the sonnet is solidly rooted. It tends to impose a helpful condensation, thus counteracting the temptation to diffuseness. Except for the narrow limits within which the acceptance of the form has restricted it, many a poem that " would have been but a loose nebulous vapor has been compressed and rounded into a star," — so Trench declared; "the sonnet, like a Grecian temple, may be limited in its scope, but like that, if successful, it is altogether perfect."

Tennyson said to a friend that " a sonnet arrests the free sweep of genius, and if poets were to keep to it, it would cripple them; but it is a fascinating kind of verse, and to excel in it is a rare distinction." And when his companion suggested that the last line should form the climax, both of thought and of expression, and that the whole should be like a wave breaking on the shore, Tennyson declared that "the whole should show a continuous advance of thought and movement, like a river fed by rillets, as every great poem should."

The sonnet is thus seen to be not only a form of verse, deliberately accepted and conscientiously filled, it is also a special type of poem, because it must have an absolute unity of its own. It must have its single and simple theme, lofty and yet not too large for its frame but exactly commensurate with this. It must move in every line toward its inevitable conclusion, which shall be full and satisfactory to the ear and to the mind. It must be ample and yet reticent ; and it must have sustained sonority, culminating impressively in the final line. It must be impeccable, beyond all other verse, in the easy perfection of its rhythm, its meter, and its rime, with an avoidance of all dissonance and jingle, and with an artful contrast of the vowel-sounds in all of its four or five rimes. Above all, it must be not only continuous but clear in its central thought, since the form itself is complicated, and therefore the ear must not have to strain itself also to ascertain the poet's message. Lowell praised Longfellow's sonnets especially for this quality of clarity : " they remind me of one of those cabinets we sometimes see, in which many drawers are unlocked by a single key. I have seen sonnets in which there is a separate lock, I may say, for every line, and in fumbling among our fourteen keys we find ourselves sometimes in certain confusion. Added to this there would be sometimes the conundrum of secret drawers."

This limpidity of Longfellow is displayed beautifully

in one of his sonnets on the "Divina Commedia" of
Dante: —

> Oft have I seen at some cathedral door
>   A laborer, pausing in the dust and heat,
>   Lay down his burden, and with reverent feet
>   Enter, and cross himself, and on the floor
> Kneel to repeat his paternoster o'er;
>   Far off the noises of the world retreat;
>   The loud vociferations of the street
>   Become an undistinguishable roar.
> So, as I enter here from day to day,
>   And leave my burden at this minster gate,
>   Kneeling in prayer, and not ashamed to pray,
> The tumult of the time disconsolate
>   To inarticulate murmurs dies away,
>   While the eternal ages watch and wait.

This is noble in tone and lofty in its simple imagery.
There is special felicity in the richness imparted to
the versification by the polysyllables in the second half.
But, if a blemish must be sought, it can be found in
the use of the same vowel-sound in both of the rimes
of the sestet. The long *a* in *gate*, *disconsolate* and
wait reappears in *day*, *pray* and *away;* and this is
not entirely pleasing to the ear, — if, indeed, it is not
even a little confusing.

The rigorous limitation to fourteen lines of prescribed and equal length, the restriction of the rimes
to four or five as the case may be, the intricate arrangement of these rimes according to the Petrarchan
pattern, and the avoiding of the terminal couplet, —
all these requirements unite to make the sonnet seem
like a difficult form. And yet this very difficulty may
be an advantage. Every true artist finds his profit in
a resolute grapple with technical obstacles, a struggle
which forces him to take the utmost pains and to put

forth his topmost strength; and he gets keen pleasure out of this tussle with his material and with his form. The very limitation of the rimes of the sonnet may be suggestive and sustaining; and the poet can attain ultimate freedom within strict bounds.

That the sonnet is not so difficult as it may seem at first sight is proved by the multitude of English sonnets which rise to a fairly satisfactory level of technical merit. Few of the major poets of our language have failed absolutely in this form. On the other hand, only a few even of the greater lyrists have attained to high distinction as sonneteers, because the sonnet at its best demands a union of imaginative inspiration, of moral aspiration, and of technical accomplishment which is very rarely achieved. And a poor sonnet is a very poor thing, indeed. As a French critic once wittily asserted, " nothing is longer than a sonnet when there is nothing in it."

Although the sonnet is best fitted for the expression of a single thought or a single emotion complete in itself, ample for the form and yet not too abundant for its limited framework, certain poets have chosen to use it almost as if it were only a stanza. They have composed a succession of sonnets on a central theme, each devoted to a single aspect of this. These sonnet-sequences, as they are termed, were particularly popular with the Elizabethans; and they have been attractive also to certain of the Victorians, especially to Rossetti and Mrs. Browning. And yet the sonnet-sequence seems to be rather contradictory, since the unique characteristic of the sonnet is that it must be the perfect expression of a single and simple thought or mood. To treat the sonnet merely as though it was a stanza is to forego this special quality, without any compensating advantage. It is to adventure on the quest for a necklace of flawless and priceless pearls, all of equal size and of equal value.

CHAPTER VIII

OTHER FIXED FORMS

The six most important of the poetic creations of old France, the rondel, the rondeau, the triolet, the villanelle, the ballade, and the chant-royal. . . . Each has a fixed form, regulated by traditional laws, and each depends upon richness of rime and delicate workmanship for its successful exercise. The first three are habitually used for joyous or gay thought, and lie most within the province of *jeu d'esprit* and epigram ; the last three are usually wedded to serious or stately expression, and almost demand a vein of pathos. — EDMUND GOSSE : *A Plea for Certain Exotic Forms of Verse.*

THE sonnet is the noblest of all fixed forms, with a special function of its own. The quatrain is inferior to the sonnet, if only by reason of its brevity; but it can serve on occasion even for imagination, although it seems better suited to fancy or to wit. There is also a five-line stanza of wide popularity which confines itself within the lower realm of playful humor, often deriving a large proportion of its effect from the inventive unexpectedness of its double and treble rimes. This is the form which has won wide recognition under the curious title of the " limerick." It is anapestic in rhythm, with its first, second and fifth lines trimeter, and its third and fourth dimeter. Sometimes the rimes are single throughout, as in this : —

> There was a young lady from Lynn,
> Who was so excessively thin
>   That when she essayed
>   To drink lemonade
> She slipped through the straw and fell in.

Sometimes the thrice-repeated rime of the trimeter lines is double, as in this: —

> There was once an ichthyosaurus,
> Who lived when the earth was all porous;
> But he fainted with shame
> When he first heard his name,
> And departed a great while before us.

And sometimes these longer lines have a triple rime which affords abundant scope for the devising of unlooked-for collocations, as in this: —

> Do you know the young ladies of Birmingham,
> And the terrible scandal concerning 'em? —
> How they took their hat-pins
> And scratched at the shins
> Of the bishop while he was confirming 'em?

This last specimen illustrates the special opportunity of the limerick, the reward it pays to the fertile rime-ster. Full advantage is not taken of the form when the fifth line merely repeats the terminal word of the first, as in this: —

> There was a small boy of Quebec,
> Who was buried in snow to his neck,
> When asked, "Are you friz?"
> He answered, "I is, —
> But we don't call this cold in Quebec."

In view of its widespread popularity wherever the English language is spoken, there is no denying that the limerick is a definite fixed form.

The humble limerick has the distinction of being the only fixed form which is actually indigenous to English. The sonnet is a transplanted exotic which has long been acclimatized in our language. And the quatrain, which was cultivated in both Greek and

Latin, has in our own tongue attained an importance not paralleled in any other modern language. There are other fixed forms of foreign growth which have also taken root in English versification, — most of them having been imported from France. They have not succeeded, any of them, in winning equality with the sonnet, but they afford to the lyrist the same opportunity for working within prescribed bounds. They have the fascination of apparent difficulty, the overcoming of which is likely to give pleasure to the listener and delight to the artist. And each of them has possibilities of its own, now serious and now comic.

Of these imported forms, the least important is the triolet. It is an artificial stanza with its brief lines and its treble repetition of the refrain; but it lends itself readily to frank fun with a flavor of personality. Although it had been known earlier in English literature, it attracted no attention until it was revived by Austin Dobson, — to whom, more than to any other poet, these imported fixed forms owe their vogue with our verse-makers. The triolet is at its best when it is used for epigram, for a single swift thrust of satire; but it can also carry playful humor with a faint hint of sentiment. Although its multiplied refrains tend to make it monotonous if heard too often, Alphonse Daudet, in French, and Austin Dobson, in English, have ventured on triolet-sequences, not without a certain measure of success in both cases.

The triolet is a stanza of eight lines, preferably brief, containing only two rimes, arranged *a*, *b*, *a*, *a*, *a*, *b*, *a*, *b*, with the first line repeated as the fourth and again as the seventh, and with the second line repeated as the eighth. Here, as an example, is one stave

of the triolet-sequence which Austin Dobson entitled
" Rose-Leaves " : —

> I intended an ode,
>> And it turned into triolets.
> It began *à la mode*.
> I intended an ode,
> But Rose crossed the road
>> With a bunch of fresh violets ;
> I intended an ode,
>> And it turned into triolets.

Here is another from the same set of little lyrics ;
and in this second example the smiling lyrist has been
able to suggest a more distinct differentiation of meaning in the several repetitions of the refrain : —

> Rose kissed me to-day.
>> Will she kiss me to-morrow ?
> Let it be as it may,
> Rose kissed me *to-day ;*
> But the pleasure gives way
>> To a savor of sorrow ; —
> Rose kissed me to-day, —
>> *Will* she kiss me to-morrow ?

Henley, borrowing the hint from Dobson's rondeau
after Voiture, rimed a triolet on the triolet itself : —

> Easy is the Triolet,
>> If you really learn to make it !
> Once a neat refrain you get
> Easy is the Triolet.
> As you see ! I pay my debt,
>> With another rime, Deuce take it !
> Easy is the Triolet,
>> If you really learn to make it !

But by its undue weight and by its condescending
bluster this example proves that the triolet is really
not so very easy, after all : — or at least it is evidence
that Henley himself could not rival the apparent ease

of Dobson. Part of the heaviness of Henley's specimen is due to the riming of *triolet* on the last syllable, which has not quite emphasis enough for this,
just as part of the lightness of the first of Dobson's
two specimens is the result of the triple-riming *triolets* and *violets*. It is sad to have to record that a
pedantic friend persuaded the poet that *triolets* was
not yet an English word, and that it therefore retained
its French pronunciation, which forbade its mating
with *violets*, whereupon Dobson transmogrified his
lightsome lyric, and despoiled it of not a little of its
levity as well as of most of its truth: —

> I intended an Ode,
>   And it turned to a Sonnet.
> It began *à la mode*.
> I intended an Ode;
> But Rose crossed the road
>   In her latest new bonnet.
> I intended an Ode,
>   And it turned to a Sonnet.

One cause of the gossamer unsubstantiality of
" Rose-Leaves " is the brevity of the line, adjusting itself to the brevity of the stanza itself. For the triolet
the meter must not be too long; and his choice of
anapestic dimeter is added evidence of the delicacy of
Dobson's intuitive feeling for propriety of rhythm.
His anapestic dimeter is far better for the purpose in
hand than Henley's trochaic tetrameter. The triolet
loses a little of its lightness even when the line is
lengthened from anapestic dimeter to anapestic trimeter, as in this triolet of Bunner's: —

> A pitcher of mignonette,
>   In a tenement's highest casement:

Queer sort of flower-pot — yet
That pitcher of mignonette
Is a garden in heaven set,
    To the little sick child in the basement—
The pitcher of mignonette,
    In the tenement's highest casement.

And there is in this example, charming as it is in
feeling, a regrettable lapse from the rigor of the rules,
in that the fourth and seventh lines are slightly varied in wording from the first. Perhaps it must be
said also that the sentiment in Bunner's triolet is almost too serious for so tricksy a form. Yet, as is
shown in these two triolets by Mme. Duclaux (A. Mary
F. Robinson), an even deeper emotion has been expressed in this stanza: —

All the night and all the day
    I think upon her lying dead,
With lips that neither kiss nor pray
All the night nor all the day.
In that dark grave whose only ray
    Of sun or moon 's her golden head;
All the night and all the day
    I think upon her lying dead.

What can heal a broken heart?
    Death alone, I fear me.
Thou that dost true lovers part,
What can heal a broken heart?
Death alone, that made the smart,
    Death, that will not hear me.
What can heal a broken heart?
    Death alone, I fear me.

It may not be fanciful to see in the triolet the
source of the captivating stanza which Swinburne devised for his lovely lyric, " A Match." He gave up the
repetition of the first line as the fourth; and he em-

ployed a third rime for the third and fourth lines
linked in a couplet: —

> If I were what the words are,
>   And love were like the tune,
> With double sound and single
> Delight our lips would mingle
> With kisses glad as birds are
>   That get sweet rain at noon;
> If I were what the words are,
>   And love were like the tune.
>
> . . . .
>
> If you were queen of pleasure
>   And I were king of pain,
> We 'd hunt down love together,
> Pluck out his flying feather
> And teach his feet a measure,
>   And find his mouth a rein;
> If you were queen of pleasure
>   And I were king of pain.

A little more substantial than the triolet and yet
closely akin in restriction of rime and in repetition
of refrain are the rondel and the rondeau. The rondel has two accepted forms in English, both of which
are due to the example set by Dobson, who has
adapted the French original to the requirements of
our English tongue with the same certainty of touch
that Horace revealed when he modified the Greek
sapphic stanza to fit the needs of Latin. In the fuller
form, the rondel consists of fourteen lines with only
two rimes, the first and second lines being repeated
as the seventh and eighth and again as the thirteenth
and fourteenth. The more serious possibility of the
rondel is revealed in Bunner's "Ready for the
Ride" [1]: —

[1] By permission from *Poems* by H. C. Bunner, copyrighted, 1884,
by Charles Scribner's Sons.

Through the fresh fairness of the spring to ride,
 As in the old days when he rode with her,
With joy of Love that had fond Hope to bride,
 One year ago had made her pulses stir.

Now shall no wish with any day recur,
(For Love and Death part year and year full wide,)
Through the fresh fairness of the spring to ride,
 As in the old days when he rode with her.

No ghost there lingers of the smile that died
 On the sweet pale lips where his kisses were —
Yet still she turns her delicate ear aside,
 That she may hear him come with jingling spur —
Through the fresh fairness of the spring to ride,
 As in the old days when he rode with her.

The other form of the rondel is exactly the same as this, except that it consists of thirteen lines only, the final repetition of the second line as the fourteenth being discarded, the poem ending with the repetition of the first line as the final line. The full value of the rondel in this slightly curtailed variation is disclosed in Austin Dobson's melodious "Wanderer" : —

Love comes back to his vacant dwelling —
 The old, old Love that we knew of yore!
 We see him stand by the open door,
With his great eyes sad, and his bosom swelling.

He makes as though in our arms repelling,
 He fain would lie as he lay before;
Love comes back to his vacant dwelling —
 The old, old Love that we knew of yore !

Ah, who shall help us from over-telling
 That sweet forgotten, forbidden lore!
 E'en as we doubt in our heart once more,
With a rush of tears to our eyelids welling,
Love comes back to his vacant dwelling.

It may be well to call attention to the unforced ingenuity with which both Bunner and Dobson, in these two rondels, have given new meaning to the first line of their charming lyrics, as this is repeated later in their poems. This is a point too often neglected by these who have chosen to express themselves in this form, although it is only by attaining this felicity that the repetition of the refrain can be made interesting to the ear. If the game is to be played at all, the poet must willingly abide by all its rules, making his profit out of them. He must know what they are when he begins; and he must do his best within the rigorous code. As Stevenson declared, " the engendering idea of some works is stylistic; a technical preoccupation stands them instead of some robuster principle of life. And with these the execution is but play; for the stylistic problem is resolved beforehand, and all large originality of treatment wilfully foregone. Such are the verses intricately designed, which we have learned to admire, with a certain smiling admiration, at the hands of Mr. Lang and Mr. Dobson." And when the pattern of the intricate design is once attempted, the execution, playful though it may be, must concord therewith.

Swinburne rejected both of the established variations of the rondel and devised a form which he called a *roundel*, and in which he composed a hundred lyrics. For this "Century of Roundels" he wrote one more in which he exemplified and explained the form he had devised to suit himself : —

A roundel is wrought as a ring or a star-bright sphere,
  With craft of delight and cunning of sound unsought,
That the heart of the hearer may smile if to pleasure his ear
    A roundel is wrought.

Its jewel of music is carved of all or of aught —
Love, laughter, or mourning, remembrance of rapture or
    fear —
That fancy may fashion to hang in the ear of thought.

As a bird's quick song runs round, and the hearts in us hear
Pause answer to pause, and again the same strain caught,
So moves the device whence, round as a pearl or a tear,
        A roundel is wrought.

This roundel Swinburne may have wrought himself
with craft of delight; but the device has failed to
charm other lyrists. Perhaps the reason may be that
the line is a little too long and too full for so light a
thing, or, that since its inventor had composed five-
score lyrics in this mold of his own, he had exhausted
all its possibilities. Of course, the failure of the roundel
may have an even simpler explanation, — that no
other poet cared to venture on a rivalry with Swinburne in a field which that master of verse had fenced
in for the exercise of his own surpassing metrical
dexterity.

The rondel is ampler than the triolet and fitted for
a wider and higher range of themes; and its sister
form, the rondeau, is perhaps still a finer instrument.
The rondeau has continually tempted English rimesters; Wyatt essayed himself in this form in his day;
and again in Canning's time it reappeared to serve as
a vehicle for partisan satire. Praed must have had
these political verses in mind when he wrote: —

    And some compose a tragedy,
      And some compose a rondo:
    And some draw sword for liberty,
      And some draw pleas for John Doe.

Yet Leigh Hunt did not know the exact form when

he composed what he called a rondeau to commemorate his being kissed by Mrs. Carlyle : —

> Jenny kissed me when we met,
>   Jumping from the chair she sat in ;
> Time, you thief ! who love to get
>   Sweets into your list, put that in.
> Say I 'm weary, say I 'm sad ;
>   Say that health and wealth have missed me ;
> Say I 'm growing old ; but add —
>   Jenny kissed me !

The true form was revived by Dobson, to whom it has owed its later popularity. He has used it more often and to better effect than any of the many minor bards who have followed in his footsteps both in Great Britain and in the United States. The rondeau consists of thirteen lines with only two rimes between them ; and it has also an unrimed refrain after the eighth line and after the thirteenth, this refrain being the first four syllables of the first line. Lope de Vega once wrote a sonnet on the difficulty of writing a sonnet ; and it was this playful Spanish lyric which probably suggested to Voiture the composition of a rondeau on the difficulty of writing a rondeau. This clever trifle of Voiture's Dobson has most cleverly adapted into English : —

> You bid me try, blue eyes, to write
> A rondeau. What ! — forthwith ? — to-night ?
>   Reflect, some skill I have, 't is true ;
>   But thirteen lines — and rimed on two —
> "Refrain" as well. Ah, hapless plight !
>
> Still, there are five lines, — ranged aright
> These Gallic bonds, I feared, would fright
>   My easy Muse. They did, till you —
>   You bid me try !

This makes them nine. The port's in sight ;
'T is all because your eyes are bright !
   Now just a pair to end with " oo "—
   When maids command, what can't we do ?
Behold ! the rondeau — tasteful, light —
    You bid me try !

In an article written in 1877, before his own examples had won favor for the form, Dobson asserted that there was " no real reason why the rondeau should not become as popular in its own line as the sonnet,"— a prophecy which has not quite been fulfilled, partly because " its own line " has less breadth of appeal than that of the sonnet. The rondeau, satisfactory as it is for the purposes for which it is fit, lacks the large variety of the sonnet, which can voice all moods of sentiment and of passion. In this same essay, Dobson declared that to learn the inner secret of the rondeau, " to give the refrain a new savor and fragrance at each repetition by some covert art of setting, and to make it seem mere bubbling over, as it were, of the eighth and thirteenth lines, — these are things which only masters of the lyre can attain to."

To vary the content of the four sounds which constitute the refrain, a daring rimester now and then has risked a play upon words. This is justified by the precedent of the French ; and yet it does not recommend itself heartily to us with our confirmed belief that the pun belongs to a subordinate order of wit. Still it may be well to give an example of this method of solving the problem ; and here is a rondeau entitled " Sub Rosa " : —

      Under the rows of gas-jets bright,
      Bathed in a blazing river of light,

A regal beauty sits; above her
The butterflies of fashion hover,
And burn their wings, and take to flight.

Mark you her pure complexion, — white
Though flush may follow flush ? Despite
Her blush, the lily I discover
Under the rose.

All compliments to her are trite ;
She has adorers left and right ;
And I confess here, under cover
Of secrecy, I too — I love her !
Say naught. She knows it not. 'T is quite
Under the rose.

That the rondeau can aspire to more than the hinted
sentiment and the external gaiety of familiar verse,
and that it can stand forth on occasion as worthy of
comparison even with the sonnet, Dobson himself has
proved in more than one of his lyrics in this seemingly
narrow form. In none has he done this with more
masterly certainty than in this : —

In after days when grasses high
O'er-top the stone where I shall lie,
Though ill or well the world adjust
My slender claim to honored dust,
I shall not question nor reply.

I shall not see the morning sky;
I shall not hear the night-wind sigh;
I shall be mute, as all men must
In after days.

But yet, now living, fain were I
That some one then should testify,
Saying — *He held his pen in trust
To Art, not serving shame or lust.*
Will none ? — Then, let my memory die
In after days !

As there are two slightly different types of rondel, so there are two varieties of the rondeau. The type observed by Voiture is that just considered; and the type used by Villon departs from it both in the reduction of the number of lines to ten and in the condensing of the refrain to a single word. Here is John Payne's English rendering of one of Villon's lyrics in this more compact type: —

> Death, of thy rigor I complain,
>   That hast my lady borne from me,
>   And yet will not contented be
> Till from me too all strength be ta'en
> For languishment of heart and brain.
>   What harm did she in life to thee,
>   Death ?
>
> One heart we had betwixt us twain ;
>   Which being dead, I too must dree
>   Death, or, like carven saints we see
> In choir, sans life to live be fain,
>   Death !

Although this is disfigured by the unnecessary and unfortunate repetition of the refrain-word at the beginning of the next to the last line, it is a fairly satisfactory example of the shorter type of the rondeau; and it exhibits the inferiority of this to the more generous type which Dobson has employed for themes both grave and gay. The briefer type seems to lack something of the "nimble movement, speed, grace, lightness of touch," which Banville held to be the foremost characteristics of the rondeau.

The villanelle has an intricacy of its own not quite of the same kind as the complexity of the triolet, the rondel, and the rondeau. The villanelle consists of five stanzas of three lines each and of a sixth stanza of four; it has only two rimes; and the last line of the first stanza recurs as the last line of the third, fifth and sixth stanzas, while the first line reappears as the final line of the second and fourth stanzas and also as the third line of the final quatrain. Here again the most successful example is one of Austin Dobson's, an alluring portrayal of fascinating maidenhood limned with the assured swiftness of an etching:—

> When I saw you last, Rose,
> You were only so high;—
> How fast the time goes!
>
> Like a bud ere it blows,
> You just peeped at the sky,
> When I saw you last, Rose.
>
> Now your petals unclose,
> Now your May-time is nigh;—
> How fast the time goes!
>
> And a life,— how it grows!
> You were scarcely so shy,
> When I saw you last, Rose!
>
> In your bosom it shows
> There's a guest on the sly;
> How fast the time goes!
>
> Is it Cupid? Who knows!
> Yet you used not to sigh,
> When I saw you last, Rose
> How fast the time goes!

In the exquisite simplicity of this lyric, with its touch of tenderness and with its glancing humor, the delicate effect is due in part to the felicity of the meter, anapestic dimeter, which here proves its appro-

priateness for this linked sequence of little stanzas.
If the meter is changed, something of the lightness
and brightness is immediately lost, as we are convinced when we compare Dobson's triumph with this
labored effort of Henley's : —

> A dainty thing's the villanelle,
>   Sly, musical, a jewel in rime.
> It serves its purpose passing well.
>
> A double-clappered silver bell
>   That must be made to clink in chime,
> A dainty thing's the villanelle;
>
> And if you wish to flute a spell,
>   Or ask a meeting 'neath the lime,
> It serves its purpose passing well.
>
> You must not ask of it the swell
>   Of organs grandiose and sublime—
> A dainty thing's the villanelle;
>
> And filled with sweetness, as a shell
>   Is filled with sound, and launched in time,
> It serves its purpose passing well.
>
> Still fair to see and good to smell
>   As in the quaintness of its prime,
> A dainty thing's the villanelle,
> It serves its purpose passing well.

In this rather lumbering attempt, the effort to be
airy is a little too obvious, and the vivacity is evidently
a little forced. But the fundamental mistake of the
writer was in the selection of his meter, iambic tetrameter, which lacks the ethereal ease of the anapestic
dimeter. Yet the iambic tetrameter is not out of
place when the theme is statelier, as Lang made plain
in this congenial appreciation of Theocritus : —

Apollo left the queenly Muse,
    And shepherded a mortal's sheep,
Theocritus of Syracuse !

With thee to lead the lambs and ewes
    Where Milon and where Battus reap,
Apollo left the queenly Muse.

With thee, he loitered in the dews,
    He slept the swain's unfever'd sleep,
Theocritus of Syracuse !

To watch the tunny-fishers cruise
    Below the sheer Sicilian steep,
Apollo left the queenly Muse.

And now with his might Time confuse
    Thy songs, like his that laugh and leap,
Theocritus of Syracuse !

To sing with thee beside the deep,
Or where Ætnæan waters weep,
Theocritus of Syracuse,
Apollo left the queenly Muse.

Of all these French forms, the noblest by far is the
ballade, the largest in its framework, the widest in
its range, and the most varied in its possibilities. It
has had the supreme advantage of serving early as
the instrument of a true poet, Villon, that " warm
voice out of the slums of Paris," as Matthew Arnold
called him. Yet the form soon lost its popularity in
France; and the poet-critics of the Pléïade were
hostile to it, although they accepted the sonnet willingly enough. The ballade crossed the channel into
England as early as Chaucer's time; and he may have
borrowed from it the stanza which he made his own
(the eight lines of iambic tetrameter riming a, b, b,

a, a, c, a, c), and which Spenser took as the foundation of his own superb stave. Yet the ballade fell out of favor in English as it had fallen out of favor in France; and not until after Théodore de Banville had revived it in Paris and exhibited anew its lyric grace and its adaptability to both pathetic and jocular themes, did the ballade regain its footing. It was Banville's book of "Trente-six Ballades Joyeuses" which moved Dobson to write "The Prodigals"; and his example was followed at once by Andrew Lang and also, after an interval, by Swinburne. It was at the beginning of the last quarter of the nineteenth century that these various French forms renewed their citizenship in English poetry; and in the years that have passed since they were gladly acclaimed, they have continued to allure many lyrists of Great Britain and the United States. When the warmth of their first welcome was chilled by the lapse of time, most of them lost a little of their vogue. But the ballade has rooted itself solidly in our poetry; it is as definitely acclimatized as the sonnet, although it has not yet taken captive as many of the major bards of our tongue. It lacks the stern compression of the sonnet and the lofty simplicity of that Italian form; but it has its own field and it serves its own purpose, less serious than the sonnet, but fitter for themes where sentiment and humor disclose themselves in turn, like twins playing hide-and-seek.

The ballade has two variations of type, of which the shorter is more characteristic of the form and is more firmly intrenched in popular favor. This consists of three stanzas of eight lines each and a final quatrain; it has only three rimes in all its twenty-eight lines, every octave abiding by the same rime-scheme, *a*, *b*, *a*, *b*, *b*, *c*, *b*, *c*, the final quatrain riming *b*, *c*, *b*, *c*. This quatrain is called the Envoy; and it was originally addressed directly to the king or prince or dignitary in whose honor the ballade had been rimed. The final quatrain and each of the three staves must end with the same line, absolutely unvaried in wording, however modified it may be in meaning. Thus, the ballade displays itself as a tiny comedy in three acts, with the envoy as an epilog spoken to the public. Here is Andrew Lang's " Ballade of Old Plays," evoked by an edition of Molière published in Paris in 1667 : —

La Cour

When these Old Plays were new, the King,
　　Beside the Cardinal's chair,
Applauded, 'mid the courtly ring,
　　The verses of Molière ;
　　Point-lace was then the only wear,
Old Corneille came to woo,
　　And bright Du Parc was young and fair,
When these Old Plays were new !

La Comédie

How shrill the butcher's cat-calls ring,
　　How loud the lackeys swear !
Black pipe-bowls on the stage they fling,
　　At Brécourt, fuming there !
　　The Porter 's stabbed ! a Mousquetaire
Breaks in with noisy crew —
　　'T was all a commonplace affair
When these Old Plays were new !

La Ville

When these Old Plays were new ! They bring
　　A host of phantoms rare :

Old jests that float, old jibes that sting,
   Old faces peaked with care :
   Ménage's smirk, de Visé's stare,
The thefts of Jean Ribou, —
   Ah, publishers were hard to bear
When these Old Plays were new !

Envoy

Ghosts, at your Poet's word ye dare
   To break Death's dungeons through,
And frisk, as in that golden air,
   When these Old Plays were new !

The other variation of the ballade employs a stanza of ten lines with four rimes, *a, b, a, b, b, c, c, d, c, d,* and it therefore lacks the couplet which links the octave together in the middle, as exemplified in Lang's lilting lyric. Banville was emphatic in asserting the importance of this internal couplet, warning the ballade-makers against composing separately the two quatrains of the octave, since this was a process likely to give the stanza a broken back. In the absence of this internal couplet in the longer variation of the ballade, the back of the stanza must bear the weight of ten lines as best it may. The increase of the number of rimes also diminishes the difficulty of the task the poet has undertaken, and thereby robs the ballade of a part of its charm. Yet this second type is not without admirers; and here is Gosse's lyric written just after the death of Théodore de Banville : —

One ballade more before we say good-night,
   O dying Muse, one mournful ballade more ;
Then let the new men fall to their delight,
   The Impressionist, the Decadents, a score
   Of other fresh fanatics, who adore
Quaint demons, and disdain thy golden shrine ;
Ah ! faded goddess, thou wert held divine

When we were young ! But now each laureled **head**
Has fallen, and fallen the ancient glorious line ;
   The last is gone, since Banville too is dead.

Peace, peace a moment, Dolorous Ibsenite !
   Pale Tolstoiat, moaning from the Euxine shore !
Heredity, to dreamland take thy flight !
   And, fell Psychology, forbear to pour
   Drop after drop thy dose of hellebore,
For we look back to-night to ruddier wine
And gayer singing than those moans of thine !
   Our skies were azure once, our roses red,
Our poets once were crowned with eglantine ;
   The last is gone, since Banville too is dead.

With flutes and lyres and many a lovely rite
   Through the mad woodland of our youth they **bore**
Verse, like an ichor in a chrysolite,
   Secret yet splendid, and the world forswore,
   One breathing space, the mocking mask it wore.
Then failed, then fell those children of the vine —
Sons of the sun — and sank in slow decline ;
   Pulse after pulse their radiant lives were shed.

Envoy

Prince-jeweler, whose facet rimes combine
All hues that glow, all rays that shift and shine,
   Farewell ! thy song is sung, thy splendor fled !
No bards to Aganippe's wave incline ;
   The last is gone, since Banville too is dead.

It is also the ten-line variation which Swinburne preferred for his buoyant and overwhelming " Ballade of Swimming," with its large long lines of anapestic heptameter : —

The sea is awake, and the sound of the song of the joy of her
    waking is rolled
From afar to the star that recedes from anear to the wastes of
    the wild wide shore.

Her call is a trumpet compelling us homeward : if dawn in her
  east be acold,
From the sea shall we crave not her grace to rekindle the life
  that it kindled before
Her breath to requicken, her bosom to rock us, her kisses to bless
  as of yore ?
For the wind, with his wings half open, at pause in the sky,
  neither fettered nor free,
Leans waveward and flutters the ripple of laughter ; and fain
  would the twain of us be
Where lightly the wave yearns forward from under the curve
  of the deep dawn's dome,
And full of the morning and fired with the pride of the glory
  thereof and the glee,
Strike out from the shore as the heart in us bids and beseeches,
  athirst for the foam.

Life holds not an hour that is better to live in : the past is a tale
  that is told,
The future a sun-flecked shadow, alive and asleep, with a blessing in store.
As we give us again to the waters, the rapture of limbs that the
  waters enfold
Is less than the rapture of spirit whereby, though the burden it
  quits were sore,
Our souls and the bodies they wield at their will are absorbed in
  the life they adore —
In the life that endures no burden, and bows not the forehead,
  and bends not the knee —
In the life everlasting of earth and of heaven, in the laws that
  atone and agree.
In the measureless music of things, in the fervor of forces that
  rest or that roam,
That cross and return and reissue, as I after you and as you after
  me
Strike out from the shore as the heart in us bids and beseeches,
  athirst for the foam.

For, albeit he were less than the least of them, haply the heart
  of a man may be bold
To rejoice in the word of the sea as a mother's that saith to the
  son she bore,

Child, was not the life in thee mine, and my spirit the breath in
  thy lips from of old ?
Have I let not thy weakness exult in my strength, and thy fool-
  ishness learn of my lore ?
Have I helped not or healed not thine anguish, or made not the
  might of thy gladness more ?
And surely his heart should answer, The light of the love of my
  life is in thee.
She is fairer than earth, and the sun is not fairer, the wind is not
  blither than she :
From my youth hath she shown me the joy of her bays that I
  crossed, of her cliffs that I clomb,
Till now that the twain of us here, in desire of the dawn and in
  trust of the sea,
Strike out from the shore as the heart in us bids and beseeches,
  athirst for the foam.

Envoy

Friend, earth is a harbor of refuge for winter, a covert where-
  under to flee
When day is the vassal of night, and the strength of the hosts of
  her mightier than he ;
But here is the presence adored of me, here my desire is at rest
  and at home.
There are cliffs to be climbed upon land, there are ways to be
  trodden and ridden : but we
Strike out from the shore as the heart in us bids and beseeches,
  athirst for the foam.

In this resonant lyric, the lines sweep forward and
swing backward like the sounding surges of the surf,
billow after billow, breaker following breaker, tum-
bling ahead till they crash at last on the shore. Yet
the line is so long-drawn and so loud-sounding that the
ear is only doubtfully conscious of the structure of the
ballade. Indeed, while this lyric of Swinburne is proof
positive that the ballade can obey the poet's behest for
amplitude of treatment and for elevation of tone, yet
it is not really characteristic of what is best in the form.

So far as its form is concerned every ballade must be arbitrary and artificial; and therein lies not a little of its fascination. It could stretch itself out at Swinburne's bidding; but it needed to make no effort when Dobson called on it for hidden tenderness of sentiment touched with a hint of humor.

The soul of the ballade is its refrain; each of the three octaves and the final quatrain lead up to this recurring line, elucidating it and justifying it. The refrain must be aptly chosen and adroitly handled, so that, as Dobson himself declared, it will " recur without the tedium of importunity and return with the certainty of welcome." Especially significant are the two contrasted refrains in the *ballade à double refrain*, wherein the fourth line of the first octave re-appears unchanged in every octave, and wherein the envoy consists of two couplets, the final line of the first couplet being the internal refrain and the final line of the second couplet being the external refrain. Here there are two refrains for the poet to provide and to set over against each other in rhythmical antithesis. And again we find a perfect example prepared for us by Austin Dobson in "The Ballade of Prose and Rime":—

> When the ways are heavy with mire and rut,
>   In November fogs, in December snows,
> When the North Wind howls, and the doors are shut,
>   There is place and enough for the pains of prose; —
>   But whenever a scent from the whitethorn blows,
> And the jasmine-stars to the casement climb,
>   And a Rosalind-face at the lattice shows,
> Then hey! — for the ripple of laughing rime!
>
> When the brain gets dry as an empty nut,
>   When the reason stands on its squarest toes,

When the mind (like a beard) has a " formal cut,"
  There is place and enough for the pains of prose ; —
But whenever the May-blood stirs and glows,
And the young year draws to the " golden prime," —
  And Sir Romeo sticks in his ear a rose,
Then hey ! — for the ripple of laughing rime !

In a theme where the thoughts have a pedant-strut,
  In a changing quarrel of " Ayes " and " Noes,"
In a starched procession of " If " and " But,"
  There is place and enough for the pains of prose : —
But whenever a soft glance softer grows,
And the light hours dance to the trysting-time,
  And the secret is told " that no one knows,"
Then hey ! — for the ripple of laughing rime !

Envoy

In the work-a-day world, — for its needs and woes,
  There is place and enough for the pains of prose ;
But whenever the May-bells clash and chime,
Then hey ! — for the ripple of laughing rime !

Here we have the finest flower of the artificial lyric,
in which the very artificiality is made to accentuate
our pleasure, as the laughing rime ripples in our
ears. In this ballade we find the crispness of rhythm,
the apparent spontaneity, the unfailing felicity of
phrase, which we demand in what Cowper chose to
call " familiar verse " and which is more often known
by the wholly inadequate and unsatisfactory French
term *vers de société*.[1]

---

[1] In almost every department of familiar verse, Austin Dobson has
proved himself a master ; and he had a right, therefore, to declare its
code in the Twelve Good Rules that he drew up many years ago for
the guidance of all who shall adventure themselves in this sort of
verse : —
1. Never be vulgar. 2. Avoid slang and puns. 3. Avoid inversions. 4. Be sparing of long words. 5. Be colloquial but not commonplace. 6. Choose the lightest and brightest of measures. 7. Let

The ballade and the rondeau are best fitted for
familiar verse, no doubt, and their obvious artifice
may prevent their use in the highest reaches of poesy,
where the lyrist must forego as many shackles as he
may. Yet they need not be restricted to the field of
vers de société alone. They may lack the sharp concision of the quatrain and the soaring elevation of the
sonnet; but their range is wider than the drawing-
room lyric only. The ballade especially has an indisputable variety; and in the hands of a true poet its
arbitrary rime-scheme and its foreordained twenty-
eight lines are not unduly cramping to the liberty of
the lyrist. If evidence must be adduced in behalf of
this contention, here is Swinburne's haunting "Ballade of Dreamland": —

I hid my heart in a nest of roses,
  Out of the sun's way, hidden apart;
In a softer bed than the soft white snow is,
  Under the rose I hid my heart.
  Why would it sleep not? why should it start,
When never a leaf of the rose-tree stirred?
  What made sleep flutter his wings and part?
Only the song of a secret bird.

Lie still, I said, for the wind's wing closes,
  And mild leaves muffle the keen sun's dart;
Lie still, for the wind on the warm sea dozes,
  And the wind is unquieter yet than thou art.
  Does a thought in thee still as a thorn's wound smart?
Does the fang still fret thee of hope deferred?
  What bids the lips of thy sleep dispart?
Only the song of a secret bird.

the rimes be frequent but not forced. 8. Let them be rigorously
exact to the ear. 9. Be as witty as you like. 10. Be serious by accident. 11. Be pathetic with the greatest discretion. 12. Never ask
if the writer of these rules has observed them himself.

The green land's name that a charm encloses
  It never was writ in the traveler's chart,
And sweet on its trees as the fruit that grows is,
  It never was sold in the merchant's mart.
  The swallows of dreams through its dim fields dart,
And sleep's are the tunes in its tree-tops heard ;
  No hound's note wakens the wildwood hart,
Only the song of a secret bird.

Envoi

In the world of dreams I have chosen my part,
  To sleep for a season and hear no word
Of true love's truth or of light love's art,
  Only the song of a secret bird.

Perhaps the best plea that has been made for the
ballade is to be found in one of the brilliant essays of
M. Jules Lemaitre, which Mr. Andrew Lang has rendered into English : " The poet who begins a ballade
does not know very exactly what he will put into it.
The rime, and nothing but the rime, will whisper things
unexpected and charming, things he would never have
thought of but for her, things with strange and re-
mote relations to each other, all united in the disorder
of a dream. Nothing, indeed, is richer in suggestion
than the strict laws of these difficult pieces ; they force
the fancy to wander afield, hunting high and low; and
while she seeks through all the world the foot that
can wear Cinderella's slipper, she makes delightful
discoveries by the way."

There is an amplified form of the ballade which is
called the *chant-royal*. It consists of five eleven-line
stanzas, riming *a, b, a, b, c, c, d, d, e, d, e*, with a
five-line envoy, riming *d, d, e, d, e*, every stanza and
the envoy ending with the refrain. Here is John
Payne's "God of Love " : —

O most fair God, O Love both new and old,
   That wast before the flowers of morning blew,
Before the glad sun in his mail of gold
   Leapt into light across the first day's dew;
Thou art the first and last of our delight,
That in the blue day and the purple night
   Holdest the hearts of servant and of king,
   Lord of liesse, sovran of sorrowing,
That in thy hand hast heaven's golden key
   And Hell beneath the shadow of thy wing,
Thou art my Lord to whom I bend the knee.

What thing rejects thy mastery ? Who so bold
   But at thine altars in the dusk they sue ?
Even the strait pale goddess, silver-stoled,
   That kissed Endymion when the Spring was new,
To thee did homage in her own despite,
When in the shadow of her wings of white
   She slid down trembling from her moonèd ring
   To where the Latmian boy lay slumbering,
And in that kiss put off cold chastity.
   Who but acclaim with voice and pipe and string,
"Thou art my Lord to whom I bend the knee ?"

Master of men and gods, in every fold
   Of thy wide vans the sorceries that renew
The laboring earth, tranced with the winter's cold,
   Lie hid — the quintessential charms that woo
The souls of flowers, slain with the sullen might
Of the dead year, and draw them to the light.
   Balsam and blessing to thy garments cling;
   Skyward and seaward, when thy white hands fling
Their spells of healing over land and sea,
   One shout of homage makes the welkin ring,
"Thou art my Lord to whom I bend the knee !"

I see thee throned aloft; thy fair hands hold
   Myrtles for joy, and euphrasy and rue:
Laurels and roses round thy white brows rolled,
   And in thine eyes the royal heaven's hue:
But in thy lips' clear color, ruddy bright,
The heart's blood shines of many a hapless wight.

Thou art not only fair and sweet as spring ;
Terror and beauty, fear and wondering
Meet on thy brow, amazing all that see:
All men do praise thee, ay, and everything;
Thou art my Lord to whom I bend the knee.

I fear thee, though I love. Who can behold
The sheer sun burning in the orbèd blue,
What while the noontide over hill and wold
Flames like a fire, except his mazèd view
Wither and tremble ? So thy splendid sight
Fills me with mingled gladness and affright.
Thy visage haunts me in the wavering
Of dreams, and in the dawn awakening,
I feel thy radiance streaming full on me,
Both fear and joy unto thy feet I bring ;
Thou art my Lord to whom I bend the knee !

Envoy

God above Gods, High and Eternal King,
To whom the spheral symphonies do sing,
I find no whither from thy power to flee,
Save in thy pinions' vast o'ershadowing,
Thou art my Lord to whom I bend the knee.

This has a lyric largeness; and yet the chant-royal
lies peculiarly open to the objection which Professor
Lounsbury has urged against all fixed forms of verse,
to the effect that " it is poetry not of art, but of artifice, though often artifice in a very high sense. Work
of this kind is usually produced by men who are artists,
and sometimes great artists, in poetry, as distinguished
from great poets. It is accordingly not so much what
they say that interests us as the way in which they say
it." It is true that this objection must also hold, to a
certain extent, even against the sonnet. In every art difficulty conquered affords an abiding source of pleasure ;
and although this is admitted ungrudgingly, there is

conviction also in Lowell's assertion that " difficulty without success is perhaps the least tolerable kind of writing." As Théodore de Banville was frank in declaring, "without poetic vision all is mere marquetry and cabinet-maker's work; that is, so far as poetry is concerned — nothing."

The case for the fixed form was never better put than by Edmund Gosse in his " Plea for Certain Exotic Forms of Verse," written when these imported types were just reappearing in our language. " But there is always the danger of using elaborate and beautiful measures to conceal poverty of thought, and my plea would be incomplete if I left this objection to it unstated. The only excuse for writing rondeaux and villanelles is the production of poems that are charming to a reader who takes no note of their elaborate form; they should be attractive in spite of, and not because of, their difficulty. The true test of success is that the poem should give the reader an impression of spontaneity and ease, and that the attention should be attracted by the wit, or fancy, or pathos, in the thoughts and expression, and not, until later study, by the form at all. Let it not, however, be for this reason imagined that the labor is thankless and the elaboration needless. Half the pleasure given to the reader, half the sense of richness, completeness, and grace which he vaguely perceives and unconsciously enjoys, is due to the labor the poet has expended."

One more exotic form remains to be considered, not French this time, but Malayan. This is the pantoum, imported but not important, which Victor Hugo called to the attention of Gautier and Banville. It is not an attractive form, and its resources are scanty. It con-

sists of a succession of quatrains, the second and fourth
lines of the first quatrain being repeated as the first
and third of the second quatrain, and the second and
fourth lines of this second quatrain serving again as
the first and third of the third quatrain ; and so on, the
final quatrain picking up again the first and third
lines of the first. Monotony is inevitable, and any
ample treatment of a theme is impossible. With his
customary tact, Austin Dobson seized on this monotony as the excuse for the lyric he prepared in this
form, thereby forcing the incessant repetition to sub-
serve the general effect of insistently recurrent lines.
He called his pantoum, the first to be attempted in
English, " In Town " : —

> Toiling in town now is " horrid "
>   (There is that woman again !) —
> June in the zenith is torrid,
>   Thought gets dry in the brain.
>
> There is that woman again:
>   " Strawberries! fourpence a pottle! "
> Thought gets dry in the brain;
>   Ink gets dry in the bottle.
>
> " Strawberries! fourpence a pottle ! "
>   O for the green of a lane ! —
> Ink gets dry in the bottle;
>   " Buzz " goes a fly in the pane !
>
> O for the green of a lane,
>   Where one might lie and be lazy !
> " Buzz " goes a fly in the pane;
>   Bluebottles drive me crazy !
>
> Where one might lie and be lazy,
>   Careless of town and all in it ! —
> Bluebottles drive me crazy:
>   I shall go mad in a minute !

Careless of town and all in it,
  With some one to soothe and to still you;
I shall go mad in a minute;
  Bluebottle, then I shall kill you!

With some one to soothe and to still you,
  As only one's feminine kin do, —
Bluebottle, then I shall kill you:
  There now! I've broken the window!

As only one's feminine kin do, —
  Some muslin-clad Mabel or May! —
There now! I've broken the window!
  Bluebottle's off and away!

Some muslin-clad Mabel or May,
  To dash one with eau de Cologne:
Bluebottle's off and away,
  And why should I stay here alone?

To dash one with eau de Cologne,
  All over one's eminent forehead; —
And why should I stay here alone!
  Toiling in town now is "horrid."

CHAPTER IX

RIMELESS STANZAS

Rime, the rack of finest wits,
That expresseth but by fits
  True conceit,
Spoiling senses of their treasure,
Cozening judgment with a measure,
  But false weight;
Wresting words from their true calling,
Propping verse for fear of falling
  To the ground,
Jointing syllables, drowning letters,
Fastening vowels, as with fetters
  They were bound.
. . . .
Greek was free from rime's infection,
Happy Greek by this protection
  Was not spoiled,
Whilst the Latin, queen of tongues,
Is not yet free from rime's wrongs,
  But rests foiled.
  BEN JONSON: *A Fit of Rime against Rime.*

In the various types of stanza which have been considered, in the sonnet and in the other fixed forms, rime serves to indicate the metrical scheme which the ear is to expect. Now and again, one line or another in the quatrain, or in a longer stanza, may be left unmated; and often a refrain is rimeless. Yet the importance of rime is indisputable; indeed one might declare that its necessity is almost undeniable. At least, this much must be admitted — that in our modern English the stanza, whatsoever its length, seems to insist upon its sequence of terminal rimes, and that

in consequence of this apparent insistence very few
lyrics have been able to sing themselves into the
memory and to capture a popularity which is at once
wide and enduring, unless they have soared aloft on
the wings of rime.

In the epic and in the drama, poetry can get along
very well without the tinkle of the terminal syllables;
in fact, English poetry of this lofty species seems to
reject rime, as needless and even enfeebling. But in
lyrical poetry, whether it is confined in a single stanza
or extended to a sequence of stanzas, rime appears
to be almost obligatory. George Meredith went so far
as to insist that " in lyrics the demand for music is
imperative, and, as quantity is denied to the English
tongue, rimes there must be." If rime is absent,
our ears are deprived of a delight which they have
learned to anticipate. Rime supplies to the stanza its
architectural outline; and it is the steel-frame for the
firm construction of the towering ode. If the rime
is lacking, our ears miss it and they have to strain to
make sure of the stanzaic form. This may be due
merely to long traditions in English verse; or more
probably it may be ascribed to some unexplored peculiarity of our modern languages. Certainly the lack
of rime does not interfere with the charm of the lyrics
of the Greeks, of the Latins, and of the Hebrews.
The French, it may be noted, are even more dependent
upon rime than we are; they have never been able
to develop blank verse; and both their epic and their
tragic poetry gladly wears the fetters of the riming
couplet, made even more galling by the rule that a
pair of masculine rimes shall always alternate with a
pair of feminine rimes.

Yet many poets have composed English lyrics in rimeless stanzas of varying length; and not a few of them have produced poems of unquestionable grace and beauty. Nevertheless, the fact remains that scarcely any poet of our language has achieved one of his major successes with an unrimed lyric; and it is always upon his lyrics adorned with chiming ends that his reputation rests. In English the rimeless lyric is sporadic and abnormal; and yet these experiments in stanzas without rime are significant and interesting.

If we limit the word *couplet*, as perhaps we should, to describe a pair of lines which rime together, we have the word *distich* to describe a pair of unrimed lines. For inscriptions, for memorial purposes, the distich has a proved fitness. In so brief a lyric the necessity for rime is less obvious. Here is a distich of Emerson's: —

> This passing moment is an edifice
> Which the Omnipotent cannot rebuild.

Here are three lines of Landor's on Shakspere: —

> In poetry there is but one supreme,
> Though there are many angels round his throne,
> Mighty, and beauteous, while his face is hid.

There is a lapidary concision like that of an Attic inscription in these three lines of Emerson's: —

> No fate, save by the victim's fault, is low,
> For God hath writ all dooms magnificent,
> So guilt not traverses His tender will.

The unrimed quatrain is infrequent in English verse; and yet a few stately specimens are available. Here is one from Emerson: —

> There is a time when the romance of life
> Should be shut up, and closed with double clasp:
> Better that this be done before the dust
> That none can blow away falls into it.

In these little lyrics, the ear has scarce time to awaken to the expectancy of rime before the poem comes to its end. But when the lyric consists of several stanzas the absence of the rime is soon noted; and although this may be forgiven, still it is likely to be more or less disconcerting, especially if the stanza chosen is familiar, as in this "Etching" of Henley's:—

> Two and thirty is the plowman;
> He's a man of gallant inches,
> And his hair is close and curly,
>   And his beard;
> But his face is wan and sunken,
> And his eyes are large and brilliant,
> And his shoulder blades are sharp,
>   And his knees.

This stanza seems to cry aloud for its customary rimes; and there is a wanton bravado in depriving us of them. The unrimed lyric is more acceptable when it avoids the well-known stanzaic forms wherein rime is traditional and when it employs a less rigid frame, freer in its movement. This Longfellow felt with his intuitive feeling for felicity of presentation. Here are the opening quatrains of his greeting "To an Old Danish Song-Book":—

> Welcome, my old friend,
> Welcome to a foreign fireside,
> While the sullen gales of autumn
> Shake the windows.
>
> The ungrateful world
> Has, it seems, dealt harshly with thee,

> Since, beneath the skies of Denmark,
> First I met thee.

This is excellent in its mating of style and substance. These unrimed quatrains justify themselves; they do not demand rime; they would not be bettered by it. There is an even bolder irregularity in the opening of " The Saga of King Olaf ": —

> I am the God Thor,
> I am the War God,
> I am the Thunderer !
> Here in my Northland,
> My fastness and fortress,
> Reign I forever !

> Here amid icebergs
> Rule I the nations ;
> This is my hammer,
> Miölner the mighty ;
> Giants and sorcerers
> Cannot withstand it !

Longfellow had an easy mastery of rime when he chose to exert it, yet he liked to forego its aid and to lift up a lyric without the assistance of the expected pairs of terminal words. His song on " The Bells of Lynn " is written in distichs, with a refrain at the end of every second line : —

> O curfew of the setting sun ! O Bells of Lynn !
> O requiem of the dying day ! O Bells of Lynn !

> From the dark belfries of yon cloud-cathedral wafted,
> Your sounds aerial seem to float, O Bells of Lynn.

> Borne on the evening wind across the crimson twilight,
> O'er land and sea they rise and fall, O Bells of Lynn !

In this lyric the stave is only two lines long and the expectancy of rime is met by the recurring re-

frain. It is by the aid of a refrain also that Charles
Lamb ties together his sequence of three-line stanzas: —

> All, all are gone, the old familiar faces.
>
> I have had playmates, I have had companions,
> In my days of childhood, in my joyful school-days,
> All, all are gone, the old familiar faces.
>
> I loved a love once, fairest among women;
> Closed are her doors on me, I must not see her;
> All, all are gone, the old familiar faces.

Tennyson succeeded in giving lightness and fluidity
to an unrimed lyric arranged in stanzas of three
lines each, which is supposed to be sung in " The Princess " : —

> O Swallow, Swallow, flying, flying south,
> Fly to her, and fall upon her gilded eaves,
> And tell her, tell her, what I tell to thee.
>
> O tell her, Swallow, that thou knowest each,
> That bright and fierce and fickle is the South,
> And dark and true and tender is the North.

And in " Tears, Idle Tears," one of his loveliest
lyrics, Tennyson again abandoned rime, but clung
to the refrain as marking usefully the limit of the
stanza : —

> Tears, idle tears, I know not what they mean,
> Tears from the depth of some divine despair
> Rise in the heart, and gather to the eyes,
> In looking on the happy autumn-fields,
> And thinking of the days that are no more.
>
> Fresh as the first beam glittering on a sail,
> That brings our friends up from the underworld,
> Sad as the last which reddens over one
> That sinks with all we love below the verge ;
> So sad, so fresh, the days that are no more.

Symonds held this to be a "perfect specimen of the most melodious and complete minstrelsy in words"; and he declared that the refrain with its "recurrence of sound and meaning is a substitute for rime and suggests rime so persuasively that it is impossible to call the poem mere blank verse."

A device not dissimilar is employed in a lyric by an American poet, untimely cut off in his youth, Charles Henry Lüders. This song is entitled the "Four Winds"[1]: and it must be given in full to show clearly how the several stanzas are kept separate and distinct, clearly perceptible to the listening ear, without the aid of the rime: —

> Wind of the North,
> Wind of the Northland snows,
> Wind of the winnowed skies and sharp, clear stars, —
> Blow cold and keen across the naked hills,
> And crisp the lowland pools with crystal films,
> And blue the casement-squares with glittering ice,
> But go not near my love.
>
> Wind of the West,
> Wind of the few, far clouds,
> Wind of the gold and crimson sunset lands, —
> Blow fresh and pure across the peaks and plains,
> And broaden the blue spaces of the heavens,
> And sway the grasses and the mountain pines,
> But let my dear one rest.
>
> Wind of the East,
> Wind of the sunrise seas,
> Wind of the clinging mists and gray, harsh rains, —
> Blow moist and chill across the wastes of brine,
> And shut the sun out, and the moon and stars,
> And lash the boughs against the dripping eaves,
> Yet keep thou from my love.

[1] By permission from *The Dead Nymph and other Poems* by Charles Henry Lüders, copyrighted, 1891, by Charles Scribner's Sons.

But thou, sweet wind !
Wind of the fragrant South,
Wind from the bowers of jasmine and of rose, —
Over magnolia glooms and lilied lakes
And flowering forests come with dewy wings,
And stir the petals at her feet and kiss
The low mound where she lies.

Although the refrain has served Lamb, Longfellow, and Tennyson to impress the form of an unrimed stanza upon the ear, other poets have done without its aid, perhaps because they did not feel any desire to isolate the successive units of construction. Thus William Watson has a sequence of quatrains in " England, My Mother," linked together by the continuity of the thought and flowing forward without any sharp division into stanzas : —

Lo, with ancient
Roots of man's nature
Twines the eternal
Passion of song.

Ever Love fans it, —
Ever Life feeds it ;
Time cannot age it,
Death cannot slay.

Deep in the world-heart
Stand its foundations,
Tangled with all things,
Twin-made with all.

In this poem of Watson's the stanzas are of uniform length and of uniform metrical construction ; but they are not separate unities. The stanza is not insisted on ; it is not integral to the movement of the ode-like lyric. Still less does our ear ask for rime when the successive stanzas are not of uniform length or of uniform metrical construction.

In Matthew Arnold's "Strayed Reveler," there is no rigorous uniformity; indeed, the rhythmical movement is so free that the ear adjusts itself at once to this freedom and has to make no effort to seize any prescribed metrical scheme: —

The Youth

Who speaks? Ah, who comes forth
To thy side, Goddess, from within?
How shall I name him?
This spare, dark-featured,
Quick-eyed stranger?
Ah, and I see too
His sailor's bonnet,
His short coat, travel-tarnished,
With one arm bare! —
Art thou not he, whom fame
This long time rumors
The favor'd guest of Circe, brought by the waves,
Art thou he, stranger?
The wise Ulysses,
Laertes' son?

Ulysses

I am Ulysses.
And thou, too, sleeper?
Thy voice is sweet.
It may be thou hast follow'd
Through the islands some divine bard,
By age taught many things,
Age and the Muses;
And heard him delighting
The Chiefs and the people
In the banquet, and learned his songs
Of Gods and Heroes,
Of war and arts,
And peopled cities,
Inland or built
By the gray sea. If so, then hail!
I honor and welcome thee.

Apparently it is only when the stanza stands out by itself that our ears expect the rime to indicate the metrical framework; and when the verse flows on avoiding equal subdivisions, our ears accept this without being in any way strained. Browning, for example, divides " One Word More," his epistle to his wife at the end of " Men and Women," into groups of lines, these metrical paragraphs containing sometimes only three or four lines and sometimes extending to more than twenty. Thus there is no suggestion of any stanzaic form, and therefore there is no need for rime or refrain or for any other device to guide the ear. Here is the first of these paragraphs, limited to four lines only : —

> There they are, my fifty men and women
> Naming me the fifty poems finished !
> Take them, Love, the book and me together;
> Where the heart lies, let the brain lie also.

And here is another paragraph, the sixth, having three lines only : —

> You and I would rather see that angel,
> Painted by the tenderness of Dante,
> Would we not ? — than read a fresh Inferno.

Part of the ease and lightness of this poem is due to its trochaic rhythm. As we examine the most satisfying of the lyrics in our language which are not adorned with rime, we cannot help remarking how strong is the tendency of the poets to end their lines with short syllables. They are prone either to employ a trochaic rhythm, or to append an extra short syllable to their iambic lines. It is an unrimed iambic heptameter with this added short syllable which Newman chose for his translation of Homer.

It is in unrimed dactylic trimeter that Dr. Weir Mitchell composed his " Psalm of the Waters," carrying over the final short syllable of every line to the beginning of the next: —

> So this is a psalm of the waters, —
> The wavering, wandering waters:
> With languages learned in the forest,
> With secret of earth's lonely caverns,
> The mystical waters go by me
> On errands of love and of beauty,
> On embassies friendly and gentle,
> With shimmer of brown and of silver.

It is in iambics, chiefly tetrameter and trimeter, that Southey wrote his " Thalaba," adding frequently a short syllable at the end of his line: —

> He found a woman in the cave,
> A solitary Woman
> Who by the fire was spinning
> And singing as she spun.
> The pine boughs were cheerfully blazing,
> And her face was bright with the flame.

In the very year, 1855, when Browning published " One Word More," Longfellow had earlier issued "The Song of Hiawatha" in a kindred trochaic rhythm. But the American poet took over from the Finnish " Kalevala " (which had suggested his meter) the device of frequent repetition of the same thought in slightly varied words. This device gave individuality to his lyrical legend, and a pervading gracefulness almost feminine in its delicacy: —

> Give me of your bark, O Birch-tree !
> Of your yellow bark, O Birch-tree !
> Growing by the rushing river,
> Tall and stately in the valley !
> I a light canoe will build me,

Build a swift Cheemaun for sailing,
That shall float upon the river,
Like a yellow leaf in Autumn,
Like a yellow water-lily !

Two other of Longfellow's longer poems are also without the assistance which rime may bestow. These are " Evangeline " and " The Courtship of Miles Standish." They are written in what may be described as English hexameters, every line consisting of five dactyls, followed by a single trochee, which supplied the final short syllable that unrimed verse appears to prefer. The choice was singularly felicitous, especially for " Evangeline." As Dr. Holmes declared, " the hexameter has been often criticized, but I do not believe any other measure could have told that lovely story with such effect, as we feel when carried along the tranquil current of these brimming, slow-moving, soul-satisfying lines. Imagine, for a moment, a story like this minced into octosyllables. The poet knows better than his critics the length of step which best befits his muse." The shrewdness of Dr. Holmes's opinion is shown by an experiment tried by Longfellow himself. The poet rewrote one of the most beautiful passages of " Evangeline," not in octosyllables, but in riming iambic pentameters. The matter was substantially identical in both versions, and only the manner was different ; yet not a little of the charm of the hexameter original has evaporated in the rewriting into rimed pentameters.

Then from a neighboring thicket the mocking-bird, wildest of
     singers,
Swinging aloft on a willow spray that hung o'er the water,
Shook from his little throat such floods of delirious music,

That the whole air and the woods and the waves seemed silent
  to listen.
Plaintive at first were the tones and sad : then soaring to
  madness
Seemed they to follow or guide the revel of frenzied
  Bacchantes.
Single notes were then heard, in sorrowful, low lamentation ;
Till, having gathered them all, he flung them abroad in derision,
As when, after a storm, a gust of wind through the tree-tops
Shakes down the rattling rain in a crystal shower on the
  branches.

This is the unrimed hexameter original; and here is
the rimed pentameter reworking : —

> Upon a spray that overhung the stream
> The mocking-bird, awaking from his dream,
> Poured such delirious music from his throat
> That all the air seemed listening to his note.
> Plaintive at first the song began, and slow;
> It breathed of sadness, and of pain and wo;
> Then, gathering all his notes, abroad he flung
> The multitudinous music from his tongue, —
> As, after showers, a sudden gust again
> Upon the leaves shakes down the rattling rain.

The immediate welcome accorded to " Evangeline "
and to its successor in the same meter, " The Courtship
of Miles Standish," is proof that the English-speaking
peoples found no difficulty in accepting this dactylic
hexameter as Longfellow handled it. Almost a novelty
in English versification, it was received at once as
pleasing to our ears. As Dr. Holmes noted, it met
with not a little adverse criticism, mostly from those
who applied a false test and who blamed Longfellow
for a failure to accomplish what he had never tried
to attempt. The dissatisfied critics complained that
these English hexameters did not conform exactly to
the strict rules of the Greek and Latin hexameter and

therefore that they did not suggest to an English ear the full effect made by the classic hexameter on the ears of the Athenians and the Romans. But nowhere did Longfellow claim that his dactylic hexameter was the equivalent in our language of the classic hexameter which depended for a large part of its weight and of its stately march on the terminal spondee, a foot which our language abhors. What Longfellow did was to establish an English hexameter, which the English ear was glad to accept. This English hexameter was un-doubtedly suggested to Longfellow by certain attempts to acclimatize in our versification the classic hexameter; but the American poet was too accomplished a metrist to have supposed that he could carry over into our accentual language the specific characteristics of any verse-form developed in a quantitative language like the Greek.

In Greek and in Latin the rhythm is the result of quantity, that is to say, it is caused by the alternation of syllables which are actually long or actually short in the duration of the time taken to pronounce them. In English, rhythm is caused to some slight extent by quantity, but more often by accent, by stress, by the emphasis with which we habitually pronounce one or more syllables in all words containing more than one syllable. An actual length of vowel-sound, a superior accent, a heightening of pitch, any of these or all of them at once, create rhythm in the ears of those who have English for their mother-tongue. Our ears are not trained to feel quantity alone or to receive a rhythm which is purely quantitative. Although it has seemed convenient in these chapters to call the more marked syllables *long* and the less marked syllables *short*, this was done only after full warning that length by itself does not account for English rhythm. So accentual is our language that the spondee, the foot composed of two longs, can hardly be said to exist in English verse. Milton was able to achieve it now and again, and so was Tennyson; but we are so habituated to accent that we find it almost impossible to give equal weight to two successive syllables.

As a result of this fundamental difference between the rhythmic basis of Greek and Latin versification and the rhythmic basis of English versification, any attempt to import into our language the classical meters (founded on quantity alone) is foredoomed to failure. Such an attempt can be only the amusement of the learned; it cannot aspire to anything else; it must be foreign to any consideration of modern English versification. And even the learned are rarely satisfied with any particular imitation in English of the specific characteristics of the classical writer. What one scholar has devised another scholar is likely to find fault with. Coleridge, for example, taking a hint from Schiller, tried to exemplify the classical hexameter and pentameter in these two lines : —

> In the hexameter rises the fountain's silvery column —
> In the pentameter aye falling in melody back.

But this distich did not meet with Tennyson's approbation; and he revised it, striving to make it quantitative rather than accentual : —

> Up springs hexameter, with might, as a fountain arising,
> Lightly the fountain falls, lightly the pentameter.

It may even be doubted whether Tennyson would have been any better pleased with Longfellow's attempt than he was with Coleridge's : —

> In hexameter plunges the headlong cataract downward,
> In pentameter up whirls the eddying mist.

In two other lines Coleridge sought not only to suggest in English verse the largeness and the force of the Homeric hexameter, but also to reproduce its metrical arrangement: —

> Strongly it bears us along in swelling and limitless billows —
> Nothing before and nothing behind but the sky and the ocean.

It is possible that these two lines were lingering in Tennyson's memory when he dismissed contemptuously the various strivings to carry over into English the " surge and thunder of the Odyssey " : —

> These lame hexameters the strong-wing'd music of Homer !
> No — but a most burlesque barbarous experiment.
> When was a harsher sound ever heard, ye Muses, in England?
> When did a frog coarser croak upon our Helicon ?
> Hexameters no worse than daring Germany gave us,
> Barbarous experiment, barbarous hexameters.

English poets of high distinction, Tennyson and Swinburne among them, have sportively toyed with the technical difficulty of writing sapphics and alcaics in English. At least one of these interesting experiments proved to be truly a poem, valuable in itself apart from the overcoming of the metrical difficulties. This is Tennyson's poem in alcaics on " Milton " : —

> O mighty-mouth'd inventor of harmonies,
> O skill'd to sing of Time or Eternity,
>   God-gifted organ-voice of England,
>   Milton, a name to resound for ages ;
> Whose Titan angels, Gabriel, Abdiel,
> Starr'd from Jehovah's gorgeous armories,
>   Tower, as the deep-domed empyrean
>   Rings to the roar of an angel onset !
> Me rather all that bowery loneliness,
> The brooks of Eden mazily murmuring,

And bloom profuse and cedar arches
    Charm, as a wanderer out in ocean,
Where some refulgent sunset of India
Streams o'er a rich ambrosial ocean isle,
    And crimson-hued the stately palm-woods
        Whisper in odorous heights of even.

For the several lyrists this exercise in exotic meters may have been a valuable gymnastic; but it means little to the lovers of English poetry. The experiments may not be burlesque and barbarous; they may be refined and delicate; but they remain experiments, none the less, and experiments doomed to ultimate failure. Perhaps the final word on the subject was uttered three centuries ago by Thomas Nash: "The hexameter I grant to be a gentleman of an ancient house (so is many an English beggar); yet this clime of ours he cannot thrive in; he goes twitching and hopping, retaining no part of that stately, smooth gait, of which he vaunts himself among the Greeks and Romans." The sapphic and the alcaic in English are no better off than the hexameter; they cannot divest themselves of the strenuous effort and of the self-conscious artifice that have gone to their making. With the aid of the refrain and of alliteration and of repetition, English lyrists have won us to accept lyrics devoid of rime; but they have been able to do this only when they have chosen metrical forms native to our tongue, or at least not hostile to our system of accentual rhythm.

Another foreign device, not transplanted from a dead language, but taken over from another modern tongue, was essayed by George Eliot in one of the songs of "The Spanish Gipsy." As her theme was Spanish she borrowed from Spanish poetry a system

of semi-riming which is known as assonance, the
vowel-sounds being repeated exactly while the consonants which follow these vowel-sounds may vary at the
caprice of the poet. Here are two stanzas : —

> Maiden, crowned with glossy blackness,
>   Lithe as panther forest-roaming,
> Long-armed naiad, when she dances,
>   On a stream of ether floating —
>   Bright, O bright Fedalma !

> Form all curves like softness drifted,
>   Wave-kissed marble roundly dimpling,
> Far-off music slowly wingéd,
>   Gently rising, gently sinking —
>   Bright, O bright Fedalma !

The long *o* of *roaming* is repeated in *floating ;* and
the short *a* and short *e* of *blackness* are echoed in
dances. To the Spanish ear, trained to catch this repetition of the vowel-sound, assonance is as acceptable as actual rime ; but to the English ear there is
scarcely a suggestion of the author's intent to marry
blackness and *dances*. To us this stanza is as though
it was absolutely unrimed. The assonance is apprehended only by those who are learned enough to know
that it is employed by the Spaniards. It is quite possible that our ears, once possessed of this knowledge,
might be trained to follow the recurring vowels ; but
this could be achieved only by an effort which would
violate the Economy of Attention. In *blackness* and
dances the assonance extends to two syllables and
thereby becomes twice as difficult for us to perceive.
In *floating* and *roaming* there is identity of the terminal short syllable ; and the long *o* might carry over
its impression from one line to another. This bolder

and more obvious assonance is akin to that with which
we are already familiar in proverbs and folk-rimes:—

> Leave them *alone*
> And they 'll come *home*.

But in these more or less accidental variations from
strict rime, the changing consonants which follow
the unchanged vowel-sound do not greatly vary. In
alone and *home*, the *n* and the *m* are easily confounded
when sung.

In Matthew Arnold's "The Future," the lines are
unrimed; but the keen ears of an accomplished student
of verse have discovered a play of assonance, that is,
of occasional identity of the final vowels of certain
pairs of lines.

> Haply, the river of *Time* —
> As it grows, as the towns on its **marge**
> Fling their wavering *lights*
> On a wider, statelier stream —
> May acquire, if not the calm
> Of its early mountainous *shore*,
> Yet a solemn peace of its *own*.
> And the width of the waters, the hush
> Of the gray expanse where he *floats*,
> Freshening its current and spotted with *foam*
> As it draws to the ocean, may strike
> Peace to the soul of the man on its breast, —
> As the pale waste widens around *him*,
> As the banks fade dimmer away,
> As the stars come out, and the night-*wind*
> Brings up the *stream*
> Murmurs and scents of the infinite *sea*.

Arnold has pleased the ear by the casual repetition
of the same vowel-sound without creating any exact
expectation of this recurrence.

In the chapter on the ballade, the rondeau and the

other fixed forms, one of these forms was omitted, the
sestina, because it was originally composed without
rime. The sestina is an awkward and uninviting form,
which is quite as effective without rime as with it.
Although it has tempted poets as variously gifted as
Swinburne and Kipling, it cannot be said to have
demonstrated its worthiness. It is so forced in its for-
mality that it takes on an aspect of freakishness; and
so cumbrous is its structure that it can be seized by
the ear only as the result of undue exertion. Edmund
Gosse has written an unrimed sestina, of which this is
the first stanza: —

> In fair Provence, the land of lute and *rose*,
> Arnaut, great master of the lore of *love*,
> First wrought sestines to win his lady's *heart*,
> For she was deaf when simpler staves he *sang*,
> And for her sake he broke the bonds of *rime*,
> And in this sabler measure had his *wo*.

The six terminal words reappear in changing order
at the line-ends of all the other five stanzas, *wo* ending
the first line of the second stanza, and the other five
words following in turn, the final line ending with
heart. And *heart* then becomes the terminal word of
the first line of the third stanza, followed by *wo*, with
the rest of them tagging after. There is an envoy of
three lines, in which we find one half of the six words
at the ends of the lines and the other half concealed
in the middle: —

> Ah ! Sovereign *Love*, forgive this weaker *rime*,
> The men of old who *sang*, were great at *heart*,
> Yet have we too known *wo*, and worn their *rose*.

Swinburne, following the example of the French-
man, Gramont, tipped the six-line staves of his sestina

with rimes; and Kipling, eschewing rime, made use of the dialect of Tommy Atkins for his "Sestina of the Tramp Royal." But rimed or unrimed, picturesquely lyrical or realistically prosaic, the sestina is never likely to win favor in the ears of listeners whose native speech is English. Its arbitrary artificiality is too subtle; and the difficulty vanquished is not here an adequate reward.

At the opposite extreme from the cumbersome restraint which is imposed by the laws of the sestina is the lawlessness which is found in the most of Walt Whitman's earlier poems. Many poets of our language have claimed the full freedom which results from rejecting the strict stanza and the exact metrical equivalence of corresponding lines. In Matthew Arnold's "The Strayed Reveler," for example, we cannot decide with certainty just what the meter may be, so large and sweeping is the rhythmical flow of the poem. Whitman went still further; he declared a revolt from all the accepted conventions of English versification. He proclaimed the right to be a law unto himself and asserted substantially that his formlessness was its own excuse for being. He believed that he had rejected all tradition, yet he had plainly come under the influence of Blake, and he had been impressed also by the mighty movement of the Hebrew rhapsodists as this had been carried over into English by the translators under King James. As a result of this theory, many passages of Whitman reveal themselves as only a little removed from prose; they fail to give us exactly the kind of pleasure which we have been in the habit of expecting from poetry. Whitman is most impressive when he comes nearest to shapeliness of structure

and when he approaches most closely to the flowing
rhythm which delights us in Arnold's poem, for example, and in some of Blake's. Desiring to break
away from all the restrictions, he has won his warmest
welcome when his verse has been most in accord with
our normal expectation. It is significant that the one
poem of Whitman's which has been taken to heart
by the American people, "O Captain! My Captain,"
is the lyric of his which unhesitatingly accepts the
current conventions of English verse; it is in stanza
and in rime, and it has a refrain. It is significant also
that those of his other poems which are most admired
are those in which he most widely departed from his
own iconoclastic theories and in which he is most
evidently following the broader current of English
poetry. Consider, for example, "When Lilacs last in
the Dooryard Bloom'd," one of his threnodies for
Lincoln: —

When Lilacs last in the dooryard bloom'd,
And the great star early droop'd in the western sky in the
     night,
I mourn'd, and yet shall mourn with ever-returning spring.

Ever-returning spring, trinity sure you bring,
Lilac blooming perennial and drooping star in the west,
And thought of him I love.

Here is another fragment from the same lofty and
aspiring lyric: —

O, how shall I warble myself for the dead one there I loved?
And how shall I deck my song for the large sweet soul that has
     gone?
And what shall my perfume be for the grave of him I love?

Sea-winds blown from east and west,
Blown from the Eastern sea and blown from the

Western sea, till there on the prairies meeting,
These and with these and the breath of my chant,
I 'll perfume the grave of him I love.

This may seem irregular, but it is scarcely more irregular than Arnold's " The Strayed Reveler " or than Southey's " Thalaba." It is free and spontaneous, but it carries at least the suggestion of a definite form. It is the utterance of deep emotion, liberal and surging, but sustained and restrained by art. It has a technic of its own, not narrow and confined, not easily declared with precision, and yet felt and appreciated. Whitman's best poetry is the work of his maturity, when he had fully mastered his new form, which, as Professor Carpenter put it, " hovered between prose and verse." He had found his instrument at last; " it was living, musical, rhythmical, impassioned speech. If it had a prototype or an origin, it may be said to have been born of the rhythm which he heard in nature and of his memories of the arias and recitatives of the Italian opera."

" A man who finds that his gloves cripple him does right in drawing them off," said Stedman; " at first Whitman certainly meant to escape all technic. But genius, in spite of itself, makes works that stand the test of scientific laws." And the keen critic added that " unrimed verse, the easiest to write, is the hardest to excel in, and no measure for a bardling." What is too easy is not worth while; and the greatest artists are those who have most eagerly accepted the specific limitations under which a given piece of work had to be done; so far from rejecting technic, they have ever been athirst for new devices; and it has been their pride always to prove that although bound,

they could be free. And this Whitman came in time
to feel, even though he may never have confessed it
even to himself. Those move easiest who have learned
to dance ; and in " When Lilacs last in the Dooryard
Bloom'd " Whitman proved he had devised a form,
loose, large and free, exactly suited to his own needs.

CHAPTER X

THE COUPLET

With the substitution of heroic for unrimed verse, the theory and practice of harmony in English composition were altered. What was essentially national in our poetry — the music of sustained periods, elastic in their structure, and governed by the subtlest laws of melody in recurring consonants and vowels — was sacrificed for the artificial eloquence and monotonous cadence of the couplet. For a century and a half the summit of all excellence in versification was the construction of neat pairs of lines, smooth indeed and polished, but scarcely varying in their form. — JOHN ADDINGTON SYMONDS: *Blank Verse.*

FOR the expression of lyrical sentiment, the poets have generally chosen some form of the stanza, — a single quatrain, an octave, a sonnet, a ballade, or a sequence of whatever unit they have deemed most fit for their purpose. For narrative, they have also employed not infrequently a succession of stanzas, notably in the ballad, which sets forth a story running over from one quatrain into another until the tale is told. But more often the poets have preferred not to cut up their narrative into equal parts and not to confine themselves within the narrow limits of any stanza-form.

If the poet decides that his story will profit by the aid of rime, he is likely to select one of three meters, anapestic tetrameter, iambic tetrameter, or iambic pentameter, generally riming in couplets. Of these three the iambic pentameter, commonly known as the "heroic couplet," has been most frequently employed. The heroic couplet has served not only for narrative, but also for contemplative, philosophic, descriptive and satiric expression. It demands more detailed consideration here than either of the other meters; and these had therefore better be discussed briefly before the heroic couplet itself is analyzed. And as the anapestic tetrameter has been less often employed than the iambic tetrameter, it may be considered first.

Although Byron has chosen to print " The Destruction of Sennacherib " in stanzas of four lines each, its movement is continuous and the unit of construction rather is the single couplet than the pair of couplets joined to suggest a quatrain to the eye. The ear would find it almost impossible to detect any break between the successive quatrains. Indeed, the three final stanzas begin each of them with an *and* which ties them closely to their predecessor : —

The Assyrian came down like the wolf on the fold,
And his cohorts were gleaming in purple and gold ;
And the sheen of their spears was like stars on the sea,
When the blue wave rolls nightly on deep Galilee.

Like the leaves of the forest when summer is green,
That host with their banners at sunset were seen :
Like the leaves of the forest when autumn hath blown,
That host on the morrow lay wither'd and strown.

For the Angel of Death spread his wings on the blast,
And breathed in the face of the foe as he pass'd ;
And the eyes of the sleepers wax'd deadly and chill,
And their hearts but once heaved, and forever grew still !

And there lay the steed with his nostril all wide,
But through it there roll'd not the breath of his pride :
And the foam of his gasping lay white on the turf,
And cold as the spray of the rock-beating surf.

And there lay the rider distorted and pale,
With the dew on his brow, and the rust on his mail ;

> And the tents were all silent, the banners alone,
> The lances unlifted, the trumpet unblown.
>
> And the widows of Ashur are loud in their wail,
> And the idols are broke in the temple of Baal ;
> And the might of the Gentile, unsmote by the sword,
> Hath melted like snow in the glance of the Lord !

The essential quality of this meter, as it is disclosed in this poem of Byron's, is swiftness; it has an irresistible onward rush, due to the anapestic rhythm itself. This is the reason why Browning used anapests in his galloping lines on " How They Brought the Good News from Ghent to Aix."

This same rapidity we find earlier, here and there, in Dryden's " Alexander's Feast," for example, in these two lines : —

> The princes applaud, with a furious joy ;
> And the king seized a flambeau with zeal to destroy.

Yet the same meter is employed by Cowper in " The Poplar Field," wherein he is striving rather for an unhurried effect : —

> The poplars are felled ; farewell to the shade,
> And the whispering sound of the cool colonnade ;
> The winds play no longer and sing in the leaves,
> Nor Ouse on his bosom their image receives.
> Twelve years have elapsed since I first took a view
> Of my favorite field, and the bank where they grew,
> And now in the grass behold they are laid,
> And the tree is my seat that once lent me a shade.

Although Cowper chose this meter for a contemplative poem, it has been employed most often in humorous verse, and more especially in satire. Its briskness, its facility, its easy brilliancy aid the versifier to make his lines glittering and pointed. There can be no bet-

ter example of this than Goldsmith's delicate and
delightful " Retaliation " : —

> Here Reynolds is laid, and, to tell you my mind,
> He has not left a wiser or better behind.
> His pencil was striking, resistless and grand ;
> His manners were gentle, complying, and bland ;
> Still born to improve us in every part,
> His pencil our faces, his manners our heart.
> To coxcombs averse, yet most civilly steering ;
> When they judged without skill, he was still hard of hearing ;
> When they talked of Raphaels, Correggios, and stuff,
> He shifted his trumpet, and only took snuff.

Possibly it was a recalling of the success with which
Goldsmith had used this meter for his gallery of por-
traits that led Lowell to choose it also for the series
of character-studies which he included in " A Fable
for Critics," in which he is as acute as Goldsmith, although a little less tolerant, as well as a little more
wilfully clever in the invention of novel rimes : —

> There comes Poe, with his raven, like Barnaby Rudge,
> Three fifths of him genius and two fifths sheer fudge,
> Who talks like a book of iambs and pentameters,
> In a way to make people of common sense damn meters,
> Who has written some things quite the best of their kind,
> But the heart somehow seems all squeezed out by the mind.

Lowell's criticism of Bryant is as candid and as acute
as his criticism of Poe ; and it is also quite as ingenious in its riming and in its rhythmic swing : —

> There is Bryant, as quiet, as cool, and as dignified
> As a smooth, silent iceberg, that never is ignified,
> Save when by reflection 't is kindled o' nights
> With a semblance of flame by the chill Northern Lights.
> He may rank (Griswold says so) first bard of your nation
> (There 's no doubt that he stands in supreme iceolation),
> Your topmost Parnassus he may set his heel on,

But no warm applauses come, peal following peal on, —
He 's too smooth and polished to hang any zeal on :
Unqualified merits, I 'll grant, if you choose, he has 'em,
But he lacks the one merit of kindling enthusiasm ;
If he stir you at all, it is just, on my soul,
Like being stirred up with the very North Pole.

These extracts from Goldsmith and from Lowell
serve to exemplify the privilege of commingling double
and treble rimes with the single rimes which are
the staple of the anapestic tetrameter. Indeed, when
this meter is used for a humorous or satiric purpose
there is an almost irresistible temptation to devise unexpected rimes and to decorate the edges with sound-
combinations never before attempted. The lyrist has
also the privilege of substituting iambics for anapests,
more often in the first foot, but also on occasion in
the second or third ; — although this privilege can be
availed of only at the peril of slackening the swift
movement. And the versifier may even inject, now
and again, a couplet of dimeters, without retarding
the flow of his lines. This is what Barham did unhesitatingly in his " Ingoldsby Legends," as will be seen
in this extract from " The Jackdaw of Rheims " : —

The Cardinal rose with a dignified look,
He called for his candle, his bell, and his book :
In holy anger, and pious grief,
He solemnly curs'd that rascally thief !
He curs'd him at board, he curs'd him in bed,
From the sole of his foot to the crown of his head !
He curs'd him in sleeping, that every night
He should dream of the devil, and wake in a fright ;
He curs'd him in eating, he curs'd him in drinking,
He curs'd him in coughing, in sneezing, in winking ;
He curs'd him in sitting, in standing, in lying ;
He curs'd him in walking, in riding, in flying ;
He curs'd him in living, he curs'd him dying !

> Never was heard such a terrible curse !
>> But what gave rise
>> To no little surprise,
> Nobody seem'd a penny the worse !

The anapestic tetrameter is thus seen to have extraordinary flexibility; it may rime in couplets or in triplets or for four and five lines in succession; it may utilize at will single or double or treble rimes; it may shrink to eight or nine syllables, as in Barham's

> In holy anger, and pious grief,

or it may expand to fourteen syllables, as in Lowell's

> As a smooth, silent iceberg, that never is ignified.

It can go on frolicking and rollicking in the utmost high spirits, with the rushing tumult of a cataract.

Certain of the same qualities, especially the swiftness, although a little relaxed, can be found also in the iambic tetrameter, particularly when it is used for satire as it was by Butler, by Churchill and by Trumbull. But what the iambic tetrameter lacks in speed, it makes up in sententiousness, as we note in the familiar couplets of " McFingal " : —

> But rogue ne'er yet felt halter draw,
> With good opinion of the law,

and

> For optics sharp it needs, I ween,
> To see what never can be seen.

The same pregnant concision is to be found in Butler : —

> Great conquerors greater glories gain
> By foes in triumph led than slain,

and

> Ay me ! what perils do environ
> The man that meddles with cold iron !

Butler indulges also in the arbitrary and inventive riming that we find later in Lowell : —

> When pulpit, drum ecclesiastick,
> Is beat with fist instead of a stick.

(Strictly speaking, this is not a true rime, since the second line merely repeats without the proper variation the terminal sound of the first line.)

The iambic tetrameter has served other purposes than satire. Chaucer employed it in "The House of Fame," Milton in "Il Penseroso," Burns in "Tam o' Shanter," Byron in "The Prisoner of Chillon," Wordsworth in "The White Doe," Scott in "Marmion" and "The Lady of the Lake," Whittier in "Maud Muller" and "Barbara Frietchie." Scott, indeed, was frank in declaring his preference for the iambic tetrameter over the pentameter for purposes of narrative, although perhaps not for descriptive poetry. He held that the tetrameter "is capable of certain varieties denied to the heroic couplet. Double rimes, for instance, are congenial to it. . . . You may also render it more or less rapid by retaining or dropping an occasional syllable. Lastly, it runs better into sentences than any length of line I know, as it corresponds, upon an average view of our punctuation, very commonly with the proper and usual space between comma and comma." And then Scott added, as a final reason for his liking, that he had "somehow a better knack at this" meter than at the longer pentameter. In other words, Scott found iambic tetrameters easy to write; and so they are; and this facility is often fatal to them, since they may flow too fast and without sufficient thought and emotion behind them. As Holmes pointed out, the iambic tetrameter does not conform to our normal breathing; it forces us to hurry and to take short breaths. It may be rapid, as indeed it is in the movement of Scott's narrative passages ; but it tends in time to be fatiguing. It lacks the broader scope of the pentameter, which is better adjusted to our natural inspiration and expiration. Yet Scott was right in thinking that it was a satisfactory meter for the bold and lusty deeds he desired to set forth in verse ; and he modified its rigidity under two influences. One of these was the old English ballad which he had absorbed so absolutely, and from which he borrowed the privilege of dropping the strict couplet, now and then, and employing a quatrain with its interlaced rimes, and with its occasional trimeter lines to relieve the monotony of the tetrameter. And the other influence was that of Coleridge's " Christabel," which he had seen or heard before its publication. Coleridge had deliberately departed from the strict eight syllables of the rigid iambic tetrameter as that had been written by his immediate predecessors. He claimed the right to vary iambics with anapests and to drop out syllables at will, if the sense explained the resulting pause ; he professed to reserve the privilege of varying the number of syllables in any line from seven to twelve as long as he retained the four long syllables which were the backbone of the meter. As a matter of fact, he went so far as to put only four syllables into one of his lines : —

> 'T is the middle of night by the castle clock,
> And the owls have awakened the crowing cock,
> Tu—whit ! Tu—whoo !

Here Coleridge is rather anapestic than iambic, whereas Scott following him is more regularly iambic, although not without an occasional anapest, which gives enhanced rapidity to his lines : —

> "Now, in good sooth," Lord Marmion cried,
> "Were I in warlike wise to ride,
> A better guard I would not lack
> Than your stout forayers at my back;
> But as in form of peace I go,
> A friendly messenger, to know
> Why, through all Scotland, near and far,
> Their king is mustering troops for war,
> The sight of plundering Border spears
> Might justify suspicious fears,
> And deadly feud or thirst of spoil
> Break out in some unseemly broil."

It is curious that Scott, brought up on the iambic pentameter, which still retained its vogue in his youth, should have abandoned it in his narrative poems, when his great predecessors in the art of story-telling in verse, Chaucer and Dryden, long familiar with the tetrameter, seem to have introduced the pentameter as an ampler instrument for the same purpose. Chaucer and Dryden are not only greater poets than Scott; they are also far more consummate metrists, far more careful and conscientious artists in verse. The explanation of Scott's reversion to the meter Chaucer had abandoned is probably to be found in the fact that he found the pentameter after it had received the impress of Pope, whereby it had lost not a little of the easy spontaneity with which Chaucer had endowed it. In Pope's hands the iambic pentameter had stiffened; it had become antithetic and artificial. There is more than a little truth in Cowper's

assertion that Pope had " made poetry a mere mechanic
art " ; — at least Pope had made the mechanism of
verse more obvious, and never more obvious than in
his handling of the heroic couplet. Perhaps the difference between this meter as Pope used it and as
Chaucer had used it can be indicated by declaring that
in Pope's hands it is strictly the heroic couplet, with
the thought firmly clamped within two riming lines,
whereas in Chaucer it is rather to be called iambic
pentameter flowing ever freely from line to line with
no rigid limitation of the sense within the successive
pairs of rimes.

Although the main purpose of the present book is
not to give the history of English versification but to
dwell on its principles and on its practice, the importance of the rimed iambic pentameter is such that
a brief chronological survey is here justifiable, — indeed, the rich variety of which this meter is capable
can best be shown by considering its development.
The easy amplitude of the iambic pentameter as
Chaucer handled it will be found also in Spenser's
treatment. It retained its fluidity and openness in
Marlowe and Shakspere; but it tightened and
stiffened in Ben Jonson's hands. Waller refined on
Jonson and Pope on Waller, until the heroic couplet
became antithetical, exactly balanced, with the meaning rigidly compacted into a single line or at most
within the pair of rimes. At its worst the heroic
couplet as Pope had sharpened and polished it justifies Lowell's assertion that " Mr. Pope's versification
was like the regular ticking of one of Willard's clocks,
in which we could fancy, after long listening, a certain
kind of rhythm or tune, but which yet was only a

poverty-stricken *tick, tick,* after all." And in "A
Fable for Critics" Lowell declared that the heroic
couplet was

> what I call a sham meter,
> But many admire it, the English pentameter.

Here Lowell is in disaccord with Holmes, who liked
to write the iambic pentameter and who loved to
praise it : —

> The proud heroic, with its pulse-like beat,
> Rings like the cymbals, clashing as they meet.

This couplet is from one of his earlier poems; and
in one of his later lyrics Holmes with even more
emphasis again declared the faith that was in him : —

> And so the hand that takes the lyre for you
> Plays the old tune on strings that once were new.
> Nor let the rimester of the hour deride
> The straight-backed measure with its stately stride,
> It gave the mighty voice of Dryden scope;
> It sheathed the steel-bright epigrams of Pope;
> In Goldsmith's verse it learned a sweeter strain;
> Byron and Campbell wore its clanking chain;
> I smile to listen while the critic's scorn
> Flouts the proud purple kings have nobly worn.

Holmes himself relished the heroic couplet as it
had been edged and pointed by Pope; and though he
cited Goldsmith and Campbell, he failed to mention
the later poets who have used the iambic pentameter
with the same large liberty that Chaucer enjoyed.
Leigh Hunt led the way in emancipating this meter,
and he was followed immediately by Keats and Shelley.
And later it was employed by Swinburne and Morris,
with a freedom from mere antithesis, which made this
measure in their hands a very different instrument

from what it had been in the hands of Pope and of
his less gifted disciples.

But the full possibilities of the iambic pentameter
can best be shown by a sequence of selections from
successive poets. Here is an extract from the pro-
log to the " Canterbury Tales " : —

> A knyght ther was, and that a worthy man,
> That fro the tyme that he first bigan
> To riden out, he loved chivalrie,
> Trouthe and honour, fredom and curteisie.
> Ful worthy was he in his lorde's werre,
> And therto hadde he riden, no man ferre,
> As wel in cristendom as in hethënesse,
> And evere honoured for his worthynesse.

These lines have the flowing ease so characteristic
of Chaucer. The rimes are not sharply emphasized
and the sense is not shut up in a line or even in a
couplet. Neither the line nor the couplet is the unit
of structure. And these same characteristics are visible also in this passage, from Spenser's " Shepherd's
Calendar " : —

> There grewe an aged Tree on the greene,
> A goodly Oake sometime had it bene.
> With armes full strong and lergely display'd,
> But of their leaves they were disarayde:
> The bodie bigge, and mightely pight,
> Thoroughly rooted, and of wonderous height,
> Whilome had bene the King of the field,
> And mochell mast to the husband did yielde,
> And with his nuts larded many swine:
> But now the gray mosse marred his rine;
> His bared boughes were beaten with stormes,
> His toppe was bald, and wasted with wormes.

This may lack the spontaneity of Chaucer's verse;
but a little awkward as it may be, it runs on with its
initial impetus, never arrested arbitrarily at the end

of a line or a couplet. The movement of the narrative is possibly a little slower than in these lines from Marlowe's "Hero and Leander": —

> On Hellespont, guilty of true love's blood,
> In view and opposite two cities stood,
> Sea-borderers, disjoined by Neptune's might;
> The one Abydos, the other Sestos hight.
> At Sestos Hero dwelt; Hero the fair,
> Whom young Apollo courted for her hair,
> And offer'd as a dower his burning throne,
> Where she should sit, for men to gaze upon.
> The outside of her garments were of lawn,
> The lining purple silk, with gilt stars drawn;
> Her wide sleeves green, and bordered with a grove,
> Where Venus in her naked glory strove
> To please the careless and disdainful eyes
> Of proud Adonis, that before her lies.

The example from Shakspere may be taken from an early play, written when he was most under the influence of Marlowe. Here is part of a speech from "Love's Labor's Lost": —

> Under the cool shade of a sycamore
> I thought to close mine eyes some half an hour;
> When, lo! to interrupt my purpos'd rest,
> Toward that shade I might behold address'd
> The King and his companions. Warily
> I stole into a neighbor thicket by,
> And overheard what you shall overhear,
> That, by and by, disguis'd they will be here.
> Their herald is a pretty knavish page,
> That well by heart hath conn'd his embassage.
> Action and accent did they teach him there;
> "Thus must thou speak," and "thus thy body bear";
> And ever and anon they made a doubt
> Presence majestical would put him out.

In all these specimens of iambic pentameter from Chaucer to Shakspere we find the sense gliding on from line to line, with no undue emphasis on the rimes and with no effort to arrest the movement within the limit of the couplet. In Ben Jonson, we begin to find the motion less easy; we catch a dawning desire for antithesis; we discover already a certain snap at the end of the line; we perceive an increasing tendency toward sententiousness; and our attention is more often called to the couplet itself. These characteristics are already visible in Jonson's epigram "To my mere English Censure": —

> To thee, my way in epigrams seems new,
> When both it is the old way, and the true.
> Thou sayst that cannot be ; for thou hast seen
> Davis and Weever, and the best have been.
> And mine come nothing like. I hope so ; yet,
> As theirs did with thee, mine might credit get.
> If thou 'dst but use thy faith, as thou didst then,
> When thou wert wont t' admire, not censure men.
> Prithee believe still, and judge not so fast :
> Thy faith is all the knowledge that thou hast.

The characteristics which we can only glimpse in Jonson are overtly revealed in Waller. Dryden declared that "the excellence and dignity of rime were never fully known until Mr. Waller taught it; he first made writing easily an art, first showed us to conclude the sense, most commonly in distichs, which in the verse of those before him runs on for so many lines together, that the reader is out of breath to overtake it." It was Waller who pointed the path to Dryden himself and after Dryden to Pope. In his hands the couplet became the obvious unit of structure ; in fact, in his verse, the poem had the unity only of a chain of which the couplets are the several links. Here is Waller's account of "His Majesty's Escape": —

While to his harp divine Arion sings
The loves and conquests of our Albion kings ;
Of the fourth Edward was his noble song,
Fierce, goodly, valiant, beautiful and young ;
He rent the crown from vanquished Henry's head,
Raised the White Rose, and trampled on the Red,
Till love, triumphing o'er the victor's pride,
Brought Mars and Warwick to the conquered side, —
Neglected Warwick, whose bold hand like fate,
Gives and resumes the sceptre of our state,
Woos for his master, and with double shame,
Himself deluded, mocks the princely dame,
The Lady Bona, whom just anger burns,
And foreign war with civil rage returns ;
Ah ! spare your swords, where beauty is to blame,
Love gave the affront, and must repair the same,
When France shall boast of her, whose conquering eyes
Have made the best of English hearts their prize,
Have power to alter the decrees of fate,
And change again the counsels of our state.

Dryden followed Waller and easily bettered his model because he was truly a poet, which Waller chanced to be only in a lyric or two, almost by accident. Dryden refused to let his meaning run on line after line. He isolated the couplet, and thus emphasized the importance of the rime. He yielded to a rhetorical temptation and used antithesis to balance his lines. His verse became compacter and more sententious, because he relied more often on his wit than on his imagination. In his hands the iambic pentameter ought rather to be described as the heroic couplet; and no one has used this implement with more certain mastery than Dryden. Here is a fragment from one of his satires, the famous portrait of the infamous Duke of Buckingham : —

Some of their chiefs were princes of the land :
In the first rank of these did Zimri stand ;

A man so various, that he seemed to be
Not one, but all mankind's epitome :
Stiff in opinions, always in the wrong ;
Was everything by starts, and nothing long ;
But, in the course of one revolving moon,
Was chemist, fiddler, statesman, and buffoon :
Then all for women, painting, rhyming, drinking,
Besides ten thousand freaks that died in thinking.
Blest madman, who could every hour employ,
With something new to wish, or to enjoy !
Railing and praising were his usual themes ;
And both, to show his judgment, in extremes :
So over-violent, or over-civil,
That every man, with him, was God or Devil.
In squandering wealth was his peculiar art :
Nothing went unrewarded but desert.
Beggared by fools, whom still he found too late,
He had his jest, and they had his estate.
He laughed himself from court ; then sought relief
By forming parties, but could ne'er be chief ;
For, spite of him, the weight of business fell
On Absalom and wise Achitophel :
Thus, wicked but in will, of means bereft,
He left not faction, but of that was left.

The heroic couplet, which seems to be best fitted for
satire, Dryden employed also in narrative, with the
same certainty of stroke. Here is his spirited description of a tourney in " Palamon and Arcite " : —

At this the challenger, with fierce defy,
His trumpet sounds; the challeng'd makes reply :
With clangor rings the field, resounds the vaulted sky.
Their vizors clos'd, their lances in the rest,
Or at the helmet pointed, or the crest,
They vanish from the barrier, speed the race,
And spurring see decrease the middle space.
A cloud of smoke envelops either host,
And all at once the combatants are lost :
Darkling they join adverse, and shock unseen,
Coursers with coursers justling, men with men;

As lab'ring in eclipse, a while they stay,
Till the next blast of wind restores the day.
They look anew; the beauteous form of fight
Is chang'd, and war appears a grisly sight.
Two troops in fair array one moment show'd,
The next, a field with fallen bodies strow'd:
Not half the number in their seats are found;
But men and steeds lie grov'ling on the ground.
The points of spears are stuck within the shield,
The steeds without their riders scour the field.
The knights, unhors'd, on foot renew the fight;
The glitt'ring fauchions cast a gleaming light:
Hauberks and helms are hew'd with many a wound ;
Out spins the streaming blood, and dyes the ground.

Pope followed Dryden as Dryden had followed
Waller, continuing and developing the tendencies which
are visible in the verse of these immediate predecessors. He lacked the bold imagination of Dryden, but
he was a more meticulous artist. There was often a
large affluence about Dryden, whereas Pope was
rather a miser than a spendthrift. He was always a
deliberate and conscientious craftsman in verse, with a
code of his own to which he conformed at whatever cost
of toil. He relied on antithesis for much of his rhetorical effect ; indeed, the suggestion might be ventured
that he is rather a rhetorician in rime than a true
poet. He preached what he practised ; and the formula
of the heroic couplet as he had perfected it was free
to all who came after. His method was so easily acquired that almost anybody could set up for a poet,
who accepted Pope's rules and trod in Pope's own
footsteps ; and thus in time the iambic pentameter itself was emptied of its vitality by dint of uninspired
imitation, until Lowell was justified in his assertion
that " the measure is so facile that one soon loses one's

sense of the difference between what sounds like something and what really is something."

In his versified "Essay on Criticism," Pope laid
down the law by which he wished to be judged. Here is
one of the cleverest and most characteristic passages
in which he adroitly exemplifies the doctrine he is declaring : —

> But most by Numbers judge a poet's song,
> And smooth or rough with them is right or wrong.
> In the bright Muse tho' thousand charms conspire,
> Her voice is all these tuneful fools admire;
> Who haunt Parnassus but to please their ear,
> Not mend their minds; as some to church repair,
> Not for the doctrine, but the music there.
> These equal syllables alone require,
> Tho' oft the ear the open vowels tire,
> While expletives their feeble aid do join,
> And ten low words oft creep in one dull line:
> While they ring round the same unvaried chimes,
> With sure returns of still expected rimes;
> Where'er you find "the cooling western breeze,"
> In the next line, it "whispers thro' the trees " ;
> If crystal streams "with pleasing murmurs creep,"
> The reader 's threaten'd (not in vain) with "sleep " ;
> Then, at the last and only couplet, fraught
> With some unmeaning thing they call a thought,
> A needless Alexandrine ends the song,
> That, like a wounded snake, drags its slow length along.
> Leave such to tune their own dull rimes, and know
> What 's roundly smooth, or languishingly slow;
> And praise the easy vigor of a line,
> Where Denham's strength and Waller's sweetness join.
> True ease in writing comes from art, not chance,
> As those move easiest who have learn'd to dance.
> 'T is not enough no harshness gives offence,
> The sound must seem an echo to the sense.
> Soft is the strain when zephyr gently blows,
> And the smooth stream in smoother numbers flows;
> But when loud surges lash the sounding shore,
> The hoarse rough verse should like the torrent roar ;

When Ajax strives some rock's vast weight to throw,
The line, too, labors, and the words move slow.
Not so, when swift Camilla scours the plain,
Flies o'er the unbending corn, and skims along the main.
Hear how Timotheus' varied lays surprise,
And bid alternate passions fall and rise !

And in one of his " Imitations of Horace," Pope described the refining of English poetry as he understood it : —

We conquer'd France, but felt our captive's charms,
Her arts victorious triumph'd o'er our arms ;
Britain to soft refinements less a foe,
Wit grew polite, and numbers learn'd to flow.
Waller was smooth ; but Dryden taught to join
The varying verse, the full resounding line,
The long majestic march, and energy divine :
Tho' still some traces of our rustic vein
And splay-foot verse remain'd, and will remain.
Late, very late, correctness grew our care,
When the tir'd nation breath'd from civil war.
Exact Racine, and Corneille's noble fire
Show'd us that France had something to admire.
Not but the tragic spirit was our own,
And full in Shakspere, fair in Otway, shone ;
But Otway fail'd to polish or refine,
And fluent Shakspere scarce effac'd a line.
Ev'n copious Dryden wanted, or forgot,
The last and greatest art, the art to blot.

Admirably adapted as Pope's methods may be for satire and for epigram, they are wholly unfitted to render the largeness of Homer, the simplicity and the nobility of his bold manner. Matthew Arnold in his lectures " On Translating Homer " quoted a passage from Pope's version : —

Could all our care elude the gloomy grave
Which claims no less the fearful than the brave,
For lust of fame I should not vainly dare
In fighting fields, nor urge thy soul to war :

> But since, alas ! ignoble age must come,
> Disease, and death's inexorable doom ;
> The life which others pay, let us bestow,
> And give to fame, what we to nature owe.

And on this Arnold made the pertinent comment that "nothing could better exhibit Pope's prodigious talent; and nothing, too, could be better in its own way. But, as Bentley said, 'You must not call it Homer.' One feels that Homer's thought has passed through a literary and rhetorical crucible, and come out highly intellectualized; come out in a form which strongly impresses us, indeed, but which no longer impresses us in the same way as when it was uttered by Homer. The antithesis of the last two lines —

> The life which others pay, let us bestow,
> And give to fame, what we to nature owe —

is excellent, and is just suited to Pope's heroic couplet; but neither the antithesis itself, nor the couplet which conveys it, is suited to the feeling or to the movement of the Homeric ἴομεν."

Arnold objected to Pope's parade of antithesis to break up the natural movement of Homer's narration. Antithesis, symmetry, balance, Pope employed to give immediate point to his lines. This trick of style is the most obvious of Pope's mannerisms. Leigh Hunt quoted a passage from "The Rape of the Lock," dividing every line in two by a dash to call attention to the wilful and persistent setting off of one half of a line against the other : —

> On her white breast — a sparkling cross she wore,
> Which Jews might kiss — and infidels adore.
> Her lively looks — a sprightly mind disclose,
> Quick as her eyes, — and as unfix'd as those :

Favors to none, — to all she smiles extends ;
Oft she rejects, — but never once offends.
Bright as the sun, — her eyes the gazers strike,
And, like the sun, — they shine on all alike.
Yet, graceful ease, — and sweetness void of pride,
Might hide her faults, — if Belles had faults to hide :
If to her share — some female errors fall,
Look on her face, — and you 'll forget 'em all.

" The reader will observe," Leigh Hunt remarked,
"that it is literally *see-saw*, like the rising and the
falling of a plank, with a light person at one end who
is jerked up in the briefer time, and a heavier one
who is set down more leisurely at the other." Here
Hunt has caught Pope in flagrant violation of his
own theory, as the author of " The Rape of the Lock "
once wrote a letter in which he asserted that " every
nice ear must, I believe, have observed that in any
smooth English verse of ten syllables, there is naturally a pause either at the fourth, fifth, or sixth syllable," and he added that " to preserve an exact
harmony and variety none of these pauses should be
continued above three lines together, without the in-
terposition of another, else it will be apt to weary the
ear with one continual tone." But even if this break
in the line is not continuously after the fourth syllable,
as it is in the passage Leigh Hunt cited, even if it is
sometimes after the fifth and sometimes after the sixth,
even this limitation becomes monotonous in time and
tends to reduce the rhythm to a mechanical tick-tack.

Scott pointed out another occasional weakness in
the heroic couplet as Pope wrote it, — the use of needless adjectives merely to fill out the five feet. Scott
was defending his own preference for the tetrameter,
and he quoted the opening lines of Pope's " Iliad,"

italicizing the adjectives which seemed to him needless: —

> Achilles' wrath, to Greece the *direful* spring
> Of woes unnumber'd, *heav'nly* goddess, sing !
> That wrath which hurl'd to Pluto's *gloomy* reign
> The souls of *mighty* chiefs untimely slain :
> Whose limbs, unburied on the *naked* shore,
> Devouring dogs and *hungry* vultures tore.

Scott said that " since it is true that by throwing out the epithets underscored, we preserve the sense without diminishing the force of the verses, and since it is also true that scarcely one of the epithets are more than merely expletive, I do really think that the structure of verse which requires least of this sort of bolstering, is most likely to be forcible and animated."

While Goldsmith inherited the heroic couplet from Pope and from the clouds of imitators who encompassed Pope about, he had more feeling than his witty predecessor ; he was less obviously clever; he was gentler and more human ; and as a result he modified the meter to suit his own needs. There is less striking antithesis ; and the lines break with less monotony. There are fewer expletive adjectives thrust in to fill out the line. The couplet is still the unit of structure ; and yet the narrative has a less jerky movement. Here is a passage from "The Deserted Village": —

> Near yonder copse, where once the garden smiled,
> And still where many a garden flower grows wild,
> There, where a few torn shrubs the place disclose,
> The village preacher's modest mansion rose.
> A man he was to all the country dear,
> And passing rich with forty pounds a year ;
> Remote from towns he ran his godly race,
> Nor e'er had changed, nor wished to change his place ;

Unpractised he to fawn, or seek for power,
By doctrines fashioned to the varying hour ;
Far other aims his heart had learned to prize,
More skilled to raise the wretched than to rise.
His house was known to all the vagrant train,
He chid their wanderings, but relieved their pain ;
The long-remembered beggar was his guest,
Whose beard descending swept his aged breast ;
The ruined spendthrift, now no longer proud,
Claimed kindred there, and had his claims allowed ;
The broken soldier, kindly bade to stay,
Sate by his fire, and talked the night away ;
Wept o'er his wounds, or, tales of sorrow done,
Shouldered his crutch, and showed how fields were won.

The heroic couplet was employed by Johnson and
by Byron in their satires; and they were content to
leave it as they found it. Even Cowper, although he
was no slavish follower of Pope, did not impress his
individuality on the iambic pentameter. After Goldsmith the next poet to handle it with any freedom
was Leigh Hunt, who blazed the trail for Keats and
Shelley. In his "Story of Rimini" there is an abandon-
ment of Pope's couplet-structure with its epigrammatic flavor and with its monotony of strict iambics.
The rhythm is more fluid and the narrative runs over
from line to line. The thought is no longer diked
between two rimes. There is again a sense of freedom
and of spontaneity, due partly to the avoidance of the
self-conscious ingenuity of Pope : —

But 'twixt the wood and flowery walks, half-way,
And formed of both, the loveliest portion lay, —
A spot, that struck you like enchanted ground ; —
It was a shallow dell, set in a mound
Of sloping orchards, — fig, and almond trees,
Cherry and pine, with some few cypresses ;
Down by whose roots, descending darkly still
(You saw it not, but heard), there gushed a rill,

Whose low sweet talking seemed as if it said,
Something eternal to that happy shade.

This harks back to Chaucer and points forward to
Keats, in whose hands the iambic pentameter was to
reveal itself again as a fit and flexible instrument for
a true poet. Keats claimed the liberty of occasional
double rimes, which helped him to avoid the temptation to end a majority of lines with bold monosyllables. He shifted the place of his pauses in the middle
of his lines with exquisite skill, varying the movement
to mate with his sentiment. Perhaps the passage that
best exemplifies this new ease of the iambic pentameter is the well-known description of beauty, in
" Endymion " : —

A thing of beauty is a joy forever :
Its loveliness increases ; it will never
Pass into nothingness ; but still will keep
A bower quiet for us, and a sleep
Full of sweet dreams, and health, and quiet breathing.
Therefore, on every morrow, are we wreathing
A flowery band to bind us to the earth,
Spite of despondence, of the inhuman dearth
Of noble natures, of the gloomy days,
Of all the unhealthy and o'er-darken'd ways
Made for our searching : yes, in spite of all,
Some shape of beauty moves away the pall
From our dark spirits. Such the sun, the moon,
Trees old and young, sprouting a shady boon
For simple sheep ; and such are daffodils
With the green world they live in ; and clear rills
That for themselves a cooling covert make
'Gainst the hot season ; the mid-forest brake,
Rich with a sprinkling of fair musk-rose blooms ;
And such too is the grandeur of the dooms
We have imagined for the mighty dead ;
All lovely tales that we have heard or read :
An endless fountain of immortal drink,
Pouring unto us from the heaven's brink.

Shelley used this meter with similar ease; and the rigidity of the heroic couplet disappeared. The way was now made straight for the poets who were to come after. Browning found the iambic pentameter available for the narrative of " Sordello "; Swinburne employed it with large luxuriance in " Tristram of Lyonesse "; and Morris took it to tell the " Life and Death of Jason."

CHAPTER XI

BLANK VERSE

That which is the glory of blank verse, as a vehicle of poetry, is also its danger and its difficulty. Its freedom from the fetters of rime, the infinite variability of the metrical structure of its lines, the absence of couplets and stanzas, — all assimilate it to prose. It is the easiest of all conceivable meters to write; it is the hardest to write well. Its metrical requirements are next to nothing; its poetical requirements are infinite. It was Byron, I believe, who remarked, that it differed from other meters in this, that whereas they required a certain proportion of lines, some more, some less, to be good, in blank verse, *every* line must be good. — SHADWORTH H. HODGSON: *English Verse.*

BLANK verse, the unrimed iambic pentameter, is the most characteristic and the most individual meter of English poetry. It has shown itself to be the best instrument for the expression of the essential energy of the English-speaking peoples in their loftiest flights of imagination. It is a nobler vehicle for the epic and for the tragic than the Alexandrine of the French encumbered as that is with its pairs of rimes, alternately masculine and feminine. It has proved itself a worthy rival of the supple and sonorous hexameter of the Greeks. It has a definite firmness of structure and, at the same time, an infinite variety within this framework. It can be swift, simple, and direct ; or it may be elaborate and luxuriant. It lends itself to all moods, and it is adequate for every kind of poetry. It can tell a story ; it can voice a purely lyric sentiment ; it can convey at will the interpreta-

tive description of external nature or the subtlest
revelation of human psychology. It can serve alike
for the witty banter of light comedy and for the soul-
stirring depths of inexorable tragedy. It demands
that the poet who essays it shall always put forth his
topmost power and that he shall always do the best that
is in him. With no support from any stanza and with
no assistance or suggestion from rime, it may seem
easy; but it is an instrument to be handled worthily
only by a master. It has a large freedom wherein a
man adventures himself only at his peril. "In hearing good blank verse," so Symonds declared, "we do
not long for rime, our ears are satisfied without it;
nor does our sense of order and proportion require
the obvious and artificial recurrence of stanzas, when
the sense creates for itself a melodious structure
and is not forced into the mold of any arbitrary
form."

In the history of English poetry, blank verse developed later than the heroic couplet, which it was to succeed as the supreme implement of the English poets,
only in its turn to be superseded for a while under the
influence of Dryden and Pope. Blank verse came into
its own slowly, influenced at first by the tradition of
the heroic couplet. In its turn, it influenced the heroic
couplet; and if rimed pentameter was able in the
nineteenth century to recapture the larger liberty it
had earlier enjoyed, this was due mainly to the inspir-
ing example of blank verse. The rimed pentameter
and the unrimed pentameter have existed side by
side for now three centuries and more, rivals for the
favor of the poets, each in turn borrowing from the
other. The heroic couplet has been dealt with first,

as the elder; and blank verse in turn demands the same chronological consideration, since it is only by following it through its development that we are able to possess ourselves of its essential principles and to discover its immense variety as its many possibilities were perceived by the poets of our language, generation after generation.

Apparently Surrey, in his translation of part of the "Æneid," was the first to write the unrimed iambic pentameter which came later to be known as blank verse. And by a happy chance the meter was taken over by Sackville and Norton for their tragedy " Gorboduc." The motive of their choice was probably threefold: first, they wanted a more dignified meter than the rimed iambic heptameter (ballad-meter), which had been generally employed in the unpretending folkdrama; second, they wished to avoid rime altogether, since that had been unknown to the Latin and Greek dramatists whom they supposed themselves to be imitating and emulating; and thirdly, they were seeking a meter which would allow them more easily to attain the concise sententiousness which they admired in the tragedies of Seneca, written rather for recitation than for actual performance. Probably this last motive was the strongest of the three; and its influence is most obvious in their blank verse, which tends to the stiffness of rhetoric and to the compacting of the thought within a single swelling line or at most within a pair of lines.

The blank verse of " Gorboduc " has prim regularity; it consists of a sequence of iambics in close accord with the exact pattern; it rarely ventures on any substitution of a trochee for an iambus, even in the first foot;

it seldom permits itself an unaccented extra syllable at
the end of the line; it hesitates to allow the thought
to run over from one line halfway into the next. As a
result of these self-imposed limitations the blank verse
of "Gorboduc" lacks melody and variety; it is characterized by a chill monotony; it seems eminently uninspired. But it was incisive at times, and emphatic; it
lent itself to declamatory rhetoric; it was not unsuited
to the purpose in hand; and it gave the English drama
a meter which later poets, more adroit and more gifted,
were able to bend to their bidding. Here, for example,
is part of a speech in the fifth act of "Gorboduc": —

> Lo, here the end of Brutus' royal line,
> And lo, the entry to the woful wreck
> And utter ruin of this noble realm!
> The royal king and eke his sons are slain;
> No ruler rests within the regal seat;
> The heir, to whom the scepter 'longs, unknown;
> That to each force of foreign prince's power
> Whom vantage of our wretched state may move,
> By sudden arms to gain as rich a realm.
> And to the proud and greedy mind at home
> Whom blended lust to reign leads to aspire,
> Lo, Britain realm is left an open prey,
> A present spoil for conquest to ensue.

In this the single line is plainly the unit of construction; and the passage as a whole is built up by successive lines most of which are end-stopt, — that is, complete in themselves. The phrase does not run on or run
over, line after line. The unity is only that of a series
of drawers, each with its own content. There is nothing
organic in a passage of this sort; it is fragmentary
and lacking in any large movement. Yet it served as
a texture for the more richly endowed Marlowe to em-
broider at will.

In Marlowe's blank verse there is more ease and
flexibility. The pause in the middle of the line is
shifted, now here and now there, thus avoiding
monotony. Trochees are substituted for iambs, more
often in the first foot, but sometimes elsewhere in the
line. Feminine endings appear occasionally, relieving
the end of the lines from rigidity. The thought is no
longer clamped into the single line; or at least the
phrase is no longer absolutely coincident with the
line. There is an obvious unity in the larger passages,
and a sweeping movement that rolls forward, wave
after wave. Here is the famous speech of Faustus
when Mephistopheles has granted his wish to behold
Helen of Troy : —

> Was this the face that launch'd a thousand ships,
> And burnt the topless towers of Ilium ? —
> Sweet Helen, make me immortal with a kiss, —
> Her lips suck forth my soul: see, where it flees ! —
> Come, Helen, come, give me my soul again.
> Here will I dwell, for heaven is in these lips,
> And all is dross that is not Helena.
> I will be Paris, and for love of thee,
> Instead of Troy, shall Wittenberg be sack'd;
> And I will combat with weak Menelaus,
> And wear thy colours on my plumèd crest;
> Yes, I will wound Achilles in the heel,
> And then return to Helen for a kiss.
> O, thou art fairer than the evening air
> Clad in the beauty of a thousand stars;
> Brighter art thou than flaming Jupiter
> When he appear'd to hapless Semele;
> More lovely than the monarch of the sky
> In wanton Arethusa's azur'd arms;
> And none but thou shalt be my paramour !

And here is the opening of the soliloquy of Faustus
when he faces his doom : —

> Ah, Faustus,
> Now thou hast but one bare hour to live,
> And then thou must be damn'd perpetually !
> Stand still, you ever-moving spheres of heaven,
> That time may cease, and midnight never come;
> Fair Nature's eye, rise, rise again and make
> Perpetual day ; or let this hour be but
> A year, a month, a week, a natural day,
> That Faustus may repent and save his soul !
> *O lente, lente currite, noctis equi!*
> The stars move still, time runs, the clock will strike,
> The devil will come, and Faustus must be damn'd.

It was due to the example of Marlowe that blank verse was accepted as the standard instrument for the English poetic drama ; and the value of this acceptance can scarcely be overstated. Symonds was not exaggerating when he asserted that " Marlowe did not merely drive the rimed couplet from the stage by substituting the blank verse of his contemporaries ; he created a new meter by the melody, variety and force which he infused into the iambic, and left models of versification, the pomp of which Shakspere and Milton alone can be said to have surpassed. . . . He found the ten-syllabled heroic line monotonous, mono-syllabic and divided into five feet of tolerably regular short and long. He left it various in form and structure, sometimes redundant by a syllable, some-times deficient, enriched with unexpected emphasis and changes in the beat. He found no sequence or attempt at periods ; one line succeeded another with insipid regularity, and all were made after the same model. He grouped his verse according to the sense, obeying an internal law of melody, and allowing the thought contained in his words to dominate their form. He did not force his meter to preserve a fixed and unalterable type, but suffered it to assume most variable modulations, the whole beauty of which depended upon their perfect adaptation to the current of his ideas. By these means he was able to produce the double effect of variety and unity, to preserve the fixed march of his chosen meter, and yet, by subtle alterations in the pauses, speed and grouping of the syllables to make one measure represent a thousand."

Marlowe gave blank verse ease and force, especially force. His lesser contemporaries Greene and Peele bestowed on it a gentleness and a sweetness which Marlowe had not sought. Here is a specimen of Greene's easy-running lines, a speech of Margaret in "Friar Bacon and Friar Bungay" : —

> Ah, father, when the harmony of heaven
> Soundeth the measures of a lively faith,
> The vain illusions of this flattering world
> Seem odious to the thoughts of Margaret.
> I lovèd once, — Lord Lacy was my love;
> And now I hate myself for that I lov'd,
> And doted more on him than on my God, —
> For this I scourge myself with sharp repents.
> But now the touch of such aspiring sins
> Tells me all love is lust but love of heaven;
> That beauty us'd for love is vanity;
> The world contains naught but alluring baits,
> Pride, flattery, and inconstant thoughts.
> To shun the pricks of death, I leave the world
> And vow to meditate on heavenly bliss,
> To live in Framlingham a holy nun,
> Holy and pure in conscience and in deed;
> And for to wish all maids to learn of me
> To seek heaven's joy before earth's vanity.

Shakspere learned much from Marlowe, and even from Peele and Greene; but he bettered his lesson. He made himself master of blank verse in all its possibilities. He used it for tragedy and for comedy, for description, for sentiment, and for pathos. But he did not tie himself down to it. Nothing is more characteristic of Shakspere's dramatic instinct than his use or avoidance of blank verse. He held himself at liberty to employ whatever metrical device best suited his immediate purpose. He unhesitatingly commingled prose and blank verse and rime. In his earlier plays, both comic and tragic, there is a large proportion of riming couplets; and on occasion, he even made use of quatrains and other stanzaic forms which he felt to be appropriate to the more or less artificial sentiment he was voicing. In his later plays, when he had ceased to be artificial, he abandoned rime, but even then he frequently dropped into prose when he felt intuitively that prose was a better implement.

It was only by degrees that Shakspere arrived at his full mastery of blank verse. At first, we find him restrained by the tradition of the less gifted poets in whose footsteps he was then treading. Many of his lines are end-stopt; — that is to say, the thought is completely expressed within the line. The longer speeches may often be described as built up of a sequence of single lines each complete in itself. There are few dropt syllables, such as we find in the later plays, where the place of a missing word may be filled out by a pause in the dialog. There are few feminine endings; indeed, Shakspere was a little slow in perceiving the value of an added unaccented eleventh syllable at the end of a line to give fluidity to a speech. But even early in his development as a dramatist and as a poet, we cannot fail to find a nice adjustment of the meter

to the character and to the situation. "Romeo and
Juliet" is a comparatively early play; and Professor
Saintsbury has called attention to its "curious alternation, or rather intermixture, of the cumulative and
the periodic styles of blank verse." The stately speech
of the Prince after the opening brawl, the longer utterances of Friar Laurence, are periodic. "But
Juliet's heart beats throughout to another tune than
their sententious clank; her lover, though less uni-
formly, is master of the better rhythm also; and
Mercutio shows that fancy can act as the solvent no
less than passion."

The same critic has also called attention to the great
patriotic speech of Gaunt in "Richard II": —

> This royal throne of kings, this scepter'd isle,
> This earth of majesty, this seat of Mars,

and he has pointed out how it is that "although almost
every line is self-enclosed, the paragraph-effect is
given in a way Marlowe hardly ever attains, by the
variation of the pause, the weighting of different parts
of the line by the quicksilver power of specially sonorous or important words, and sometimes by a cunning
parenthetic device, which makes the voice hurry over
parts of a line, or whole lines, so as to connect rhythmically as in sense, what comes after with what comes
before." The great agency in giving variety to Shakspere's blank verse is the shifting of the pause, which
his predecessors (Marlowe chiefly excepted) tended to
retain more or less in the middle of the line. Another
agency, almost equally effective in the avoidance of
rigidity, is the separation of the phrase from the exact
line or sequence of lines; the thought is no longer
contained in a series of drawers; it may begin in the

middle of one line, flow on through two or three or
more, and end at last in the middle of yet another, without departing in the least from the normal decasyllabic
division.

Perhaps no better example can be quoted to exhibit
the infinite modulation of which dramatic blank verse
is capable in Shakspere's hands, after he made himself absolute master of his instrument, than a speech
of Prospero's in the "Tempest" (which we know to
be one of his very latest plays) : —

> Our revels now are ended. These our actors,
> As I foretold you, were all spirits, and
> Are melted into air, into thin air ;
> And, like the baseless fabric of this vision,
> The cloud-capp'd towers, the gorgeous palaces,
> The solemn temples, the great globe itself,
> Yea, all which it inherit, shall dissolve
> And, like this insubstantial pageant faded,
> Leave not a rack behind. We are such stuff
> As dreams are made on, and our little life
> Is rounded with a sleep.

This exquisite passage justifies Symonds's assertion
that the characteristic of Shakspere's blank verse is
"that it is naturally, unobtrusively, and enduringly
musical. We hardly know why his words are melodious, or what makes them always fresh. There is a
subtle adjustment of sound to sense, of lofty thoughts
to appropriate words ; the ideas evolve themselves with
inexhaustible spontaneity, and a suitable investiture
of language is never wanting, so that each cadenced
period seems made to hold a thought of its own, and
thought is linked to thought and cadence to cadence in
unending continuity. Inferior artists have systems of
melody, pauses which they repeat, favorite termina-

tions, and accelerations or retardations of rhythm, which they employ whenever the occasion prompts them. But there is none of this in Shakspere. He never falls into the commonplace of mannerism."

And this is what could not be said of any of Shakspere's immediate followers. There is abundant power in the blank verse of Webster and even of Ford; but there is rarely the variety and the ease which characterize Shakspere's lines. As for Fletcher and Massinger, it can scarcely be denied that they come near to falling into "the commonplace of mannerism." Indeed, Fletcher employed a feminine ending so frequently that his style often approached to the very verge of effeminacy. But he is undeniably a poet; and his lines have constant melody and sweetness. Massinger, on the other hand, is less poet than he is psychologist and rhetorician; and his blank verse, direct as it generally is, tends to be a little pedestrian; and it has marked peculiarities, which lend themselves easily to imitation. Coleridge declared that Ben Jonson's blank verse is "very masterly and individual"; and Symonds added that it was the blank verse of "a scholar — pointed, polished and free from the lyricisms of his age," lacking harmony and often labored; but "vigorous and solid it never fails to be."

Even the less richly endowed playwrights of that inspired period, Marston and Heywood, Dekker and Shirley, are all of them capable on occasion of blank verse of fine quality. The secret of it seems then to have been a common property. Upon all of them, each in his own degree, had been bestowed the ability now and again to write plaintively or melodiously or nobly. And moreover all of the dramatic poets of that splendid epoch seem to have understood instinctively the necessity which the playwright is under of always adjusting his lines to oral delivery. The dramatist wrote his speeches to be actually spoken in the theater and not merely to be read in the library. His appeal was not to the eye of the reader but to the ear of the hearer through the mouth of the actor. Therefore the Elizabethan playwright-poets composed blank verse which is fundamentally dramatic, not lyric in temper or narrative in leisurely movement.

Symonds pointed out that Webster, for example, "no doubt imagined his actors declaiming with great variety of intonation, with frequent and lengthy pauses, and with considerable differences in the rapidity of their utterances"; and the same thing might be said of all the others, — above all, of Shakspere, whose lines are always phrased for easy delivery by the actor and reveal always a delicate adjustment of the rhythm to the dramatic situation. He, and in a less degree his contemporaries, possessed the true secret of blank verse, which is to be found in "the proper adaptation of words and rhythms to the sense contained in them." It has been well said that the apparent irregularities of meter in the plays of the foremost Elizabethans furnish an unerring index "to the inflections which the actors must have used, to the characters which the poets designed, and to the situations which they calculated." The result of these endeavors was to give ease and variety and rapidity to blank verse and to make it flexible for the expression of every word.

Thus perfected by the playwrights, blank verse was ready for the use to which Milton was to put it. The stately narrative of his noble epic, with its intermittent dialog and its occasional set debate, demanded a change of method. It was written to be read in the study and not to be declaimed on the stage; and yet it is also adjusted to the voice, — indeed, it does not disclose its full beauty until it is uttered aloud. Although it was printed for the eye, its appeal was to the ear as well, for Milton was never one to overlook the fact that poetry is always to be said or sung. Even the purely narrative passages reveal added felicities of rhythm when they come to us through the ear. In Milton's verse, as Lowell asserted, "the music makes part of the meaning. . . . No one before or since has been able to give to simple pentameters the majesty and compass of the organ. He was as much composer as poet."

The iambic pentameter may be defined as a sequence of five alternate short and long syllables. When it achieved this exact regularity, it concorded with the practice of Pope and it won the approval of Johnson. But to apply any rigid standard of this sort to Milton's blank verse is to misapprehend absolutely the principle upon which he worked. He accepted the strict succession of iambics only as a norm; he accustomed the ear to the alternate shorts and longs; and then, this expectation having been thus established, he adventures numberless variations, as daring as they are successful. With him the line is no longer the unit and his large poetic phrase is not coincident with any single line or sequence of lines. It has an ampler architecture; and it sweeps forward irresistibly, with bold licenses of substitution which immediately justify themselves to the ear, however much they may disconcert unsympathetic critics like Johnson, trained to count off the succeeding shorts and longs on their fingers. In some of Milton's superbly organized passages, it may be a little difficult to scan any single line taken by itself, since this line thus isolated may seem irregular or even rugged. But if the whole passage is read aloud with due regard to its meaning and with care to give the emphasis which the thought demands, the difficulty disappears and the ear is satisfied by the majestic sweep of the rhythmic movement.

The opening lines of "Paradise Lost," elevated and sonorous, are also firm in their regularity. There is an occasional substitution of a trochee for an iambus, but even the thick-fingered Johnson ought to have found little difficulty in measuring all the successive feet by his unmusical yardstick : —

> Of Man's first disobedience, and the fruit
> Of that forbidden tree whose mortal taste
> Brought death into the World, and all our woe,
> With loss of Eden, till one greater Man
> Restore us, and regain the blissful Seat,
> Sing, Heavenly Muse, that, on the secret top
> Of Oreb, or of Sinai, didst inspire
> That Shepherd who first taught the chosen seed
> In the beginning how the heavens and earth
> Rose out of Chaos; or, if Sion hill
> Delight thee more, and Siloa's brook that flowed
> Fast by the oracle of God, I thence
> Invoke thy aid to my adventrous song,
> That with no middle flight intends to soar
> Above the Aonian mount, while it pursues
> Things unattempted yet in prose or rime.

Compare this with the opening of one of Satan's speeches : —

> Fall'n Cherub, to be weak is miserable,
> Doing or suffering : but of this be sure —
> To do aught good never will be our task,

> But ever to do ill our sole delight,
> As being the contrary to His high will
> Whom we resist.

In the first line the first foot (" Fall'n che ") is a rather forced trochee; and the last foot (" serable ") lacks the weight which might be expected in its final syllable. In the second line the first foot (" Doing ") is plainly a trochee; and the third foot (" fering; but ") is plainly an anapest. But when this speech is spoken aloud, the ear takes no account of these divergences from rigid regularity. The substitutions impose themselves upon us, without demur on our part. They have given variety to these first two lines; and they have not diverted our attention to themselves. If we disregard the satisfactory impression made on the ear and study the passage with the eye, we discover that the single line is not here the dominant unit of measure. Nor was it generally in Milton's epics; he composed his passages as integral wholes, in which the line plays a part but in which it is not allowed to force itself on the attention. Of course, there are instances not a few where we discover Milton to achieve a subtle effect by isolating a single line and charging it with a full and complete message of its own.

Symonds pointed out that Milton's " most sonorous passages begin and end with interrupted lines, including in one organic structure, periods, parentheses, and paragraphs of fluent melody, that the harmonies are wrought by subtle and most complex alliterative systems, by delicate changes in the length and volume of syllables, and by the choice of names magnificent for their mere gorgeousness of sound " ; and he insisted that " in these structures there are many pauses which

enable the ear and voice to rest themselves, but none
are perfect, none satisfy the want created by the opening hemistich, until the final and deliberate close is
reached." And he cited in evidence this passage : —

> And now his heart
> Distends with pride, and, hardening in his strength,
> Glories : for never, since created Man,
> Met such embodied force as, named with these,
> Could merit more than that small infantry
> Warr'd on by cranes — though all the giant brood
> Of Phlegra with the heroic race were join'd
> That fought at Thebes and Ilium, on each side
> Mix'd with auxiliar gods; and what resounds
> In fable or romance of Uther's son,
> Begirt with British and Armoric knights;
> And all who since, baptized or infidel,
> Jousted in Aspramont, or Montalban,
> Damasco, or Marocco, or Trebisond,
> Or whom Biserta sent from Afric shore
> When Charlemain with all his peerage fell
> By Fontarabbia.

"Milton's use of pause is unique," so Professor
Saintsbury has insisted; "like Shakspere, he will put
it anywhere or nowhere." And the varied effect of
his constant shifting of the pause and of his refusal
to place it frequently in the middle of the line, he
heightened by abundant variations from the strict succession of iambics. He substituted trochees at will, in
any one of the five feet, even in the last. He called
in the aid of the anapest whenever he felt the need of
that swifter and lighter foot : —

> Because thou hast hearkened to the voice of thy wife.

He achieved the spondee on occasion, a foot almost
impossible in our sharply accented tongue : —

> Caves, rocks, lakes, fens, bays, dens, and shades of death.

His intimate familiarity with the Greek and Latin poets helped him to attain metrical effects rare in English because they were due mainly to quantity, to the contrast of syllables not only stressed but actually long or short in duration of utterance. If his metrical daring does not always justify itself, — and it might be possible to pick out a very few instances where this must be admitted, — this may be due to his absorption of the Italian poets, which tempted him to give an Italianate accent to an English word, an accent which the English reader recognizes only by an effort.

After Milton blank verse went under a cloud. Dryden and Pope preferred the heroic couplet and polished it to suit their several needs. It is true that Dryden could write bold blank verse; but he rarely chose to do so. Addison's blank verse serves to show how completely the poets had forgotten the lessons of Shakspere and Milton; it is not only uninspired and monotonous, but it returns to the earlier and easier structure, wherein the line coincides with the sentence, or at least with a clause of the sentence, and whereby the several lines may be said to have each an almost independent existence. The influence of the riming heroic couplet, metrically identical and yet wholly different in spirit and in opportunity, weighed down blank verse and kept it from soaring aloft. In time, Thomson and Cowper recovered much of its freedom; and they opened the doors for Coleridge and Wordsworth. In his turn, Keats recaptured a portion of the Miltonic melody, not the majesty of his mighty predecessor, but something of the music. And here in America Bryant — not a great poet, not foremost even among our own bards — found in blank verse a meter which exactly suited his large stateliness. Here is the opening passage of the austere and lofty " Thanatopsis ": —

> To him who in the love of Nature holds
> Communion with her visible forms, she speaks
> A various language. For his gayer hours
> She has a voice of gladness, and a smile
> And eloquence of beauty, and she glides
> Into his darker musings, with a mild
> And healing sympathy, that steals away
> Their sharpness, ere he is aware. When thoughts
> Of the last bitter hour come like a blight
> Over thy spirit, and sad images
> Of the stern agony, and shroud and pall,
> And breathless darkness, and the narrow house
> Make thee to shudder, and grow sick at heart; —
> Go forth, under the open sky, and list
> To Nature's teachings.

Brian Hooker has justly called attention to " the subtile grading of the stresses, the vigorous contrast of scansion and phrase-rhythm, and the tireless variety of the pauses "; and then he asked us to consider also " how all this opposition is held under just sufficient control, so that the equilibrium of the normal scansion, continually and seductively threatened, is never for one moment overthrown." And it must be remembered to Bryant's credit that although this was written after Wordsworth and Keats had reinvigorated blank verse, it was composed before Tennyson and Browning.

Tennyson early made himself a master of blank verse. In his hands it has melodious flexibility, varied cadences, richness of alliteration and of colliteration, and deliberate sweetness of tone. The workmanship is exquisite, but a little cloying and a little self-conscious. The beauty of Tennyson's blank verse strikes us as studied rather than spontaneous. The effects he aimed at he attained; but we often are aware of the effort. His style is sweetly lyric rather than boldly epic or pregnantly dramatic. His blank verse lacks largeness of sweep and inevitability of phrase. It is graceful, charming, idyllic; it suggests a Tanagra figurine rather than the Hermes of Praxiteles.

Browning's blank verse is less artificial, indeed it rarely calls attention to itself, rushing forward as though it was the poet's natural expression. It is devoid of all marquetry of beautiful sounds; it may even be termed harsh or at least rugged; and in its frankly dramatic march it is tense and masculine. Here are a few lines from "An Epistle, containing the Strange Medical Experience of Karshish": —

> The very God! think, Abib: dost thou think?
> So, the All-Great, were the All-Loving too —
> So, through the thunder comes a human voice
> Saying, "O heart I made, a heart beats here!
> Face, my hands fashioned, see it in myself!
> Thou hast no power nor mayst conceive of mine,
> But love I gave thee, with myself to love,
> And thou must love me who have died for thee!"
> The madman saith He said so: it is strange.

CHAPTER XII

POETIC LICENSE

This poetical license is a shrewd fellow, and covereth many faults in a verse; it maketh words longer, shorter, of more syllables, of fewer, newer, older, truer, falser; and to conclude it turneth all things at pleasure. — GEORGE GASCOIGNE: *Certain Notes of Instruction concerning the Making of Verse.* (1575.)

THERE is advantage always in beginning any discussion with a sharp definition of the thing to be discussed. Here, then, is a pertinent characterization of license which we find in the latest edition of Webster's Dictionary: "That deviation from strict fact, form, or rule in which an artist or writer indulges, assuming that it will be permitted for the sake of the advantage or effect gained." And this warrants us in declaring that a poetic license is a departure from strict form, which the verse-writer permits himself in the belief that it will be pardoned for the sake of some effect he may thereby gain or of some advantage he could not otherwise attain. In other words, poetic license may be described as a privilege claimed by the poet of sacrificing something that seems to him relatively unimportant to secure something else that he holds of superior value. He may feel, for example, that he cannot express himself fully, unless he is permitted, once in a way, to depart from the strict rules of grammar or rhetoric, to employ an arbitrary contraction, a forced accent or a disconcerting inversion of the natural order of words, or to avail himself of a so-called allowable rime,— which is of a truth no rime at all.

When the case is thus stated, the question as to the permissibility of any poetic license is easy to answer. In the specific instance, was the poet right in his feeling as to the importance of the two things one of which he sacrificed to the other? And was he justified in his belief that he could attain his advantage and gain his effect in no other way than by departing from the letter of the law? If his decision was sound, then will he be forgiven his violation of form, even though we cannot help being more or less conscious of his departure from the normal use of language. Every single instance of poetic license must needs be examined by itself; and the poet can claim no general permit to do as he pleases. His poem is always intended to be said or sung; its appeal is ever to the ears of those to whom it is addressed; it arouses in us a certain expectancy both of content and of form, and if for any reason, good or bad, the poet chooses to disappoint that expectancy, he can do so only at his peril, — at the risk of breaking the circuit which must bind together the listener and the singer.

If the verse-writer has seen fit to disappoint the expectancy he has created in the ears of his hearers, by an awkward inversion, by an unwonted contraction, by the use of a so-called " allowable " rime, by an ungrammatical employment of words, or by any other license, his sole excuse must be that this was necessary or at least profitable in that special instance, since only by the aid of that license could he attain the effect he was seeking at the moment. This is akin to what the lawyers call a plea of confession and avoidance ; and the burden of proof is on the poet to show that he was justified in his faith. That is to say, do we, his hearers, unhesitatingly pardon his departure from strict rule, because of the ultimate result? If we do, then there is nothing more to be said, and an insistence upon the letter of the law is beside the mark. Our own ears are the final court of appeal, and when they are satisfied the poet may depart without a stain on his character. The jury will refrain from all censure if they have been charmed by an "intuitive phrase where the imagination at a touch precipitates thought, feeling and image in an imperishable crystal," — to borrow Lowell's suggestive words. The more inspired the poet may be and the loftier the theme, the less likely are we to turn the crystal over in search of flaws. When we are rapt out of ourselves we fail to notice any little liberties the poet may have taken with the language, and we are ready enough to pardon them if they happen to attract our attention.

But only a true poet can do this unerringly, and he can do it only on occasion when he is sweeping us away with surging emotion or lifting us on high with ethereal imagination. His eye in fine frenzy rolling will profit him nothing, unless he weaves an incantation about our ears also. For those who are not assured that they are true poets there is only one counsel of perfection, — to abide sturdily by all the rules of the game and to refuse resolutely to apply for any license to break the law at will. As the younger Tom Hood declared in his useful little treatise on the "Rules of Rhyme," "the poet gives to the world his sublime thoughts, diamonds of the purest water"; and it would be petty "to quibble about minor points of the polishing and setting of such gems," whereas the writer of mere verse does not pretend to give us diamonds. "He offers paste brilliants, and therefore it the more behooves him to see to the perfection of the cutting, on which their beauty depends." This is well put; and yet attention may be called to the significant fact that the poets who have had the sublimest thoughts have generally been the most careful in their craftsmanship. No one would deny sublimity to Dante and Milton, who are both of them impeccable artists in the cutting, the polishing, and the setting of their diamonds of the purest water. It is not from the "Divine Comedy" or from "Paradise Lost" that we can most easily quote examples of poetic license. These great poets did their best always, sparing no pains and delighting in the labor which was to insure faultlessness of expression.

If the strictness of the law did not crib, cabin and confine Dante and Milton, if these major bards were willing to be bound that they might be free, still more strongly does the obligation lie upon all lesser poets, upon all mere verse-writers, upon all who make the confession we find in Browning's "One Word More,"

Verse and nothing else have I to give you.

In fact, the humbler the task and the more modest the versifier the more inexorable should he be with himself. Especially is this conscientiousness imposed upon the writers of familiar verse. As Locker-Lampson asserted, "however trivial the subject-matter may be — indeed, rather in proportion to its triviality — subordination to the rules of composition, and perfection of execution, should be strictly enforced." Locker-Lampson always practised what he preached, so does his friendly rival, Austin Dobson; and a large part of the ease and grace of their delightful lyrics is due to their unfailing acceptance of the highest standards of workmanship. Both of them profited by the example of the French, whose versification is generally sustained at a lofty level. Indeed, Lowell once asserted that very often in French verse "only the high polish keeps out the decay."

It was for the apprentice poets of his own language that Théodore de Banville composed his little treatise on French versification. And in that very entertaining volume he declared that his chapter on "poetic licenses" contained only a single sentence: "There are none": — "What!" he cried, "under the pretence of writing in verse, that is to say in a tongue which demands rhythm and orderliness above all else, you claim the right to be disorderly and to violate the rules. And this on the pretext that it would have been too difficult to get into your verse what you wanted to put into it exactly as you wanted to put it. But that is precisely what the art of versification is, and it cannot consist in not doing what you have undertaken to do." This may sound like a hard saying, and, in fact, another French poet, Auguste Dorchain, writing on the "Art of Verse" has boldly called it a paradox. But it contains the root of the matter; and it recognizes the fact that the true artist, poet or painter, sculptor or architect, never shrinks from apparent difficulty. On the contrary, he glories in vanquishing it. He grapples with it gladly, knowing that then only can he put forth his full strength. His desire is not merely to express himself amply, but also always to make a good job of the expression itself.

And he accepts the conditions of the job, whatever they may be, and however arduous they may appear at first glance. No doubt, Michael Angelo might have asked to have false flat surfaces cover the curved ceiling of the Sistine Chapel, and certainly this would have made his task easier; but we may be sure that no such thought ever entered his mind. He found himself face to face with a new problem in painting, and he yielded himself joyfully to its fascination, snatching the flower, safety, out of the nettle, danger. He would have scorned to plead for any license of any kind, just as Milton would have scorned to append a fifteenth line to a sonnet. Strong men like Michael Angelo and Milton are never tempted to plead the baby act. They never beg off: they would smile with contempt at the weaklings who are content with the easiest way.

> Yes; when the ways oppose —
>   When the hard means rebel,
> Fairer the work out-grows, —
>   More potent far the spell.
>
> O Poet, then, forbear
>   The loosely-sandaled verse,
> Choose rather thou to wear
>   The buskin, straight and terse;
>
> See that thy form demand
>   The labor of the file;
> Leave to the tiro's hand
>   The limp pedestrian style.
>
> .   .   .   .   .   .
>
> Paint, chisel, then, or write;
>   But, that the work surpass,
> With the hard fashion fight, —
>   With the resisting mass.

Thus Austin Dobson has rephrased in compact English Gautier's declaration of the creed of all true artists. They relish the hard fight for perfection of form; and they enjoy the long siege which shall force a rebellious matter to surrender itself at last in the fittest manner. They would scoff at the suggestion which Walker made in his "Riming Dictionary" that the mating of two words not identical in their terminal sounds may be forgiven on the ground that even "if these imperfect rimes were allowed to be blemishes it would still be better to tolerate them than to cramp the imagination by too narrow boundaries of exactly similar sounds." The worthy Walker herein revealed his total misunderstanding of the fundamental condition of all art, which is ever a wrestle with difficulty and an ultimate conquest, after valiant striving and impending defeat. The struggle with stubborn expression is only the stimulus to a final triumph; and no real artist ever finds it cramping to the imagination. It is only by incessant overcoming of obstacles which may seem for a season insuperable that the master measures his full strength, training his muscles and his nerves to obey his will. The poet who shrinks timidly from strenuous effort, and who is lazily willing to avail himself of the traditional poetic licenses for fear of cramping his imagination, may be likened to a man playing patience who should feel himself at liberty to depart from the rules in order to compel the cards to come out right. We cannot help despising any creature so weak of character as to cheat himself into a belief that the game can be won in this way. And we have a stern respect for the stronger poets who hold with the whist-loving

Mrs. Battle in her liking for " A clear fire, a clean hearth and the rigor of the game."

The rigor of the game, the letter of the law, the full submission to the rules, — these are terms which will be misleading if they seem to suggest that there is any arbitrary code promulgated by some superior power and imposed upon the poet. Of course, the poet is under no other compulsion than so to express himself that he can transmit his thought and communicate his emotion instantly to his hearers. For his own sake, and under obligation only to himself, the poet must avoid all impediment to this conveying of his meaning to us. Whatever calls away our attention from his message is a hindrance to our swift and complete reception of it. The principle of Economy of Attention is even more imperative in the rhetoric of verse than in the rhetoric of prose. A certain proportion of the reader's attention is necessarily absorbed by the effort of following the means whereby the writer sets forth what he has to say, and therefore that style is best which calls least attention to itself, which offers least resistance to the sending of the message, and which leaves the most attention free for its reception. In other words, a writer must so guard the manner of his utterance that we can get his matter with the slightest possible friction. And this is the only law that all writers must obey, whether they work in prose or in verse.

They violate it only at their own risk; and every poetic license is a violation of this law. What are the various kinds of poetic license? Inversions, arbitrary accents, imperfect rimes, unusual contractions, and departures from accepted grammar; — and every

one of these is likely to interrupt the current, to interfere with the poet's purpose, to call attention to
itself if only for a fleeting moment, and thus to take
away some part of our attention — however little it
may be — from the thing which he is telling us.
Some of these arbitrary variations from normal
speech, some of these contractions, some of these
inadequate rimes, may seem to the poet to be consecrated by tradition. But he cannot claim precedent,
because he has no right to suppose that all his hearers
are familiar with the earlier poets, whose practices he
would cite as authorizing his own wilfulness. As a
matter of fact, a few of these hearers of his may be
familiar with the poets of the past, and those may or
may not be disposed to tolerate a poetic license sanc-
tified by convention. On the other hand, many of them
will surely lack this acquaintance with earlier bards;
and these are likely to be annoyed by his failure to
satisfy the expectation he has created. If a poet is
seeking to reach the heart of the people, he must deny
himself the poetic licenses that earlier poets indulged
in; and he is in error if he thinks that in verse-making
"freedom slowly broadens down from precedent to
precedent."

Of all the various departures from the proper use
of language which constitute the several kinds of
poetic license, perhaps the most defensible are inversions. The rhythmic march of stately verse often calls
for a change in the natural order of words and often
justifies it to the ear. In the opening lines of "Paradise Lost" we find an example of this justifiable
inversion or rather of inversion which is actually
helpful: —

> Of Man's first disobedience, and the fruit
> Of that forbidden tree whose mortal taste
> Brought death into the World, and all our woe,
> With loss of Eden, till one greater Man
> Restore us, and regain the blissful Seat,
> Sing, Heavenly Muse!

The ear easily carries the meaning as it is unrolled until the phrase ends with the words "Sing, Heavenly Muse!" which logically should come first. And many other examples as illuminating could readily be selected from the same epic. Indeed, this is not really an instance of poetic license, since the inversion here does not interfere with the Economy of Attention; indeed, it may even heighten this. So the two inversions in one of the stanzas of Wordsworth's noble "Ode to Duty" justify themselves at once, because they are congruous to the temper of the poem as a whole: —

> To humbler functions, awful Power!
> I call thee : I myself commend
> Unto thy guidance from this hour ;
> Oh, let my weakness have an end!

In these two examples, Milton's and Wordsworth's, the eye of the reader may detect the inversion ; but the ear of the hearer would accept them without notice. It is said that certain of the horses in the frieze of the Parthenon have legs only on the outer side and that the legs on the inner side have been suppressed unhesitatingly by the sculptor, a departure from nature which can be detected only by careful observation ; and this can scarcely be termed a license since it is but the suppression of something non-essential to the purpose of the artist. This suppression in no wise calls attention to itself ; and thus it is parallel with the inversions just quoted from Milton and Words-worth.

Closely akin to awkward inversions are arbitrary contractions, such as *ta'en* for *taken*, *o'er* for *over* or *'gainst* for *against*. Here again, the sole question is whether these departures from normal language call attention to themselves. Do they interfere with our Economy of Attention, as the lines fall upon our ears? If they do not, then they justify themselves. As a matter of fact, *'gainst* is so slight a variation from *against* that most ears would fail to notice it, while on the other hand *ta'en* for *taken* would be likely to annoy the ordinary hearer not acquainted with the traditions of English poetry. The Elizabethan poets, especially the dramatists, were free in their contrac-tions. They risked *'stroy* for *destroy*, *'cide* for *decide*, *'stall* for *instal* ; and all of these licenses would jar on our ears to-day, whatever they may have done long ago. The Elizabethans also were wont to use *'twixt* for *betwixt* and *'neath* for *underneath* ; and here they seem to have anticipated our modern use of the shorter form as an accepted contraction so familiar that it opposes no friction to the thought.

It is to be noted that the later poets of the classi-cist period made many contractions which now seem to us unnecessary ; they accepted a theory of rigid regularity of rhythm and did not allow themselves to profit by the privilege of substituting frankly an anapest for an iamb, which the ear usually admits without cavil. Thus they felt themselves forced to write *whisp'ring* for *whispering*, *tim'rous* for *timor-ous*, *mis'ry* for *misery*, — contractions imposed upon them by their narrow theory of verse and yet not of-

fensive to us to-day because they are evident only to
our eyes and not audible in our ears, which unconsciously supply the missing syllable.

Where some versifiers have forced a word to fit
into their metrical schemes by violently mangling it,
others have been able to accomplish the feat only by
altering its ordinary accent. They have wrenched the
pronunciation of a single word to compel it to fit into
the rhythm of their lines. Sometimes this seems to be
mere wilfulness, as in Walt Whitman's "O Captain!
My Captain!" noble as that is in its elevation and firm
as it is in its structure. The poet was so unused to rime
that he required us to accent the insignificant *ing* twice
in order to get a semblance of rime that he needed; and
he is guilty of this in two stanzas out of three: —

The port is near, the bells I hear, the people all exult*ing*,
While follow eyes the steady keel, the vessel grim and dar*ing*,

and again

For you bouquets and ribbon'd wreaths — for you the shores
    a-crowd*ing*,
For you they call, the swaying mass, their eager faces turn*ing*.

Sometimes, however, the poet is not really falsify-
ing the accent, although he may seem to do so to the
eye of the pedantic reader. Milton, for example, in his
famous line describing the fallen angel's descent,

Burned after him to the bottomless pit,

did not intend that the word *bottomless* should have
an arbitrary stress on its second syllable. He dared
the natural pronunciation of the word here, because
he needed the unexpected variation in the meter to
suggest, at once boldly and subtly, the irresistible
slipping down into the fathomless depth. The license

here, if there is any, is not a question of pronunciation, but of meter; and if the passage is read aloud
with due regard to mass and weight, the ear is not
offended by the departure from regularity. Rather,
indeed, is this departure an element in the power and
beauty of the poetic narrative.

Now and again in English poetry we come across
a colloquial looseness which may seem to some persons
a blunder in grammar. On occasion we discover this
to have been intentional, indulged in as a stroke of
humor, as, for example, in Prior's playful epistle: —

> Then finish, dear Chloe, this pastoral war;
>   And let us like Horace and Lydia agree:
> For thou art a girl as much brighter than *her*,
>   As he was a poet sublimer than *me*.

But there is apparently no intent in a grammatical
perversity of Byron's, —

> And send'st him, shivering in thy playful spray,
>   And howling, to his Gods, where haply lies
> His petty hope in some near port or bay,
>   And dashest him again to earth: — there let him *lay*.

With all his great gifts Byron often lacked art. In
his verse he was not willing always to take the trouble
to put his best foot foremost. Probably he would have
approved of Coleridge's saying that " poetry, like
schoolboys, by too frequent and severe correction,
may be cowed into dulness." And yet there is no
denying that to be content to move along the line of
least resistance is as demoralizing and as dangerous in
verse-writing as it is in character-building.

Byron has often the brisk celerity of the impro-
viser; and he shrank from the labor of the file. In
his graver verse he was ready enough to take what-

ever rimes might run off the end of his pen. And the most frequent of all poetic licenses is that which is supposed to permit the linking of two words which do not chime with precision. Byron was willing to begin his " Stanzas " with

> Could Love for *ever*
> Run like a *river*.

And later in the same lyric he is content to set down

> When lovers *parted*
> Feel broken-*hearted*
> And, all hopes *thwarted*,
> Expect to die.

Ever does not rime with *river*, unless we are expected to pronounce it *iver ;* and *thwarted* does not rime with *parted*, unless we force it to do so by varying from the accepted pronunciation. The poet who tries to link together uncongenial words like these is impaled on the horns of a dilemma : either the words do not sound alike and then our ears are cheated of the expectation of rime, or they are made to sound alike, by forcing the pronunciation of one of them, and then our attention is distracted by this departure from the normal use of language. In either case the poet has violated the principle of Economy of Attention. These misguided attempts at rime may be tolerated by some ears, but others will hold that a rime which is only tolerable is about as unsatisfactory as a tolerable egg.

Mortimer Collins's charming lyric, the " Ivory Gate," is marred for many a hearer by several false rimes. One of them is so slight a departure from identity of terminal sound that it may not arrest the attention as it falls upon the ear : —

> Then the oars of Ithaca dip so
>   Silently into the sea
> That they wake not sad Calypso,
>   And the Hero wanders free ;
> He breasts the ocean *furrows*
>   At war with the words of fate,
> And the blue tide's low *susurrus*
>   Comes up to the Ivory Gate.

But in another stanza there are two false rimes, one of which surely calls attention to itself even if the other was covered by customary slovenliness of pronunciation : —

> Or down from green *Helvellyn*
>   The roar of streams I hear,
> And the lazy sail is *swelling*
>   To the winds of Windermere :
> That girl with the rustic *bodice*,
>   'Mid the ferry's laughing freight,
> Is as fair as any *goddess*
>   Who sweeps thro' the Ivory Gate.

To mate *furrows* and *susurrus*, *bodice* and *goddess* may be a blemish only, but to link together *Helvellyn* and *swelling* is little short of a crime. We may be willing enough to overlook the blemishes and even to pardon the crime, for the sake of the buoyancy and brilliancy of the little lyric as a whole. But the pity of it ! We cannot but grieve that a poem which came so near perfection in its kind should fall so far short of it. Even in Keats and in Tennyson we stumble on false rimes, more frequently in Keats than in Tennyson ; and they stand out as needless defects. They may be only spots on the sun, which is none the less glorious ; but none the less are they spots.

In English a pair of rimes must have identity of the accented vowel-sound and of all the following sounds and at the same time it must have different sounds preceding the accented vowel. That is to say, a word cannot rime with itself, even if the meaning is wholly different. In French and in Italian verse this rule does not obtain; but in English our ears refuse to accept *sense* and *innocence* as a fitly mated pair, although Wordsworth has chosen to marry them in a couplet. Milton linked together *ruth* and *Ruth*, probably misled by Italian precedents; and Tennyson ventured to follow

> The holly by the cottage *eave*

with

> And sadly falls our Christmas *eve*.

To many English ears these departures from the usual practice might be annoying, in that they would arrest attention to themselves. They might disappoint the expectation of the hearer; and they would be the more likely to do this the closer they came together, — that is, the more emphatically they forced themselves upon our notice. But they would probably be overlooked in the course of a lyric in which the same riming sound recurred frequently, as in a ballade, for example, wherein a dozen lines rime together. In Austin Dobson's "Ballade of the Armada" we can discover, if we take the trouble, that he has *back us* and *Bacchus, tack us* and *attack us.* Yet this repetition does not call attention to itself as it occurs in different stanzas. It can be detected by the eye, of course, but the ear would probably fail to perceive it: —

> King Phillip has vaunted his claims;
>   He had sworn for a year he would sack **us**;
> With an army of heathenish names
>   He was coming to fagot and stack **us**;

Like the thieves of the sea he would track us,
And shatter our ships on the main ;
    But we had bold Neptune to back us, —
And where are the galleons of Spain ?

His caracks were christened of dames
    To the kirtles whereof he would tack us ;
With his saints and his gilded stern-frames,
    He had thought like an egg-shell to crack us ;
    Now Howard may get to his Flaccus,
And Drake to his Devon again,
    And Hawkins bowl rubbers to Bacchus, —
For where are the galleons of Spain ?

Let his Majesty hang to St. James
    The ax that he whetted to hack us;
He must play at some lustier games
    Or at sea he can hope to out-thwack us ;
    To his mines of Peru he would pack us
To tug at his bullet and chain ;
    Alas ! that his Greatness should lack us ! —
But where are the galleons of Spain ?

Envoy

GLORIANA ! — the Don may attack us
Whenever his stomach be fain ;
    He must reach us before he can rack us, . . .
And where are the galleons of Spain ?

" Art in its perfection is not ostentatious ; it lies hid
and works its effect, itself unseen," so Sir Joshua Reynolds asserted, paraphrasing Horace. And in another
of his suggestive discourses the English painter amplified the same thought in a passage which is as appli-
cable to poetry as it is to painting : "The great end
of the art is to strike the imagination. The painter
therefore is to make no ostentation of the means by
which this is done ; the spectator is only to feel the result in his bosom. An inferior artist is unwilling that

any part of his industry should be lost upon the spectator. He takes as much pains to discover, as the greater artist does to conceal, the marks of his subordinate assiduity." While this is true of one class of inferior artists, there is another class who are deficient in this "subordinate assiduity," and who have not taken the trouble to master the means whereby they must strike the imagination. They are prone to assert a claim to that poetic license which can be allowed only to the greater artists and which the greater artists very rarely ask us to excuse.

In the Mexico of Montezuma, when the natives first caught sight of the cavalrymen of Cortez, they thought that horse and man were one, and they were astonished when they chanced to behold a trooper dismounting from his steed. When a poet soars aloft upon Pegasus he ought to be one with his winged steed; he may guide it at will as it soars aloft; but he must not let the spectator see him dismount.

APPENDIX

A : SUGGESTIONS FOR STUDY

THE student who comes to the consideration of English versification without any previous acquaintance with its principles will do well to begin by training himself to recognize the various rhythms and meters. He should take a good collection of poetry, — Palgrave's *Golden Treasury*, Stedman's *Victorian* or *American Anthologies*, — and go through its pages identifying the rhythm and the meter of the successive poems until he has attained certainty of decision. At the same time he can investigate the various forms of the stanza employed by the leading British and American lyrists. These anthologies contain only the more popular and more representative poems of the several authors ; and the student will do well to select two or three poets and to examine their complete works to see if he can perceive in the lyrics omitted from the anthologies any technical reason for the comparative failure to please the public. Sometimes he will be able to discover that an undue length of line or an awkwardness of rhythm or a monotony of rime may be responsible for the lack of success.

Then as he becomes more familiar with the technic of versification and more responsive to its delicate effects, he may consider more highly specialized collections of poetry, each devoted to a single type : Child's *English and Scottish Popular Ballads, Cambridge Edition*, Main's *Treasury of English Sonnets*, Gosse's *English Odes*, Gleeson White's *Ballads and Rondeaux*, Locker's *Lyra Elegantiarum*. Some of these volumes are devoted to poems in the same rigid form and others are confined to lyrics animated by the same spirit.

But if the student really wishes to attain an intimate understanding of the art of verse he must attempt verse-making himself. The result of his effort may be negligible, but the effort will be its own reward. He may begin very modestly by taking any simple passage of prose — for example, a newspaper account of a fire or of any other accident — and rephrasing this in a succession of iambs, running on without any division into lines. Another passage may be turned into trochees, a third into anapests and a fourth into dactyls. The iambs and the trochees ought to be achieved with no great difficulty; but the succession of dactyls and of anapests will not be so easy. When a fair facility has been conquered a passage may be chosen from some public address — Webster's *Bunker Hill Oration* or Lincoln's *Gettysburg Speech* — to be recast into blank verse, unrimed iambic pentameter. Another passage might be taken from a novel to be turned into trochaic tetrameter, the meter of *The Song of Hiawatha*.

Then the student may undertake a task calling for more or less command of form. He may find a simple story either in a newspaper or excerpted from a play or a romance; and this simple story he may turn into a ballad. The kind of ballad which he decides to experiment in ought to be consonant with the character of the theme. That is to say, the story may be treated with the naïf simplicity of the old English ballads, such as *Sir Patrick Spens*; it may be told with the narrative leisureliness of Longfellow's *Paul Revere's Ride*; it may have the swift terseness of Scott's *Young Lochinvar*, and of Macaulay's *Battle of Ivry*; it may glow with the dramatic intensity of Rudyard Kipling's *Ballade of East and West*; or it may be cast in couplets with the quaint color of Whittier's *Maud Muller*, or with the picturesque flavor of Austin Dobson's *Ballad of Beau Brocade*.

Other exercises of the same sort will easily suggest themselves to the student. For example, there would be profit in taking a critical statement from any one of Arnold's *Essays in Criticism*, and rewriting this in heroic couplets in the manner of Pope's *Essay on Criticism*. In like manner a brilliant paragraph might be picked out of one of Lowell's prose essays, — that on Thoreau, for instance, — and this might be rephrased in the rapid riming anapests of his own *Fable for Critics*.

The composition of what the French term *bouts rimés* is also an admirable gymnastic. This requires the writing of a poem to a set of rimes arbitrarily chosen in advance. The student may open a book anywhere and pick out any two words; he must find a rime to each of these words; and then with these two pairs of rimes he must write a quatrain, as best he can and on any theme that the riming words may suggest to him. Of course he can borrow a commonplace thought to fill out his four lines, if the riming words do not happen to be suggestive. After a little practice with quatrains and octaves in *bouts rimés*, the student may venture on the composition of a sonnet to a set of prescribed lines. He must choose six words, well contrasted in their vowel-sounds. Then he must find three other words to rime with the first word of his five and with the second; — these will give him the rimes for his octave, *a, b, b, a, a, b, b, a.* He needs only one rime for each of the other three of his original five words; and these will give him the sextet, *c, d, e, c, d, e.* Here again it is quite possible that the rimes themselves may suggest a topic for the sonnet.

Owing to the apparent complexity of their structure the various French forms are very useful to the student in his search for technical dexterity, — especially the rondeau and ballade. But the full profit of the grapple with their complexity is to be had only when the student abides by all the rules of the form and denies himself any privilege. A charade may be cast in the form of a ballade, with the first syllable in the first octave, the second syllable in the second octave, the third syllable in the third octave, and the whole word in the envoy.

Parody is also to be recommended, or at least deliberate

imitation, the wilful copying of the method of the chosen poet, perhaps with a playful exaggeration of his mannerisms. But useful as may be the conscious imitation of several poets having sharply diverging principles, it is not more advantageous than translation. A piece of Latin or French prose may be turned into English verse, or a foreign poem may be rendered into English as faithfully as possible with due respect for the metrical structure of the original.

These are but scattered hints to be improved by the student himself, or by the instructor. Just as the college teacher of rhetoric compels his pupils to attain to an average of facility in composition by requiring them to prepare daily themes, so the student of versification must supple his muscles by attempting all sorts of metrical exercises. But these exercises are intended chiefly to increase his appreciation and his understanding of the masterpieces of the major poets; and he must continue the constant and careful study of these poets, spying out their metrical secrets, and never failing to observe their rhythmical variety.

B: BIBLIOGRAPHICAL SUGGESTIONS

A classified list of the more important treatises on English versification will be found in Chapter VII of Gayley and Scott's *Introduction to the Methods and Materials of Literary Criticism* (Boston: Ginn & Co., 1899); and a chronological list of books and articles in English only is presented in T. S. Omond's *English Metrists* (Tunbridge Wells: Pelton, 1903).

The two most elaborate treatises in English are Guest's *History of English Rhythms*, new edition by W. W. Skeat (London: Bell, 1882), and Saintsbury's *History of English Prosody*, in three volumes (London and New York: Macmillan, 1906–1910). To be noted also are two other investigations, Verrier's *Principes de la Métrique Anglaise*, in three volumes (Paris: Welter, 1909–1910), and Jakob Schipper's *Englische Metrik*, in three volumes (Vienna,

1881–1888). A single volume condensation of Schipper's book was issued in Vienna in 1895, and the author prepared an English version of this which he called *A History of English Versification* (Oxford: Clarendon Press, 1910).

There are shorter text-books better fitted for the beginner, written from varying points of view. The names of a few of these may be given here, although an exhaustive list would be impossible: Gummere's *Handbook of Poetics* (Boston: Ginn, 1891); Corson's *Primer of English Verse* (Boston: Ginn, 1892); Parsons's *English Versification* (Boston: Leach, Shewell and Sanborn, 1894); Mayor's *Chapters on English Meter* (Cambridge: University Press, 1886); Omond's *Study of Meter* (London: Richards, 1903); Bright and Miller's *Elements of English Versification* (Boston: Ginn, 1910), and Richardson's *Study of English Rimes* (Hanover, N. H., 1909). Alden's *English Verse* (New York: Holt, 1903) contains a well-arranged collection of examples. John Addington Symonds's papers on *Blank Verse* are now available in a separate volume (New York: Scribner, 1895).

Poe's three papers on the *Rationale of Verse*, the *Philosophy of Composition* and the *Poetic Principle* can be found in any edition of his works. The influence of Poe is obvious in Lanier's *Science of English Verse* (New York: Scribner, 1880), just as the influence of Lanier is obvious in Dabney's *Musical Basis of Verse* (New York and London: Longmans, 1901). Dr. Holmes's very suggestive paper on the *Physiology of Versification* is included in his *Pages from an Old Volume of Life* (Boston: Houghton, Mifflin and Company, 1883). In my own *Parts of Speech, Essays on English* (New York: Scribner, 1901) will be found *An Inquiry as to Rime* and a paper *On the Poetry of Place-Names*.

INDEX

THE CAMBRIDGE POETS — STUDENTS' EDITION

Robert Browning's Complete Poetical and Dramatic Works.

Burns's Complete Poetical Works.

Dryden's Complete Poetical Works.

English and Scottish Ballads.

Keats's Complete Poetical Works and Letters.

Longfellow's Complete Poetical Works.

Milton's Complete Poetical Works.

Pope's Complete Poetical Works.

Shakespeare's Complete Works.

Shelley's Complete Poetical Works.

Spenser's Complete Poetical Works.

Tennyson's Poetic and Dramatic Works.

Whittier's Complete Poetical Works.

Wordsworth's Complete Poetical Works.

ANTHOLOGIES : POETRY AND DRAMA

The Chief Middle English Poets. Translated and Edited by JESSIE L. WESTON.

The Chief British Poets of the Fourteenth and Fifteenth Centuries. Edited by W. A. NEILSON and K. G. T. WEBSTER.

The Leading English Poets from Chaucer to Browning. Edited by L. H. HOLT.

A Victorian Anthology. Edited by EDMUND CLARENCE STEDMAN.

The Chief American Poets. Edited by C. H. PAGE.

An American Anthology. Edited by EDMUND CLARENCE STEDMAN.

Little Book of Modern Verse. Edited by JESSIE B. RITTENHOUSE. R.L.S. No. 254.

Little Book of American Poets. Edited by JESSIE B. RITTENHOUSE. R.L.S. No. 255.

High Tide. Edited by Mrs. WALDO RICHARDS. R.L.S. No. 256.

A Treasury of War Poetry. Edited by GEORGE H. CLARKE. R.L.S. No. 262.

The Chief Elizabethan Dramatists. Edited by W. A. NEILSON.

Chief European Dramatists. In Translation. Edited by BRANDER MATTHEWS.

Chief Contemporary Dramatists. Edited by THOMAS H. DICKINSON.

HOUGHTON MIFFLIN COMPANY
BOSTON   NEW YORK   CHICAGO
1714

FOR COURSES ON THE DRAMA

DRAMATIC TECHNIQUE
By GEORGE PIERCE BAKER, Harvard University.

THE TUDOR DRAMA
By C. F. TUCKER BROOKE, Yale University.
An illuminating history of the development of English Drama during the Tudor Period, from 1485 to the close of the reign of Elizabeth.

CHIEF CONTEMPORARY DRAMATISTS
Edited by THOMAS H. DICKINSON, University of Wisconsin.
This book presents within one volume those plays apart from the works of Ibsen which may be considered landmarks in the field of modern contemporary drama.   No compilation of a like nature has been previously made.

CHIEF EUROPEAN DRAMATISTS
Edited by BRANDER MATTHEWS, Columbia University, Member of the American Academy of Arts and Letters.
This volume contains one typical play from each of the master dramatists of Europe, with the exception of the English writers.

A STUDY OF THE DRAMA
By BRANDER MATTHEWS.
Devoted mainly to an examination of the structural framework which the great dramatists of various epochs have given to their plays; it discusses only incidentally the psychology, the philosophy, and the poetry of these pieces.

THE CHIEF ELIZABETHAN DRAMATISTS
Edited by W. A. NEILSON, Professor of English Literature in Harvard University.
This volume presents typical examples of the work of the most important of Shakespeare's contemporaries, so that, taken with Shakespeare's own works, it affords a view of the development of the English drama through its most brilliant period.

A HISTORY OF THE ELIZABETHAN DRAMA
By FELIX E. SCHELLING, University of Pennsylvania. 2 vols.

SHAKESPEAREAN PLAYHOUSES
By JOSEPH QUINCY ADAMS, Cornell University.
A History of English Theatres from the Beginnings to the Restoration.   Fully illustrated.

SHAKESPEARE QUESTIONS
By ODELL SHEPARD, Trinity College.   *Riverside Literature Series*.   No. 246.
An outline for the study of the leading plays.

HOUGHTON MIFFLIN COMPANY
BOSTON   NEW YORK   CHICAGO
1422